The Excellent Wife

A Biblical Perspective

By Martha Peace

The Excellent Wife:
A Biblical Perspective
by Martha Peace

Tenth Anniversary Edition

Scripture taken from the New American Standard Bible,
© 1960, 1962, 1963, 1971, 1972, 1973, 1975, 1977
by The Lockman Foundation.
Used by permission.

Cover design by Robert A. Yuretich

ISBN 1-885904-08-8

PRINTED IN THE UNITED STATES OF AMERICA
BY
FOCUS PUBLISHING INCORPORATED
Bemidji, Minnesota

This book is dedicated
to
my husband, Sanford

ACKNOWLEDGEMENTS FOR
THE REVISED EDITION

Dr. George Zemek and Dr. Dave Deuel (former seminary professors at The Master's Seminary and currently pastors at Grace Bible Church in Brandon, Florida) critiqued *The Excellent Wife* and shared their notes with me. Dr. Zemek also personally, patiently explained several of the passages to me. Their notes were immensely valuable and the basis for many of the revisions in the new edition. Also, my pastor, John Crotts, helped me with the revisions as well as helped me understand Dr. Zemek's and Dr. Deuel's critique notes (some of which were written in Hebrew or Greek!).

In addition, I want to thank Lynn Crotts who "proofed" the revised edition and Barb Van Thomma from Focus Publishing who carefully made the changes.

Acknowledgements

I believe that the Lord gave me a desire to write this book. Then He gave me people to help me. One of those people is my husband, Sanford. I had been talking about writing a book for quite a while. He told me to stop talking about it, prioritize my life, and write the book! Since he wasn't asking me to sin, I had to do it. Sanford didn't just tell me to write it, he helped me. He is my computer person and my comforter when I am discouraged. He loves me and believed from the beginning that God wanted me to persevere in this project. He was wonderful throughout the process.

We have two former pastors to whom I am indebted. One is Howard Dial who taught me the Bible and nourished the love God has given me for His Word. The other is Ed Sherwood. Ed was instrumental in leading me to the Lord. Much later, as I was thinking of starting the book, Ed greatly exhorted me and then offered to help me. For a year, he met with me weekly and helped me organize the material. At the same time, he began to teach me to write. I am grateful to the Lord for the time Ed and I worked on *The Excellent Wife*. It was so exciting when we mailed the proposal and sample chapters! If it weren't for Ed, I'd probably still be talking about writing a book someday.

In addition to Howard and Ed, the Lord gave me Lou. Lou Priolo is the former director of the Atlanta Biblical Counseling Center. He taught me how to counsel biblically, and he put me to work. This material is so much a part of what Lou has taught me, I wouldn't know where to begin to give him credit. Lou *diligently* edited every word and put up with me in the process! In addition to helping me with this book, Lou has had a tremendous impact on my growth as a Christian. I will be eternally grateful to the Lord for bringing Lou into my life.

Stuart Scott is another dear friend and biblical counselor. He is also the author of *The Exemplary Husband*. Stuart contributed greatly to this book through suggestions and freely sharing his material and ideas with me.

Our daughter Anna has been an especially bright spot in this process. She has cheerfully managed to read and correct the chapters before I sent them to the publisher. She did all this while caring for her husband and three very small children. She, like Ed, helped teach me to write and encouraged me. She has persevered to correct all of my many vague pronoun references!

Mort Patterson, our friend, drew all the original illustrations inside the book. He patiently helped me think of ideas when I was completely blank. He greatly encouraged me to continue in the process by telling me some of what his mother encountered when she wrote a Christian book years ago. He was enthusiastic about this project and always interested in what was happening next.

John Crotts, our new pastor, became involved near the end. I'm sure he had no idea what he was getting into when he agreed to read the manuscript and make comments! John has been a stickler for context, clarity, and the big picture. He gently has explained and re-explained certain points to me. In only a few weeks, he has taught me a lot, and I am looking forward to working with John under his pastoral care in the future.

We have many other friends who have taken such an interest in this project and have prayed for me as well as teased me greatly! Some of them are Maribeth Standring, Franklin and Jane Lawrence, Cindy Waddell, Cindy Carson, Mike Robinson, and our entire church family. I love them all and do thank God for them.

I would be remiss not to mention the wonderful people at Focus Publishing. Don Winters and Stan Haley gave me a chance. Don even teased me about the *southernisms* in the book. Jan Haley and Barb Smith labored faithfully in editing. They had much enthusiasm for the material and saw a great need for it. I have enjoyed working with them all.

I also want to thank Jay Adams for reading the manuscript and for his helpful comments. I am so pleased to be associated with him through the National Association of Nouthetic Counselors. His ministry has greatly enhanced mine.

I am so grateful to the Lord for all those He sent to help me, teach me, and encourage me. I feel like the Apostle Paul must have felt when he wrote to the church at Philippi:

> *I thank my God in all my remembrance of you, always offering prayer with joy in my every prayer for you all, in view of your participation in the gospel from the first day until now.*
>
> *Philippians 1:3-4*

Preface to Anniversary Edition

June 17, 2005
Peachtree City, Georgia

Dear Ladies,

Editing this book for the Tenth Anniversary Edition has resulted in a flood of memories for me. The project began thirteen years ago. Originally each chapter was a lecture I had written for a class I taught at Carver Bible College in Atlanta. The lectures were handwritten in outline form and none of it was on a computer. My pastor at that time, Ed Sherwood, helped me organize the material and he taught me how to write. In fact, Ed met with me for two hours every Tuesday afternoon for a year. During that year we wrote the table of contents and five chapters. Then I was on my own until the end when several pastors and biblical counselors read and critiqued it. It took me two more years to finish it and find a publisher.

Ten years ago I was an unknown author and Focus Publishing was a brand new company. We were like the "blind leading the blind." I remember when Jan Haley, President of Focus Publishing, called and asked what I wanted on the cover. I did not have a clue and neither did she. After the book came out, Jan would call me all excited because they had received an order for five books! Well, many more have been sold since then and Jan and I are both *well aware* that it is the Lord who has blessed this effort and used it for His glory.

There were two main reasons I wrote this book and those reasons have not changed. One was to help women in difficult marriages and the other was, Lord willing, to present a biblically accurate view of submission. It is God's grace and God's mercies that have made this book possible and my prayer was and continues to be that He will use it to bless you and for His glory.

In His Wondrous Grace,
Martha

The Excellent Wife
A Biblical Perspective

Part One - A Wife's Understanding
Foundational Truths for the Excellent Wife

Part Two - A Wife's Responsibility
Faithful Commitments of the Excellent Wife

Part Three - A Wife's Submission
Fulfillment of the Excellent Wife

Part Four - A Wife's Special Concerns
Sin Problems of the Excellent Wife

Introduction

The Excellent Wife began nine years ago in "seed form" as I taught a ladies' Sunday School class. Later, when I began counseling women at the Atlanta Biblical Counseling Center, I saw the need for homework material to
supplement the counseling sessions. So, I developed *The Excellent Wife* workbook and tape series. Two years ago, Lou Priolo (Director of the Atlanta Biblical Counseling Center), Sanford Peace (my husband), and Ed Sherwood
(our friend and former pastor) began to encourage me to put this material
into book form.

I wrote this book to be a comprehensive resource for pastors, counselors,
teachers, missionaries, and Christian women to use for themselves or to teach
others what it *really* means to be a godly wife. I begin the first chapter with
my testimony because the change that God has wrought in me is positively
astounding and should give anyone hope!

Chapters Two through Six cover foundational truths about God, sin, and
marriage. Beginning in Chapter Seven, the focus of the book narrows to the
individual wife's responsibilities to Christ, in her home, and to her husband
(to love him, to respect him, and to respond sexually).

Chapters Thirteen through Fifteen are the heart of this book — the wife's
submission. Chapters Sixteen and Seventeen help a wife overcome any
unbiblical communication or conflict-solving habits she may have. The last
section addresses special concerns and specific sin problems such as anger,
fear, loneliness, and sorrow.

Whether the focus is broad or narrow, each chapter is a part of the complete picture of being the wife that God desires, *The Excellent Wife*.

Part One

A Wife's Understanding

Foundational Truths for the Excellent Wife

Chapter One

The Excellent Wife
Who Can Find?

The Wife That I Was

"Submissive!? Me, be a submissive wife?" With an angry yell, I picked up the Bible and threw it directly at my long-time friend. Ed and his wife Jackie had been witnessing to my husband Sanford and me for weeks. Ed had just shown me 1 Peter 3:5 which says, **"For in this way in former times the holy women also, who hoped in God, used to adorn themselves, being submissive to their own husbands."** He didn't have to wait long for my response. Of all the things I wanted to be in my life, submissive was not one of them.

Thankfully, though the memory is still vivid, the above incident occurred over fifteen years ago. It is an accurate portrayal of my early views on submission. Soon afterwards, however, I did become a Christian and submitted my life to the Lord Jesus Christ and to my husband. Alma, another good friend, once remarked after hearing my testimony that my conversion was like *The Taming of the Shrew!* How right she was! But, let me start at the beginning.

My parents loved and indulged me as an only child. I was spoiled rotten! Imagine my shock at age 19 when my high school sweetheart and I married and I discovered that the world did not revolve around me after all! I was selfish, willful, and easily angered. In hindsight, I know that if Sanford had not loved me enough to "put up" with me, our marriage would have failed in the early stages.

I wrongly thought that getting married and having children would make me happy. It did pacify me for a while, but soon I was looking for something more. So I sought happiness in community organizations, education, jobs, and partying. Each of these entertained me for a while, but I was always yearning for something more. I could not be satisfied. As time went on, I decided to commit myself to a career. I felt sure that a career would solve my problem. So I pursued an advanced degree in the field of nursing and eventually taught nursing at a local college.

I really did enjoy teaching nursing, but all my efforts were centered on pleasing myself and pursuing my career. Soon, my marriage began to break down. I had become a full blown feminist who was going to make my mark on the world — my way. About the time that I began teaching, we began to build our dream home, a two story yellow Victorian with a large porch on three sides. As time went by, we found out that our builder was stealing large sums of money from us. We were left with an unfinished house that had over $15,000 in liens against the property. I tried to escape all of the mounting pressure by drinking and partying. Finally, I decided that what I really needed was freedom. I secretly began to make plans to leave my family. Because Sanford was much more stable than I was, I justified in my mind leaving the children with him. Fortunately for me, God had another plan.

God intervened by sending three people into my life. One was my now dear Christian friend Katrina with whom I shared an office at the college. I felt like I was chained to the Apostle Paul! I made fun of her Christian faith and yelled at her when she tried to talk to me about the Lord. She went home in tears on more than one occasion because of me. It was while I shared an office with Katrina that the Lord sent Ed and Jackie back to Atlanta. We renewed our friendship which had begun in college many years earlier. But, I will admit that I wondered about them because I had heard through the grapevine that they had "gotten religion." Boy had they! Between the two of them and Katrina, there was no getting away from talk about God or His Word.

Coming Under Conviction

As my plans to leave my family developed, I became more and more uneasy. I soon began to have full blown anxiety and what the world calls "panic attacks." Drowning my emotional pain with alcohol only left me more depressed and anxious. Ed kept telling me to pray and read the Gospel of John. Finally, out of desperation, I took his advice. I was "cracking up" and thought I needed psychiatric help. I wouldn't make an appointment, though, because I knew the medications a psychiatrist would prescribe for me would keep me from doing my nursing instructor job. Sanford insisted. Thinking that I was about to be hauled out of the house in a straight jacket, I finally agreed to go on one condition: Sanford must first let me talk with a pastor of a local church. He was reluctant, but agreed.

Soon we were attending a local church with our friends, Jackie and Ed. During this time, I continued to read the Gospel of John over and over again. Most of what I read I already knew and believed — Jesus was God, the only Savior, and He had died on the cross to pay the penalty for my sins. I had been taught these facts as a child, but I didn't really know God personally. Although I wanted to, I didn't know how. One night, however, while Sanford was at work and our children, Anna and David, were asleep, I was in bed reading John as I had done on many nights. That night it was to be different.

When I came to John 14, I read what had become the very familiar words of Jesus: **"And whatever you ask in my name, that will I do..."** (John 14:12). Aloud I said, "That's not true. I've been asking and asking for Him to take my anxiety away, to give us our money back that the builder has stolen, and put our marriage back together." He had done none of those things! But I recalled Ed saying, "Keep reading, Martha." So, I read the verse again. This time I read the *entire* verse. **"And whatever you ask in My name, that will I do, that the Father may be glorified in the Son"** (John 14:13). Suddenly, I understood. All of my prayers had been self-centered. Nothing I wanted had been for the glory of God. I bowed my head in submission and received Christ as my Savior and Lord. Confessing my sins took a long time. Then I prayed, "Lord, now I know that You have the power to take my anxiety away, but whether You do or whether You don't, You decide. I want my life to glorify You!" I turned out the lights and went to sleep.

The next morning, instead of the anxiety which for months had been flooding over me, I awoke to an incredible sense of God's peace. I got up and walked across the room, paused to flip on the light switch and thought, "My life will never be the same." I had finally found what I had been looking for. Jesus Christ, not I, was now the Lord of my life.

How My Life Changed

My life has changed dramatically because of what I have learned over the years about being a godly wife. I wish I could tell you that I am now the perfect wife. Of course I'm not, but God has given me a deep desire to be the wife that He wants me to be. Even though I fail miserably sometimes, He is in the process of molding me in that direction. God has not only given me a deep love for my husband, but also a passion for His Word and for teaching younger women to be the excellent wife described in Scripture. By God's grace, this book is my "labor of love" for you. My prayer is that God will give you the same love for Christ and His Word and the same desire to do His will that He has given me.

The Will of God for Every Wife

God's will for every Christian wife is that her most important ministry be to her husband (Genesis 2:18). After a wife's own personal relationship with the Lord Jesus Christ, nothing else should have greater priority. Her husband should be the primary benefactor of his wife's time and energy, not the recipient of what may be left over at the end of the day. Whether her husband is a faithful Christian man or an unbeliever, God wants every Christian woman to be a godly wife — an excellent wife. This truth is so important to God that He has clearly and completely revealed it in His Word, the Bible. Indeed, the Scriptures alone are sufficient to provide the wisdom wives need for living the Christian life. One of the most important Scripture passages concerning God's will for the Christian wife is Proverbs 31. Notice that in this chapter of Proverbs are the words of King Lemuel **"which his *mother* taught him"** Proverbs 31:1 (emphasis added). In verse 10, King Lemuel asks the question:

> *An excellent wife, who can find? For her worth is far above jewels.*

Who can find an excellent wife? What is an excellent wife? How is she recognized? What is she like? What does she do? These questions and more are answered in Proverbs 31:10-31. My life was radically changed by the application of these and other Scriptures. Because God gave me a heart to obey God's Word and will for my life, I am becoming the godly wife that He wants me to be. He can do this in your life, too, if you are a Christian. You can, with God's help, become a godly wife, an excellent wife! That's the purpose of this book — that you might first consider what it means to be an excellent wife and then faithfully commit yourself to that end, so that you will become the wife God wants you to be! The purpose of this chapter is to give you a glimpse of what an excellent wife is in the hope that you, too, may become one. Let's start by looking at ...

The Traits of the Excellent Wife

In Proverbs 31 verses 10-31, God describes twenty traits of an excellent wife. As these traits, or excellencies, are developed in a woman, her life will begin to glorify God. As a beautiful flower in the light of the morning sun reflects the glory of God's creation, an excellent wife reflects God's glory by her attitudes and actions. She might look something like this:

What a glorious reflection of God a woman becomes as she develops her ministry as a godly wife! You should ask yourself, "Are these the qualities I want in my life?" If the answer is, "Yes!" you may be thinking...

But Who Can Be That Excellent?

Many women have a desire to be the excellent wife of Proverbs 31. They just don't think it is possible, at least not for them. These twenty traits, however, can characterize any Christian woman's life. These traits are given in Proverbs as general truths. Any Christian woman who knows and obeys them can become a godly woman, an excellent wife! Her ministry can grow under the nurturing hand of a faithful and loving God because:

> *...His divine power has granted to us everything pertaining to life and godliness, through the true knowledge of Him who called us by <u>His Own</u> glory and EXCELLENCE.*
> *2 Peter 1:3, emphasis added*

God has called every Christian wife to His excellence! Any flower can bloom when it is tended by God's hand. A wife's responsibility is to learn to put her confidence in the faithfulness of God and His Word — to do what He says. She can become what He wants her to become if she does what He wants her to do. There is no other way! But, there is one major problem to deal with first...

The Problem of Sin

Sin is the only thing that will keep a woman from becoming a godly wife. Sin is lawlessness, a transgression from any of God's standards (1 John 3:4). It is failing to trust in and do what God's Word says. Sin is wanting to do things her own way rather than God's way. It is presuming God will help her even when she is neglecting His truth. Sin is thinking she can get by without God's help. The bad news is that there are a number of ways to sin. The good news is that God Himself has provided a remedy for sin. **"He (God) made Him (Jesus Christ) who knew no sin to be sin on our behalf that we might become the righteousness of God in Him"** (2 Corinthians 5:21). When a wife trusts in Jesus Christ as her Savior and Lord, He saves her from sin. He frees her from the death grip of sin. She is no longer a slave to sin, **"...knowing this that our old self was crucified with Him, that our body of sin might be done away with (rendered powerless), that we should no longer be slaves to sin..."** (Romans 6:6). The Lord Jesus put it this way, **"Truly, truly, I say to you, everyone who commits sin is the slave of sin... If, therefore, the Son shall make you free, you shall be free indeed"** (John 8:34,36). There is help available for every wife's struggle against sin.

The Help Wives Need

If a wife truly is a Christian, God has provided everything she needs **"pertaining to life and godliness."** God has broken the grip of sin in her life, and He has given her the supernatural power of the indwelling Holy Spirit to enable her to obey His Word and submit to His way and His will. In the following chapters we will examine the details (specifics) of what God tells us in His Word, and how to apply what we learn to our lives and marriages. Further, Jesus told His disciples not to worry, because God the Father would send us help:

> *And I will ask the Father and He will give you another Helper, that He may be with you forever, that is the Spirit of Truth; whom the world cannot receive, because it does not behold Him or know Him, but you know Him because he abides with you, and will be in you.*
>
> John 14:16-17

If this is true (and of course it is if the Lord Jesus Christ is her Savior,) then ...

Wives Are Without Excuse

Because God has so richly provided for a Christian wife in her battle against sin, she is without excuse. Her loving, merciful, and holy God has truly provided everything she needs to become a godly wife — to become the excellent wife that God wants her to be. And even when she falls short, she can be forgiven. **"If we confess our sins, He is faithful and just to forgive us our sins and cleanse us from all unrighteousness"** (1 John 1:9). The only question which remains is...

Are You Ready to Begin?

If you are, you may bow your head right now and confess to God that you have not been the wife God wants you to be. Ask God to help you by His grace to become the excellent wife He wants you to be. You might want to pray a prayer similar to the following one:

> *"Dear Lord, I confess that I have not been the wife that You want me to be. I need your help to become that wife. I now commit myself to make my ministry to my husband the primary ministry of my life. Teach me what I need to know. I want my life and my relationship with my husband to glorify You. In Jesus' Name, Amen"*

If you just prayed that prayer and meant it, you can know that God has heard you and will answer your prayer because 1 John 5:14 says, **"And this is the confidence which we have before Him, that, if we ask anything according to His will, He hears us."**

Chapter Two

A Wife's Understanding of God
God's Protective Authority

In talking with people, I frequently encounter their misperceptions of God. For instance, some feel that God is a lofty version of Santa Claus and think that, if they are good enough, God is obligated to give them presents. Those presents can be whatever the person wishes. Some wish for a godly, romantic, or rich husband. Some desire physical beauty, good health, or your basic, everyday, ordinary hurt free/pain free life. Others believe that God is like a kind, old "Grandfather in the sky" who winks at sin and thinks it is little more than mischief or child's play. Their god loves everybody and is happy with them as long as they are sincere about whatever they believe. Still others believe that God is foremost a god of wrath. Their god is always angry and always punishing them. He is hard hearted and poised to "zap" them at any given moment. He is impossible to please, and they live in hopeless despair of what will happen next. For them, the Christian life is virtually miserable.

Unlike a make believe god, however, the God of the Bible is the sovereign, just, and loving Ruler over all the earth and all His creatures. He is **God Most High** who is the potter and we are His clay (Romans 9:19-21). We are to bow in humble submission and adoration before Him. Our view of life is to be God-centered, not self-centered. We are here to serve Him, rather than Him being here to serve us. He alone is worthy to be praised. Understanding your proper position as a creature serving the Creator is foundational to clearing up any misperceptions you may have about God and His protective authority over you.

This chapter begins to build on the glimpse of the excellent wife you saw in Chapter One. It explains some of what you need to know about God and about yourself. Knowing these things, you will then see how you can trust God to protect you and why you need that protection. Let's begin with what you, as a wife, need to know about God.

What Wives Need to Know About God

1. God has planned a ministry for you.

> *Then the LORD God said, "It is not good for the man to be alone; I will make him a helper suitable for him.*
> *Genesis 2:18*

God created a wife for Adam who was to be his helper suitable. If you are a wife, He has also determined your primary ministry and role in life. Yours and every wife's chief end in life is to glorify God, but it is to glorify Him in the manner in which God planned. You are to be a **helper suitable for your husband** (Genesis 2:18). (See Chapter Six for a thorough explanation of this principle.)

2. God is gracious, righteous, and compassionate.

> *I love the LORD, because He hears My voice and my supplications. Because He has inclined His ear to me, therefore I shall call upon Him as long as I live... Gracious is the LORD, and righteous; yes, our God is compassionate.*
> *Psalm 116:1, 2, 5, emphasis added*

Because God is gracious and compassionate, He cares about your struggles and the hurts that you feel. As is His gracious way, God will walk with you through whatever circumstances you encounter. He will listen to you when you cry out to Him. He will shower you with His care. Because God is holy, His care over you will always be good and righteous. You can completely trust Him.

3. God's strength and understanding are unlimited.

> *He heals the brokenhearted, and binds up their wounds... Great is our Lord, and abundant in strength; His understanding is infinite.*
> *Psalm 147:3, 5*

Because God's strength and understanding are unlimited, He knows what you want, feel, desire, and need. He considers all the possible ramifications. There is no limit in His understanding. This enables Him to determine what is best for you and how you may glorify Him the most. Nor is there a limit in His strength to care for you. He can heal your heart even if it is broken.

4. God is purposefully working in your life.

> *And we know that God causes all things to work together*
> *for good to those who love God, to those who are called*
> *according to His purpose. For whom He foreknew, He also*
> *predestined to become conformed to the image of His Son,*
> *that He might be the first-born among many brethren...*
> *Romans 8:28-29, emphasis added*

God promises to use all of your life experiences, including any evil that has been done against you, for your good. One example of good that comes from adversity is changes in your character as you become more like the Lord Jesus Christ. Another example of good that comes from adversity is that God is tremendously honored (glorified) if you respond biblically. God promises to use all things for your good if you love God. You love God by being an obedient Christian (John 14:15).

5. God wants you to be a joyful and fulfilled wife.

> *She looks for wool and flax, and works with her hands*
> *in delight... She senses that her gain is good; her lamp*
> *does not go out at night... Strength and dignity are her*
> *clothing, and she smiles at the future... Her husband*
> *also, and he praises her saying, "Many daughters have*
> *done nobly, but you excel them all.*
> *Proverbs 31:13,18,25,28, 29, emphasis added*

Joy will come to you as you look forward in anticipation to what God has planned for you. A delight from doing your work, a sense of fulfillment that what you are accomplishing is good, and a husband who praises you are just part of the joy and fulfillment that God would like for you to experience.

So we can see that God does care about each and every wife — including you. With His unlimited understanding and heart of compassion, He has devised a perfect plan by which you are to live. There is purpose in whatever situation you may experience, and God wants you to experience fulfillment in your role as a wife. Living out your God-intended role is not a bad thing, but a good thing. God is good and He does all things well, including rule over His creatures. In addition to having a biblical view of God, however, you also need to know some things about yourself and the works that God would like for you to do.

What Wives Need to Know About Their Works and Themselves

1. God has prepared good works for the Christian wife to do.

> *For we are His workmanship, created in Christ Jesus for good works, which God prepared beforehand, that we should walk in them.*
>
> *Ephesians 2:10*

The works that God has prepared for you to do include not only what you do in your relationship with your husband, but also your heart's motive or attitude. It will help you to have the right attitude if you focus on what *you* are supposed to be doing, not on what your husband is supposed to be doing. Certainly, it is easy to get caught up in seeing whether other people (especially your husband) are doing their jobs right. However, the issue for the Christian wife is "am *I* doing the good works that God intended for *me*?"

2. The Christian wife's good works have eternal worth!

> *For we must all appear before the judgment seat of Christ, so that each one may be recompensed for his deeds in the body according to what he has done, whether good or bad.*
>
> *2 Corinthians 5:10*

God promises Christians eternal rewards for their good works in Christ. As in other areas of godliness, your ministry to your husband is **"profitable**

for all things, since it holds promise for the present life and also for the life to come" (1 Timothy 4:8, emphasis added). What a wonderful reward this will be!

3. The Christian wife does not have to be afraid.

> *Thus Sarah obeyed Abraham, calling him lord, and you have become her children if you <u>do what is right without being frightened by any fear.</u>*
> *1 Peter 3:6, emphasis added*

God is the determiner of what is right. He has clearly revealed right and wrong throughout His Word. So, why might you or any Christian wife be afraid to do the right thing? Perhaps you are afraid that you will be hurt, disappointed, embarrassed, or "taken advantage of." Perhaps you may be unsure of what is right. However, the most likely reason that you may be afraid to do what God wants is that you are afraid you won't have your own way. There are all kinds of wrong reasons why you might use *your* means to try to accomplish *your* end. For example, you might desire for your husband to do well at work (your end result), so you lie to his boss about why he is late to work (your means). Instead of taking matters into your own hands, do the *right thing* by telling the truth and not giving in to your fear.

4. The focus of the Christian wife is to be on God rather than herself.

> *Therefore, since we have so great a cloud of witnesses surrounding us, let us also lay aside every encumbrance, and the sin which so easily entangles us, and let us run with endurance the race that is set before us, <u>fixing our eyes on Jesus, the author and perfecter of faith, who for the joy set before Him endured the cross, despising the shame, and has sat down at the right hand of the throne of God.</u>*
> *Hebrews 12:1-2, emphasis added*

Note that the focus of Christ was on the **"joy set before Him."** He did the work that God sent Him to do in spite of the humiliation. His focus was on carrying out the Father's plan and the work before Him. He showed perfect love by enduring the agony and shame of the cross. If the Lord Jesus had reacted in a selfish way, we would have no hope. There would be no Savior for anyone. If you take your eyes off of Jesus and react in a selfish way, you will be miserable trying to fulfill your God-intended role. Focus on the Lord Jesus and His purpose for your life rather than on yourself. Put your husband first doing it "for the joy set before you."

5. A Christian wife does not have to sin.

> *...knowing this, that our old self was crucified with Him, that our body of sin might be <u>done away with</u>, that we should no longer be slaves to sin; for he who has died is freed from sin.*
> *Romans 6:6-7, emphasis added*

Christian wives, as well as all Christians, do continue to sin after salvation. However, the phrase "done away with" in Romans 6:6 means to be "rendered powerless." In other words, the power grip that sin had over them has been broken by Christ. If you are a Christian, you are now free to think and do the right thing, and God will help you by His empowering grace. You do not have to sin. It is your choice.

God does care about you and your struggles, and His understanding of your full circumstances is unlimited. He has a special plan for you and every wife. God's plan includes good works. In addition, he wants you to "do what is right" and to be joyful and fulfilled. The way for you to experience this fulfillment is for you to actively choose to place yourself under the authority of your husband. Thereby, you are really placing yourself under...

God's Protective Authority

God *is* perfect and we can completely trust that He knows what is best for us even though husbands are *not* perfect and many may not be saved. In spite of the husband's imperfections, God has chosen to place the wife under the authority of her husband. There are two passages in the New Testament which clearly state this:

> *But I want you to understand that Christ is the head of every man, and the man is the head of a woman, and God is the head of Christ.*
> *1 Corinthians 11:3*

> *For the husband is the head of the wife, as Christ also is the head of the church, He Himself being the Savior of the body.*
>
> *Ephesians 5:23*

No husband has absolute authority over his wife because God is the absolute authority. For example, if your husband asks you to lie for him, you must refuse because God's authority overrides your husband's. Consider the following passage:

> *For in Him all the fullness of Deity dwells in bodily form, and in Him you have been made complete, and He is the <u>head over all rule and authority</u>...*
>
> *Colossians 2:9-10, emphasis added*

Therefore, when you are under your husband's (limited by God) authority, you are really putting yourself in the safest possible place - in God's will. God loves you and He is good. You need not be afraid. Also, there are many additional provisions God has given in His Word to protect you. We will cover them in detail later in this book.

Even though God's authority is protective, this does not guarantee that your husband will always do the wisest or most godly thing. It does mean, however, that regardless of what he does, God is working in your life to **"conform (you) to the image of His Son"** (Romans 8:29) and God can be glorified. God does not look at life the way we do. His perspective is eternal and perfect. Unfortunately, ours is temporal and marred by sin. That's why God has given us clear guidelines to protect us. But...

Why Does The Wife Need Protection?

There are at least three reasons in Scripture why a wife needs protection.

1. The influence that the world has on her.

> *For all that is in the world, the lust of the flesh and the lust of the eyes and the boastful pride of life, is not from the Father, but is from the world.*
>
> *1 John 2:16*

Undeniably, all of us have been wrongly influenced by the world's way of thinking, humanistic worldly values, and worldly goals. All of these things are hostile to God's ways. One example of worldly values is the feminist belief that a woman's identity and fulfillment come from her education and career. The Bible says that being a **"worker at home"** is a virtue (Titus 2:5). Unfortunately, the feminist philosophy on the role of the woman has permeated every aspect of our culture including our churches. Perhaps you have been influenced in subtle ways of which you are not aware. God wants to protect you from the influence of the world.

2. The Devil

Finally, be strong in the Lord, and in the strength of His might. Put on the full armor of God, that you may be able to stand firm against the schemes of the devil. Therefore, take up the full armor of God, that you may be able to resist in the evil day, and having done everything, to stand firm.

Ephesians 6:10-11,13

Satan is against everything that God establishes. So, he tries to undermine the home and the wife's role. You are to stand firm against the schemes of the devil by being an *obedient* Christian. One biblical requirement of your obedience is for you to graciously place yourself and remain under your husband's authority (unless he asks you to sin). If you do not, you are out of God's will and have not done everything biblically possible to **"stand firm"** (Ephesians 6:13).

3. Women are often more easily deceived.

But I do not allow a woman to teach or exercise authority over a man, but to remain quiet. For it was Adam who was first created, and then Eve. And it was not Adam who was deceived, but the woman being quite deceived, fell into transgression.

1 Timothy 2:12-14, emphasis added

It is not uncommon for women today to be upset by these verses. If they are, they may not have been taught what these verses mean, or they may be reacting from a prideful heart that has been influenced by the world's way of thinking. These verses in no way mean that a woman is less valuable or less intelligent than a man. In fact, the Bible assumes women's intelligence when it instructs the older women to teach the younger, less mature women (Titus 2:3-5). What these verses do mean, however, is that God, in His infinite wisdom, restricted the woman's role in the local church partially because she could be more easily deceived. There are simply some responsibilities and burdens that God does not intend for women to have. A truly wise woman will accept that, appreciate it, and submit graciously to God's plan of protection for her.

God's protection covers you by means of the authority structure God has set up for you. His plan was devised from His perfectly pure heart of love. Even though a small child may never understand all the reasons why his mother takes him to the doctor when he is ill, it's all right because she is doing what is best for her child. It seems rather inconsequential to a mother whose child is sick that the child doesn't understand why. Like the mother of the sick child, God does His very best to protect wives. You may never comprehend all the reasons why God does what He does, but you can trust that He knows better than you what you really need. Keep in mind that you will *never* be what God wants you to be until you place yourself under God's plan by coming under the authority of your husband.

Chapter Three

A Wife's Understanding of Sin
God's Provision

Once I knew a lady who was committing adultery. She told me that she was a Christian. When I asked her on what basis God should let her into heaven, she declared, "Because I've been so kind." She may have been a kind person, but she was deceived about her sin and salvation. The fact is that no one can be kind enough or good enough to merit God's gift of salvation. In spite of what the "kind" lady believed, she did not know the God of the Bible or His provision for her forgiveness of sin. Perhaps you are like she is and need a biblical understanding of sin and God's provision for eternal life with Him. If so, this chapter explains four characteristics of sin and God's provision through the Lord Jesus Christ to deal with past sin as well as present sin.

When God created Adam and Eve, He gave them the ability to think, feel, respond to others, and know right from wrong.

> *God created man in His own image, in the image of God He created him; male and female He created them.*
> *Genesis 1:27*

The abilities that God gave Adam and Eve were declared to be good by God.

> *And God saw all that He had made, and behold, it was* <u>*very good*</u>*.*
> *Genesis 1:31, emphasis added*

That's the way man was until Adam and Eve sinned. Since then, all people have had sin in their lives. These good abilities that God gave them have been perverted by sinful man. For example, God gave man the ability to think. Men use this ability to plan and carry out bank robberies. God gave man the ability to feel and have emotions. Women feel tense, and nervous, and then scream at their children. God gave man the ability to respond in a kind and patient way. People often respond in an unkind, impatient, or unwholesome manner (Ephesians 4:29). God gave man a conscience to know right from wrong (Hebrews 10:22). Hundreds of full to over-flowing prisons show us what choices some people have made! The fact is that there is no portion of God's creation that sinful man has not perverted.

Man's tendency to sin has affected every area of life including the relationship between husband and wife. But before we can see how our tendency to sin has affected wives in a practical way, we must first understand the basic characteristics of sin.

Four Characteristics of Sin

1. Sin is universal. No one is exempt.

> *...for all have sinned and fall short of the glory of God.*
> *Romans 3:23*

2. Sin may be open and obvious to others.

> *Now the deeds of the flesh are <u>evident</u>, which are: immorality, impurity, sensuality, idolatry, sorcery, enmities, strife, jealousy, outbursts of anger, disputes, dissensions, factions, envying, drunkenness, carousing, and things like these, of which I forewarn you just as I have forewarned you that those who practice such things shall not inherit the kingdom of God.*
> *Galatians 5:19-21, emphasis added*

3. Sin cannot be hidden from God.

> *Then God said to Samuel, "Do not look at his appearance or at the height of his stature, because I have rejected him; <u>for God sees not as man sees, for man looks at the outward appearance, but the LORD looks at the heart.</u>*
> *1 Samuel 16:7, emphasis added*

> *And there is no creature hidden from His sight, but all things are open and laid bare to the eyes of Him with whom we have to do.*
>
> *Hebrews 4:13*

4. Sin is justly penalized.

> *For the <u>wages of sin is death</u>, but the free gift of God is eternal life in Christ Jesus our Lord.*
>
> *Romans 6:23, emphasis added*

> *My Servant (the Lord Jesus Christ), will justify the many, as He will bear their iniquities.*
>
> *Isaiah 53:11*

All men sin. Their sin may be open and obvious or be hidden thoughts and motives. Because God is omniscient, He knows every thought and deed of man. Because He is holy, He has to punish sin. Fortunately for mankind, God, out of His heart of love and mercy, provided a payment for the penalty of sin. God's provision was the *Lord Jesus Christ*.

Our Provision Through Christ

Jesus Christ incurred punishment from God for sin as He died in our place on the cross of Calvary. He was our substitute. We deserve death. Instead, Christ was punished for us. The prophet Isaiah expressed it this way, **"The chastening for our well-being [the punishment we deserved] fell upon Him"** (Isaiah 53:5, parenthetical comment added). Anyone can be forgiven of their sins and justified (declared <u>"righteous" by God based on the work of Christ</u>) if they, **"...believe on the Lord Jesus Christ..."** (Acts 16:31). The Apostle Paul elaborated on what he meant by **"...believe on the Lord Jesus Christ"** when he wrote Romans 10:9. There Paul explained, if you **"...confess with your mouth Jesus as Lord, and believe in your heart that God raised Him from the dead, you shall be saved."**

Perhaps you have known about Jesus all your life. You may be a member of a church and have been baptized. You may be the Sunday School Superintendent, but if you have never trusted Jesus Christ, then you only have the outward form of religion. If you like, you may bow your head right now in humble contrition before God, ask Him to have mercy on your soul, confess your sin and ask God's forgiveness, and in your own words confess Jesus as the Lord and Master of your life.

If you have placed your faith (trust) in Jesus Christ and Him alone as your Lord and Savior, you are no longer under the wrath of God. All of your sins have been forgiven — past, present and future. Not only are you cleansed of your sin, but you are also placed by God in supernatural union with Christ. Next, God wants you to have assurance of your salvation.

> *These things I have written to you who believe in the name of the Son of God, in order that you may <u>know</u> that you have eternal life.*　　　　*1 John 5:13, emphasis added*

If you are a Christian, what a joy to know you have been forgiven by God for your sin! In addition to knowing you are forgiven of your sin, you need to know...

How to Deal with the Consequences of Former Sin

But what if you have some especially grievous sin in your past that you have never told your husband? What if you were immoral? What if you had an abortion or were a homosexual or a thief? It is important that you understand God's perspective of your past. The Apostle Paul wrote his first letter to the church at Corinth to people who had committed moral sins. Remember, he was writing to Christians.

> *Or do you not know that the unrighteous shall not inherit the kingdom of God? Do not be deceived; neither fornicators, nor idolaters, nor adulterers, nor effeminate, nor homosexuals, nor thieves, nor the covetous, nor drunkards, nor revilers, nor swindlers, shall inherit the kingdom of God. And such <u>were some of you; but you were washed, but you were sanctified, but you were justified in the name of the Lord Jesus Christ, and in the Spirit of our God.</u>*
> 　　　　*1 Corinthians 6:9-11, emphasis added*

Certainly, if you are a Christian, you need to believe God when He says, **"...and such *were* some of you."** In Him, **"...old things have passed away; behold, new things have come"** (2 Corinthians 5:17). If you are saved, you have been forgiven of all your sin and declared righteous before God; however, if there is something that might possibly affect your present marriage, you may need to clear your conscience with your husband. If in doubt, consult with your pastor.

If you are a Christian and have biblically dealt with past sin, I am sure that you are aware that you still sin. So, how does God want you to ...

Deal with Present Sin

Sin permeates every aspect of man's behavior, including marriage. God provides forgiveness of sin through the Lord Jesus Christ. Therefore, man can be forgiven by God and can live in harmony with other men. (This includes husbands and wives!) Christians should graciously accept the forgiveness that they have in Christ and graciously bestow forgiveness upon their spouses **"...forgiving each other, just as God in Christ has forgiven you"** (Ephesians 4:32). (For more information on the process of forgiveness, see Chapter Nine.) God has provided Christ for us, but what is our responsibility? We are responsible to repent. If our sin has become a long-standing habit, then our fruits of repentance will take time and much work to develop. In fact, repentance begins as ...

A Process of Diligence

Not all sin is as devastating to a marriage relationship as the previous example of immorality, but any sin will erode the oneness that God intends for Christian couples to have. All Christians bring into marriage old sinful habit patterns of thinking and responding that hurt their marriage and grieve their Lord. Repentance is a process that usually involves more than just confessing to God and your spouse. It may take work and time. That's why we are instructed in Scripture to **"...*discipline* yourself for the purpose of godliness"** (1 Timothy 4:7, emphasis added).

The New Testament Greek word for discipline is *gymnazo* which means "to exercise or to train."[1] In other words, it means do it over and over until you get it right. We get our English words gymnastics and gymnasium from this Greek word. How godly we become depends on how hard we work at it. Old habits of sinful thoughts and responses do not just disappear. They have to be replaced with new, godly ways of thinking and responding. Christians have to be **"...transformed by the renewing of their minds"** (Romans 12:2). As we work at it, the Holy Spirit supernaturally enables us. Eventually the godly response becomes the automatic response. This process is described in Ephesians four and Colossians three and is called...

The Biblical Process of Change

PUT OFF	PUT ON
"...put aside the old self" *Ephesians 4:22*	*"...put on the new self..."* *Ephesians 4:24*
"Lay aside falsehood..." *Ephesians 4:25*	*"...speak truth, each one of you, with his neighbor."* *Ephesians 4:25*
"Let him who steals steal no longer." *Ephesians 4:28*	*"Let him labor that he may share with those in need."* *Ephesians 4:28*
"Let all bitterness and wrath and anger and clamor and slander be put away from you..." *Ephesians 4:31*	*"And be kind, tender-hearted, forgiving each other, just as God in Christ has forgiven you."* *Ephesians 4:32*

Overt sin begins in your heart with what you desire. What you want, in part, determines how you talk to yourself. A person may be somewhat successful at modifying outward behavior, but the only real way to glorify the Lord Jesus Christ is to *think* according to His Word (Romans 12:2). The following are examples of how a wife might think wrong, sinful thoughts contrasted with her "putting-on" right, godly thoughts.

WRONG, SINFUL THOUGHTS	RIGHT, GODLY THOUGHTS
1. *"I hate him!"*	1. *"I don't feel love for him right now, but I choose to love him by responding in a kind way."*
2. *"There is no hope for this marriage!"*	2. *"If he repents, there is nothing that I cannot forgive and that we cannot work through."*

3. "I can't be what God wants me to be because my husband is not a righteous man."	3. "He may be a complete failure before God, but I do not have to be. I can be pleasing to God whether he is or not."
4. "I can't take the pressure any more!"	4. "I can take the pressure since **'There is no temptation but such as is common to man and God is faithful who will not allow me to be tempted beyond what I am able to bear.' "** ***1 Corinthians 10:13***
5. "I wish I could be with my friend's husband. He's so kind to her."	5. "Thank you Lord for my husband. What can I do for him to show him that he is special to me?"
6. "I don't dare tell him what I am thinking. If I do, he will think badly of me."	6. "I can learn to speak the truth in love. God will give me the grace to respond to his reaction whatever it is."
7. "I wish he would leave me alone."	7. "Thank you Lord for a husband who does want to be with me."
8. "If he loved me, he would be romantic."	8. **"Love does not seek its own** (way). What can I do to show love to him?" (1 Corinthians 13:5)

Changing sinful thoughts begins with recognizing thoughts that are self-ish or unloving, vengeful or bitter, or in any way unbiblical. After realizing that your thought is wrong, confess it to God (agreeing with God that the thought was sinful). However, since repentance means to change your mind, the repentance process is not complete *until* you replace it with a godly, righteous thought. Then you will have "put off" a self-honoring thought and will have "put on" a God-honoring thought. It is a process that takes work. How hard you work at putting on the right thoughts and actions will directly affect how much like the Lord Jesus Christ you become in this life. If you work at it, you will be **"...training yourself for the purpose of godliness"** (1 Timothy 4:7).

Summary

Thus we've seen that sin can be hidden or open. It is a universal characteristic of fallen man. Only the sinless Son of God, Jesus Christ, could have provided a means to satisfy God's righteous demands against sin. God does all of the work of man's salvation. Salvation is by His grace, not based on any merit (however "kind") within man. God's provision for sin begins at the cross and continues with **"grace to help"** us grow and mature as Christians (Hebrews 4:16). With God's grace, we can work diligently at "putting off" wrong, sinful thoughts and "putting on" biblically right thoughts and actions.

> *...conduct yourselves in fear during the time of your stay upon earth; knowing that you were not redeemed with perishable things like silver or gold from your futile way of life inherited from your forefathers, but with precious blood, as of a lamb unblemished and spotless, the blood of Christ.*
>
> *1 Peter 1:17-19*

Chapter Four

A Wife's Understanding of Relationships
God's Pattern

(The concepts in this chapter have been adapted with permission from material by Dr. Stuart Scott, Professor of Biblical Counseling of Southern Seminary & Boyce College in Louisville, KY)[2]

In counseling women, I frequently hear the complaint, "I have a problem with a relationship" or "I need help to know what to do about a particular relationship." Her relationship "problem" may be with her mother, her brother, her child, her friend, her pastor, her co-worker, or her husband. As a counselor, I look for examples from Scripture that will help the wife to see a godly pattern of relationships for her to follow. By far the best example we have of this pattern is found in the Trinity. The members of the triune Godhead are living examples to us of a perfect relationship.

God designed relationships. He walked with Adam in the cool of the day. He took Enoch to be with Him. He bestowed on Noah His favor. He ate with, talked with, and made a covenant with Abraham. He comforted Hagar in the desert and gave her hope. He providentially brought Joseph to Egypt and prepared him for a future day. He even let Moses see His glory in a round-about way. He made David a King and gave him a whole heart for God. And He provided the means for sinful man to be reconciled to a right relationship with Him through the atoning work of Jesus Christ on the cross.

Shortly before His arrest and crucifixion, Jesus prayed to the Father for those who would eventually put their faith and trust in Him. He based His prayer on the work that He was about to do on their behalf on the cross and how that would glorify the Father. He prayed that God would **"...sanctify them in the truth,"** and Jesus prayed that believers would become one with God that **"...they may *all be one; even as Thou, Father, art in Me, and I in***

Thee, that they also may be in Us; that the world may believe that Thou didst send Me" John 17:21 (emphasis added).

Jesus also prayed that believers would have perfect and complete unity in their relationships with each other. **"And the glory which Thou hast given Me I have given to them;** *that they may be one, just as We are one; I in them, and Thou in Me, that they may be perfected in unity,* **that the world may know that Thou didst send Me, and didst love them, even as Thou didst love Me"** John 17:22-23 (emphasis added).

All Christian men and women supernaturally have the positional unity Jesus prayed for in John seventeen. If they are husband and wife, they are also united by God into **"*one* flesh"** (Genesis 2:24). The Hebrew word for "one" is *echad* which means "one, alike, altogether, or all at once."[3] The very same word is used in Deuteronomy 6:4 for **"the Lord is *one*."** In other words, somehow God makes the husband and wife into "one" as the Trinity is one, a compound unity.

The unity God intends for people to have in relationships is possible only through Jesus Christ. Much of what was lost at the fall of man can be regained in union with Christ. Only in Christ can the relationship of a husband and wife be godly, good, and righteously intimate.

The Godhead's relationship is our model of relationships. From eternity past God (Trinity) has set the pattern for relationships. The relationship within the Trinity is intimate and close. As there is harmony in the God-head, there can be harmony in a marriage relationship. God intends and desires for us to experience it. We are to look to God for this perfect pattern.

Within the Trinity there are certain ingredients that blend together to comprise their perfectly harmonious and intimate relationship. These ingredients are the godly character qualities that each member of the Trinity inherently possesses. God intended for man to have many of these same characteristics. Unfortunately though, sinful man has perverted each and every godly characteristic originally given to Adam and Eve. As you study the following comparison chart you can readily see how man's relationship with man so easily breaks down.

Characteristics of the Trinity (result in perfect harmony and intimacy)	Characteristics of Fallen Man (result in lack of harmony and intimacy)
1. Tender, compassionate, and merciful.	1. Not gentle, unmerciful, and cruel.
2. Open and transparent.	2. Closed, private, and self-protective.
3. Goodness towards the other shown by glorifying the other.	3. Malice towards the other shown in tearing the other down to build up self.
4. Love — sacrificial actions for the other.	4. Self-seeking — actions for self.
5. Perfect communication with each other.	5. Hurt each other by not communicating biblically.
6. Honest and truthful, commitment to a righteous standard.	6. Deceitful, lying, and committed to self.
7. Perfect knowledge and understanding of each other.	7. Limited knowledge and revelation of each other.
8. Reliable and faithful in their relationship.	8. Unreliable, unfaithful, and lacking in trust due to the conditional basis of their relationship. ("If you will, then I will...")
9. When working on a task, there is order, purpose, and voluntary subordination of the Son and Spirit to the Father. (No power play over "my rights.")	9. Likely to manipulate with anger, tears, threats to have own way. (May desperately cling to "my rights.")

As you can see, the Trinity has perfect unity and harmony. "In fact, the three members of the God-head are so interrelational, they appear to be one person, when in truth, they are three."[4] Since the three members of the God-head are our perfect example, take some time to read carefully the following explanation of how the members of the Trinity relate to one another.

> *The Trinity is a relationship in which three eternal persons (each being perfect in character and totally equal in being, power, and glory) reveal, know, and love each other tenderly and perfectly for the other's good within the context of an eternal commitment. When they decide to set and accomplish a goal, for the purpose of order and economy, God the Son and God the Spirit voluntarily subordinate themselves to God the Father in order to function according to their perfect plans. As they work together, they are totally unified in desire, thought and action until the goal's completion. Thus, they are a plurality within a unity.*[5]

Husbands and wives would do well to learn from God's pattern and strive to achieve (by God's grace) these same character traits. This again is God's goal and desire for us (Ephesians 5:22-33). Take special note of how much godly love there is within the Trinity. Also, notice their humility. Even though they are equal in being, the Son and the Spirit voluntarily submit themselves to the Father. They communicate intimately with each other. There is no confusion, but only harmony and perfect unity. Perfect unity is God's norm within the Trinity.

What, However, Is God's Norm For Mankind Within Relationships?

God's norm for man within relationships is to be like and act like the Lord Jesus Christ. We have already seen that Jesus prayed in the garden of Gethsemane that **"they (believers) may be one, just as We are one; I in them, and Thou in Me, that they may be *perfected in unity*..."** John 17:22-23 (emphasis added). Our Lord's prayers for us have not ceased. **"Hence, also, He is able to save forever those who draw near to God through Him, since He always lives to make intercession for them"** (Hebrews 7:25).

In order to be perfected in unity, you must stop asking yourself questions like "What will it do *for me?*" or "What will *I* get out of it?" or "How will it meet *my desires* (needs)?" Instead, ask yourself "How can we *glorify*

God?" or "How can we *walk in a pleasing manner* with God *enjoying Him* as we go?" Let your ambition be like Paul's which was **"to be pleasing to Him"** (2 Corinthians 5:9). In fact, Paul felt so strongly about pleasing God that he described his entire purpose in life with the words **"to live is Christ..."** (Philippians 1:21).

We naturally exalt ourselves, and when we do we are like the Chaldean King Belshazzar to whom God said through the prophet Daniel, **"You have exalted yourself against the Lord of heaven... the God in whose hand are your life-breath and your ways, you have not glorified"** (Daniel 5:23). Shortly after this warning, Belshazzar looked on in terror as a hand sent from God wrote an inscription on the wall. The inscription told of the impending end to Belshazzar's kingdom. Later that night, Belshazzar was slain. Was it a worse affront to God when King Belshazzar did not glorify Him than when we do not? I think not. God wants us to glorify and serve Him now, to think and act like the Lord Jesus Christ would, and to actively participate in the process of becoming **"conformed to the image of His Son"** (Romans 8:29; see also Romans 12:1-2).

God wants us to stop living for ourselves, to stop destroying relationships, and to start living for Him. Paul wrote to the church at Corinth saying, **"...that they who live should** *no longer live for themselves, but for Him* **who died and rose again on their behalf"** 2 Corinthians 5:15 (emphasis added). It is easy to live for yourself, but ultimately unfulfilling and empty. You may be thinking, "I'm willing to work at having a close relationship with my husband, but he is not." If he is unwilling to communicate or is cruel and yet you respond in a godly manner, you will be suffering for righteousness sake and God will meet your needs. God is the one to look to. (For more information on a husband sinning, see Chapter Fourteen.)

As you look to God and desire to have a normal relationship with your husband, you must become like and act like Jesus. (For more information on becoming like Jesus, see Chapter Five.) In order to be like Christ, you must think as well as act like Christ. To accomplish this goal, your motivation must change from "What can I get out of this?" to "What can I give?" (1 Corinthians 13:5; Philippians 2:2-3). Hence you should expect no thanks or recognition. You are just doing your minimal duty to God. Jesus compared us to the slave who was only doing what he ought:

> *So you too, when you do all the things which are commanded you, say, 'We are unworthy slaves; we have done only that which we ought to have done.'*
> *Luke 17:10, emphasis added*

Giving of yourself to your husband is not going above and beyond the call of duty. It is only doing as you ought. You ought to be kind to your husband. You ought to be open, transparent, and honest with him. Perhaps you struggle with openness, transparency, and honesty. If you do, the reason is that a sinful man:

... seeks to be *isolated*.

... seeks to be in *control*.

... seeks to *hide, cover up* from hurt/pain.

... seeks to be *self-protective*.

... tends to be *self-focused*.

Because our natural tendency is to "self," it is important to be daily in God's Word which is **"living and active"** and **"able to judge the thoughts and intentions of (your) heart"** (Hebrews 4:12, adaptation added). The Holy Spirit will use the Holy Word of God to convict you at your deepest level so that your motivation in your relationship with your husband may be for the glory of God instead of self.

In your relationship with your husband, God wants you to communicate in love and experience a righteous intimacy through sharing thoughts, present and future desires, aspirations, goals, struggles, and spiritual insights. He wants you to be open, honest, and transparent. Your words are to be edifying. Your tasks sacrificial. Your motive for the glory of God. Remember that your pattern for oneness is the Trinity. He wants you to be not only like the Lord Jesus, but He also wants you to help your husband become as much like Him as is possible. Your becoming more and more like Jesus is the process of progressive sanctification. You and your Christian husband helping each other become more like Jesus is the process of mutual sanctification. Sanctification and mutual sanctification are explained in the next chapter.

Hebrews 4:12

Chapter Five

A Wife's Understanding
of Marriage
God's Purpose

Recently, I attended my thirty year high school reunion. There I had the opportunity to reacquaint myself with several classmates including one who had been with me in the same carpool. We have both changed a lot since the eighth grade! As we were talking, he told me about an experience he had had with the school counselor while we were in high school. The counselor told my friend that he would never be accepted into a prestigious engineering school in our town. He also told my friend that if he did get accepted, he would never graduate. I, however, remember the day when he *was* accepted. He and his family were so excited! He had a goal, he diligently pursued it, and four years later he graduated. Thirty years later, he was still reaping the fruit of his pursuit as he drove up to the reunion in a Mercedes with a tag bearing the insignia of the Georgia Institute of Technology!

Just as my high school friend had a goal and pursued it, husbands and wives should have a biblical goal for their relationships and pursue it. Previously, we learned God's pattern for oneness in marriage - the example of the Trinity. Now we will learn how *both* the husband and wife are to minister to each other through pursuing God's purpose or goal for marriage.

God's Goal for Marriage

The goal of the Christian husband and wife in their marriage is to have a oneness that is characterized by a loving spiritual and physical bond that glorifies God and thereby *enhances personal spiritual growth* (Genesis 2:24; Ephesians 5:22-33; Galatians 6:1; Hebrews 13:4). Oneness and spiritual growth are achieved as each partner helps the other become as much like the Lord Jesus Christ as possible. This spiritual growth and oneness in marriage does not happen by chance. It happens in direct proportion to how diligent a couple is in pursuing it.

Drawing closer together and growing spiritually occurs in measurable, concrete, practical ways. For example, a wife stops being sarcastic and harsh in her tone of voice to her husband and begins to respond in a kind, tender-hearted, and patient manner. Not only does that kind of change promote oneness, but it also glorifies God because she is obeying His Word. Likewise, the Holy Spirit is showing the power and grace of God by His enabling of the wife to change. Rarely is any goal achieved by happenstance. Attaining the oneness that God intends involves commitment, perseverance, diligence, and the grace of God.

There is no quick, instant means for a Christian couple to achieve spiritual growth and the kind of close, loving oneness in marriage that truly glorifies God. However, there are at least four specific means by which that goal may be obtained:

Biblical Means to Achieve the Goal of Oneness and Spiritual Growth

1. Make your marriage a matter of faithful prayer.
2. Commit to a biblical course of action.
3. Take personal responsibility for your own failures and repent.
4. Submit to and participate in the process of "mutual sanctification."

Let's look at each of these points in more depth.

Begin by regularly and faithfully praying that your marriage will glorify and please God. Be specific in your requests to God. Humble yourself before Him. Name your weaknesses, confess your sin, and ask God to change your and your husband's weaknesses into strengths. Do not lose heart. Know that God hears you and that He will respond. As you pray, commit to the Lord to pursue a biblical course of action. A biblical course of action is simply a plan based on Scripture. You begin by taking personal responsibility for your own failures.

In their testimonies to the Lord, many Christian husbands express gratitude for the influence that their wives have had on them. Even if your husband is an unbeliever or is uninterested in spiritual growth, you can still glorify God and probably have a positive effect on your husband. Begin by praying and asking God to show you the sin in your life. Achieving God's purpose in marriage begins with one partner **"getting the beam out of his or her eye"** (Matthew 7:3). The Lord Jesus explained it this way:

> *And why do you look at the speck that is in your brother's eye, but do not notice the log that is in your own eye? Or how can you say to your brother, "Let me take the speck out of your eye," and behold, the log is in your own eye? You hypocrite, **first** take the log out of your own eye, and then you will see clearly to take the speck out of your brother's eye.*
>
> *Matthew 7:3-5, emphasis added*

The Lord Jesus is *not* saying to never pursue the speck in your husband's eye. He *is* saying that you must *first* make sure your life is in order. Then, you will be able to see clearly enough to confront your Christian husband with the sin in his life.

When you pray, "Lord, take the log out of my eye by showing me the sin in my life," God will answer that prayer. It is a prayer of humility, and therefore glorifies Him. Prepare yourself to respond to God's answers by becoming more discerning about how God might answer such a prayer.

How God Shows You Your Sin

1. By convicting you when you read or hear God's Word.

For the word of God is <u>living and active and sharper</u> than any two-edged sword, and <u>piercing</u> as far as the division of soul and spirit, of both joints and marrow, and <u>able to judge the thoughts and intentions of the heart</u>.

Hebrews 4:12, emphasis added

2. By having someone tell you.

Better is an open rebuke than love that is concealed. Faithful are the wounds of a friend, but deceitful are the kisses of an enemy.

Proverbs 27:5-6

Husbands, love your wives, just as Christ also loved the church ...

Ephesians 5:25

When you find that someone believes you have a sin problem in your life, you have a choice about how to respond. You can respond with a grateful heart, confessing your sin and turning from that particular sin or you can respond with a prideful heart that is embarrassed, angry, defensive, resentful, or vengeful. If you respond in the latter manner, you are guilty of sinful pride. Sinful pride causes strife and embarrassment since **"Through pride comes nothing but strife..."** (Proverbs 13:10). In addition, the Scriptures say that **"Pride goes before destruction, and a haughty spirit before stumbling"** (Proverbs 16:18). It is never pleasant to see blind-spots, but responding sinfully only compounds your sin. Getting the beam out of your own eye is where you must begin in the practical working out of mutual sanctification.

Mutual sanctification in marriage is the biblical process of helping each other become as much like the Lord Jesus Christ as possible.

The husband as spiritual leader of the family and **"fellow heir to the grace of life"** is to help his wife grow and mature as a Christian (1 Peter 3:7). The wife as a **"helper suitable"** is also to help her husband grow and mature as a Christian (Genesis 2:18).

In order to really understand the concept of mutual sanctification, we will begin by explaining sanctification. The word sanctification in the Bible comes from a root word *hagios* which means to be holy. There are three main categories of sanctification taught in Scripture: positional, progressive, and future.

The first category is positional sanctification. Positional sanctification occurs at the moment of a person's salvation. It is all the work of God. God draws the sinner to Himself, gives the sinner a desire to seek Him, convicts him of his sin, cleanses him of his sin, and saves his soul.

> *But we should always give thanks to God for you, brethren beloved by the Lord, because God has chosen you from the beginning for salvation <u>through sanctification by the Spirit</u> and faith in the truth.*
> *2 Thessalonians 2:13, emphasis added*

The last category of sanctification is future sanctification. This, too, is completely the work of God. It will occur when the Lord Jesus returns for His church, takes the church to be with Him, and in the process, gives each member a new, sanctified body that is pure and holy.

> *Now to Him who is able to keep you from stumbling, and to <u>make you stand in the presence of His glory</u> blameless with great joy...*
>
> *Jude 24, emphasis added*

The other category of sanctification is progressive sanctification. We will look at it in more detail. This aspect of sanctification begins at the moment of salvation and ends when you go to be with the Lord. In this process, you grow and mature as a Christian, becoming more like the Lord Jesus Christ. It is not only a work of God as He convicts, disciplines, and enables you, but it is also a work of man as you are responsible to **"...*grow* in the grace and knowledge of our Lord and Savior Jesus Christ"** (2 Peter 3:18. Note: "grow" is an imperative verb. This means it is a command.) You are also responsible to **"pursue love"** (1 Corinthians 14:1), to **"...set your mind on ...the things of the Spirit"**, (Romans 8:5, the "things of the Spirit" are what God desires), to **"flee immorality"** (1 Corinthians 6:18), and **"to discipline *yourself* for the purpose of godliness"** (1 Timothy 4:7, emphasis added). You have work to do to become more like Christ. God will enable you to grow spiritually by the power of the Holy Spirit. He will mold you into His image through specific tests and pressures. In fact, Scripture gives us many opportunities for growth.

Ways God Helps Us Become More Like Christ

TESTING OR PRESSURES	SCRIPTURE REFERENCES	POTENTIAL CHARACTER QUALITIES
1. Getting along with your husband	Ephesians 4:1-3	Humility, forbearance, love, diligence, patience
	Philippians 4:2,3	Living in harmony
2. Suffering for the Lord's sake	1 Peter 4:12,13	Joy, gratefulness, deeper trust in God
3. Other's sin (possibly your husband's)	1 Peter 3:8,9	Harmoniousness, sympathy, brotherliness, kindheartedness, humility
4. Financial pressures	Philippians 4:11,12	Contentment
5. Daily work	Colossians 3:23	Working heartily from the heart
	1 Thessalonians 4:11,12	Behaving properly, financially responsible
6. Illness (due to sin)	James 5:14,15	Repentance

7. Trials (temptations, testings)	James 1:2,3,12	Joy, endurance
8. Providentially hindered	James 4:13-16	Mindful of God's sovereignty
9. Death of a loved one	1 Thessalonians 4:13-18	Hopeful in the Lord
10. Bearing other's burdens	Galatians 6:2	Love
11. Admonished by others	Romans 15:14 1 Thessalonians 5:14 Colossians 1:28,29 Colossians 3:16	Perseverance, patience, wisdom, diligence, gratefulness, humility

Just as God helps us as individuals become more like Christ, He also helps couples to grow and mature and help each other become more like Christ. This process is called "mutual sanctification" and comes under the category of "admonishment by others" in the previous chart. As a result, both husband and wife must learn how to properly receive and give reproofs.

A reproof is an expression of censure or rebuke. A biblical reproof is telling someone what they are doing wrong with the intent to restore them to a right relationship with God. When a Christian husband or wife reproves their partner, they are pointing out sin in that person's life. There are specific Scriptural guidelines to follow when giving a reproof.

> *If your brother sins, go and reprove him in __private__; if he listens to you, you have won your brother.*
> *Matthew 18:15, emphasis added*

> *Brethren, even if a man is caught in any trespass, you who are spiritual, <u>restore such a one in a spirit of gentleness, each one looking to yourself,</u> lest you too be tempted.*
> *Galatians 6:1, emphasis added*

When a reproof is done privately with gentleness and with the motive of restoring the other person, then the reproof is loving. When a person won't reprove their partner, they are, most likely, more concerned about "What effect is this going to have on me?" rather than being concerned about help-ing their partner. This kind of reaction is selfish and unloving. If they love God and their partner, they will, in a righteous way, biblically reprove each other in love.

How you respond to your husband's reproof is a reflection of your de-sire to become more godly. Begin with considering his reproof to be, at the least, possibly valid. Next, consider the following right ways to respond to reproof.

1. Take the time to think about what you have been told.

> *The heart of the righteous ponders how to answer, but the mouth of the wicked pours out evil things.*
> *Proverbs 15:28*

2. Search the Scriptures to determine what the sin is and how to "put it off."

> *...lay aside the old self, which is being corrupted in accor-dance with the lusts of deceit, and that you be renewed in the spirit of your mind, and put on the new self...*
> *Ephesians 4:22-24*

3. Ask your husband to give some specific examples of how you could have better responded to his reproof.

> *The wisdom of the prudent is to understand his way, but the folly of fools is deceit.*
> *Proverbs 14:8*

4. Confess your sin.

> *If we confess our sins, He is faithful and righteous to forgive us our sins and to cleanse us from all unrighteousness.*
> **1 John 1:9**

5. Show the fruit of repentance. Stop doing the sin and start doing the right thing.

> *All discipline for the moment seems not to be joyful, but sorrowful; yet to those who have been trained by it, afterwards it yields the peaceful fruit of righteousness.*
> **Hebrews 12:11**

6. Do not justify or defend yourself.

> *I will bear the indignation of the Lord, because I have sinned against Him, until He pleads my case and executes justice for me.*
> **Micah 7:9**

If you know that your husband's reproof is valid or even partially valid, then heed his advice and change your sinful way. It may help you to think about the following benefits of a right response to reproof:

> *A fool rejects his father's discipline, But he who regards reproof is <u>prudent</u>.*
> **Proverbs 15:5, emphasis added**

> *Poverty and shame will come to him who neglects discipline, But he who regards reproof will be <u>honored</u>.*
> **Proverbs 13:18, emphasis added**

> *He whose ear listens to the life-giving reproof will dwell <u>among the wise</u>.*
> **Proverbs 15:31, emphasis added**

> *He who neglects discipline despises himself, But he who listens to reproof <u>acquires understanding</u>.*
> **Proverbs 15:32, emphasis added**

Listen and learn from the reproof. Think, "What is God trying to teach me?" Learn to see each other's reproofs from God's perspective and be grateful that your husband is telling you his complaint instead of clamming up and becoming embittered because of your sin. Perceive the rebuke from this viewpoint: **"Faithful are the wounds of a friend..."** (Proverbs 27:6) and **"Better is open rebuke than love that is concealed"** (Proverbs 27:5). Take a moment and think about what God may be trying to convey to you. Listen to your husband's rebuke, learn from it. The results will be growth and maturity as a Christian. Be wise rather than foolish. Make glorifying God your dearest heart's desire. If you have to suffer some humiliation in the process, you'll just have to suffer the humiliation. It will be uncomfortable, even painful for the moment; but if you learn from God's pruning, afterwards you will bear fruit for Him (John 15). How you respond is the difference between a maturing, growing Christian and an immature Christian. In fact, it is probably the paramount mark of maturity.

What if, however, the shoe is on the other foot, and it is your husband who needs the reproof?

1. Choose the right time.

> *There is an appointed time for everything. And there is a time for every event under heaven... A time to tear apart, and a time to sew together; a time to be silent, and a time to speak.*
>
> *Ecclesiastes 3:1,7*

The wrong times are when you are in front of others, when you have a sinful attitude, or when he cannot give you his undivided attention. The right times are when you are alone together, feeling well and rested, there is plenty of time to talk, and you are in control of yourself and reliant upon the Holy Spirit and God's Word for directing your thoughts and actions.

2. Choose the right wording.

> *The heart of the righteous ponders how to answer, But the mouth of the wicked pours out evil things.*
>
> *Proverbs 15:28*

Begin by thinking about what you want to say. It may even be wise to write it out and then practice it aloud. If you are in doubt about the content or how you are expressing the reproof, ask an objective, godly person such as an older woman in the church, who can be trusted, to read it and give her opinion.

3. Comfort him as you correct him.

> *I know your deeds and your toil and perseverance, and that you cannot endure evil men, and you put to the test those who call themselves apostles, and they are not, and you found them to be false; and you have perseverance and have endured for My name's sake, and have not grown weary.*
>
> *Revelation 2:2-3*

In His letter to the church at Ephesus, the Lord Jesus reproved the church members for losing their first love. He threatened severe discipline if they did not repent. It is interesting to note, however, that before the Lord Jesus reproved the church members, He comforted them by telling them what they had done right. In a similiar way, you also may comfort your husband and praise him for what you can before you give the reproof. It will give him hope and make the reproof easier for him to accept. One word of caution, comforting or praising him is not required nor should it be done in a manipulative way. It is simply an act of kindness.

4. Be specific regarding his sin and offer a biblical solution. Examples of Scripture that might be appropriate to use:

> *...in everything give thanks; for this is God's will for you in Christ Jesus.*
>
> *1 Thessalonians 5:18*

> *Therefore, laying aside falsehood, speak truth, each one of you, with his neighbor, for we are members of one another.*
>
> *Ephesians 4:25*

Be anxious for nothing, but in everything by prayer and supplication with thanksgiving let your requests be made known to God.

Philippians 4:6

This you know, my beloved brethren. But let everyone be quick to hear, slow to speak and slow to anger; for the anger of man does not achieve the righteousness of God.

James 1:19-20

It feels safer to give vague, indirect hints than straightforward, clear specifics regarding your husband's sin. However, people are oblivious to vague, indirect hints! Speak the truth in love to him, and he will be much more likely to understand and possibly repent. Give him hope by offering a biblical solution. For example, "Honey, I have noticed that you have been irritable and harsh with Susie lately. I know she is at a difficult age and needs to be disciplined, but '**...the anger of man does not achieve the righteousness of God'** (James 1:20). Is there anything I can do to make it easier for you? If you would like, I can quietly point it out to you when I notice that you are getting frustrated."(If he does not receive your reproof in a loving, humble manner, see Chapter Fourteen.)

5. Communicate a spirit of unconditional love.

> *But God demonstrates His own love toward us, in that while we were yet sinners, Christ died for us.*
>
> *Romans 5:8*

Tell him something like this, "Sweetheart, I will always love you no matter what." In addition, show him your love by being patient, kind, etc. It is not easy to give a loving reproof. It is easier just to pray about it. However, Scripture is clear that Christians are supposed to help each other become as much like the Lord Jesus Christ as possible. If your husband is a Christian, then you are responsible before God to gently, lovingly tell him his fault. After all, **"Love rejoices in the truth, it does not rejoice in unrighteousness"** (1 Corinthians 13:6).

As difficult as it is to give someone a reproof, it is usually more difficult to humbly receive one. How you receive reproof will be one measure of your maturity in Christ.

1. You become angry and lash out at him.

> *Through presumption (pride) comes nothing but strife, But with those who receive counsel is wisdom.*
>
> > *Proverbs 13:10*

2. You feel hurt, resentful, and unforgiving.

> *Let all bitterness and wrath and anger and clamor and slander be put away from you, along with all malice. And be kind to one another, tender-hearted, forgiving each other, just as God in Christ also has forgiven you.*
>
> > *Ephesians 4:31-32*

3. You focus on the things he is doing wrong.

> *You hypocrite, first take the log out of your own eye, and then you will see clearly to take the speck out of your brother's eye.*
>
> > *Matthew 7:5*

4. You suffer intense personal hurt.

> *...He (God) disciplines us for our good, that we may share His holiness. All discipline for the moment <u>seems not to be joyful</u>, but sorrowful; yet to those who have been trained by it, afterwards it yields the peaceful fruit of righteousness.*
>
> > *Hebrews 12:10-11, emphasis added*

Any reproof may be humiliating and may make you feel badly. However, do not add to your personal hurt by reacting sinfully. If you do not respond with humility and gentleness, you will compound your sin. Even if your husband reproves you in an angry and unkind manner, you are still responsible before God for how you respond back. (For more information on what to do when he is angry and unkind, see Chapter Fourteen, Resource # 5.)

It is never pleasant to realize that other people see you as less than perfect. It is humiliating. However, "**...all discipline for the moment seems not to be joyful, but sorrowful; yet to those who have been trained by it, after-**

wards it yields the peaceful fruit of righteousness" (Hebrews 12:11). The "yield" of the fruit will depend in a large measure in how humbly a husband and wife give and receive reproof. If they love the Lord Jesus Christ, they will participate in and submit to the process of mutual sanctification. Helping each other become more like Christ so that they can glorify Him more is God's purpose in marriage.

Chapter Six

A Wife's Understanding of Her Role
God's Perfect Plan

Our son, David, is a fire fighter and a paramedic. He and the others he works with are highly trained professionals. Once, David had to crawl under an overturned vehicle to assess and help the young man who was trapped. It took them about thirty minutes to extricate the injured man. Meanwhile, David was under the vehicle while there was gasoline dripping all around them. David called out for someone to be ready in case a fire started. His Captain, who was standing beside the car, answered, "If I were any more ready, you'd be wet!" Fortunately for David, all of the EMS personnel were working together as a "team."

Team work is obviously critical in an emergency situation. Each one of the emergency personnel that night knew their jobs. They understood their particular role. They functioned together as a team with one goal in mind — a good outcome for the victim and for David. Just as our local fire department assigns roles, God has assigned a particular role for the wife. The Fire Department's goal was to save the patient without injuring David. A Christian wife's goal is to glorify God. If your desire as a Christian wife is to glorify God, you must first understand God's perspective. He is the only one who has the insight of Creator and Redeemer. What is God's plan for the role of husbands and wives from His perspective? There are at least five issues to consider.

God's Perspective

1. Men and women are created in the image of God.

> *And God created man in His own image, in the image of God He created him; male and female He created them.*
> *Genesis 1:27*

As a result of being created in God's image, you have certain tasks as His "image-bearer." For example, you are to be in charge of God's creation and to glorify God.

> *Then God said, "Let us make man in our image, according to our likeness, and let them <u>rule over</u> the fish of the sea and over the birds of the sky and over the cattle and over all the earth, and over every creeping thing that creeps on the earth."*
> *Genesis 1:26, emphasis added*

> *Whether, then, you eat or drink or whatever you do, <u>do all to the glory of God</u>.*
> *1 Corinthians 10:31, emphasis added*

Because you were created by God, you are accountable to God. Therefore, you have the task of making responsible choices.

> *...<u>choose</u> for yourselves today whom you will serve...*
> *Joshua 24:15, emphasis added*

> *...that every mouth may be closed, and all the world may become <u>accountable</u> to God.*
> *Romans 3:19, emphasis added*

Mr. Buck Hatch, retired professor from Columbia Bible College, diagrams man's being created in God's image this way:[8]

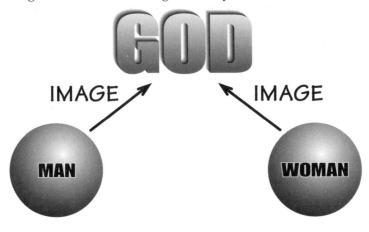

The Bible teaches that the essential natures of both men and women are the same. Both are made in the image of God although there are differences, of course, in their physical bodies.

2. In the order of creation, man was created first.

> *Then the LORD GOD formed man of dust from the ground, and breathed into his nostrils the breath of life; and man became a living being... Then the LORD GOD said, "It is not good for the man to be alone; I will make him a helper suitable for him." ...So the LORD GOD caused a deep sleep to fall upon the man, and he slept; then He took one of his ribs, and closed up the flesh at that place. And the LORD GOD fashioned into a woman the rib which He had taken from the man, and brought her to the man.*
> *Genesis 2:7, 18, 21-22*

> *For it was Adam who was first created, and then Eve.*
> *1 Timothy 2:13*

The order of creation has significance in the role of the husband and the wife. The husband was created to rule over the earth; the wife, later, was created to be a "helper" that would be suitable for him. Both, none-the-less, were created in God's image, but each one was created to carry out a different role.

3. Woman was created for the man, not man for the woman.

> *For a man ought not to have his head covered, since he is the image and glory of God; but the woman is the glory of man. For man does not originate from woman, but woman from man; for indeed man was not created for the woman's sake, but woman for the man's sake.*
> *1 Corinthians 11:7-9*

The Apostle Paul is making reference to God's original intent. Man is to glorify God and woman is to glorify the man. Mr. Hatch illustrates it this way:

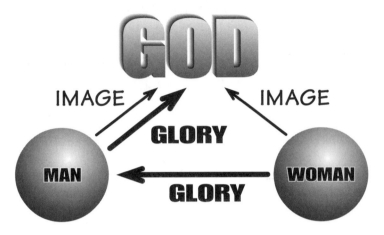

Mr. Hatch elaborates by using the Trinity as the role-model. Within the Trinity, there are three distinct roles:

The planner who makes the plans — God the Father.

The one who carries out the plans — God the Son.

The one who also carries out the plans as well as keeps and empowers Christians — God the Spirit.

In the Trinity, of course, there is perfect harmony. All are satisfied with their roles. There are no "power plays" or role confusion. Note how the Lord Jesus describes both His work and His role as well as that of the Holy Spirit:

> <u>We must work the works of Him who sent Me</u>, *as long as it is day; night is coming, when no man can work.*
> *John 9:4, emphasis added*

> *Jesus therefore said, "When you lift up the Son of Man, then you will know that I am He, and I do nothing on My own initiative, but I speak these things as the Father taught Me. And He who sent Me is with Me; He has not left Me alone, for I always do the things that are pleasing to Him."*
> *John 8:28, 29, emphasis added*

> *But the Helper, the Holy Spirit, <u>whom the Father will send</u> in My name, He will teach you all things, and bring to your remembrance all that I said to you.*
> *John 14:26, emphasis added*

Also, within the Trinity, it is interesting to note who gets the glory. The Holy Spirit did not come to call attention to Himself but to Jesus.

> *Jesus said, "But when He, the Spirit of truth, comes, He will guide you into all the truth; for He will not speak on His own initiative, but whatever He hears, He will speak; and He will disclose to you what is to come. <u>He shall glorify Me</u>; but He shall take of Mine; and shall disclose it to you."*
> *John 16:13-14, emphasis added*

In addition, Jesus did not come to call attention to Himself but to the Father.

> <u>*I glorified Thee on the earth,*</u> *having accomplished the work which Thou hast given Me to do.*
> *John 17:4, emphasis added*

So, just as Christ glorified the Father by doing the Father's "work," you are to glorify your husband by doing the husband's "work." Your role is to glorify your husband. You were created for him.

4. The effects of the fall of man.

In the beginning, God created man as ruler over the earth. Man's wife was created as a **"helper suitable"** for him. As a result of their sin, God pronounced judgment or a curse on them both. There were many painful effects of their rebellion and disobedience: death, thorns and thistles in the ground, pain in childbirth, and a power struggle between the man and his wife.

> *Yet your desire [to control or overtake] shall be for your husband, And he shall rule [to have power] over you.*
> *Genesis 3:16, emphasis and*
> *parenthetical comment added*

Whereas before the fall there was harmony between Adam and Eve in fulfilling their roles, now there would be a power-play as they both sought to dominate the other. It soon resulted in much grief, turmoil, bitterness and misery. Indeed, one of the impacts of the fall was the beginning of sinful conflict. Subsequently, Christ came to redeem us from the curse and if you are "in Christ" (as Christians), you and your husband have the potential to regain much of what was lost at the fall of man. Therefore, you do have the capacity to have the harmony in your marriage that God intended.

Originally, Adam and Eve were naked and unashamed, *completely open* with each other. As a result of the fall, they became ashamed, hid from God and were perhaps embarrassed to be seen by each other. Christ is the only one who could have reconciled them to a restored, intimate, unashamed relationship with God and with each other. Certainly, the deep unity and intimacy that God intended between husband and wife has been marred by the fall of man. This is but one area that God intends to set right through His plan of redemption.

5. The husband was and still is to be the head of his wife.

> *For the husband is the head of the wife, as Christ also is the head of the church, He Himself being the Savior of the body...*
>
> Ephesians 5:23

Your husband is the one in charge. Being in charge does not mean that he has to do everything. It does mean that he is *responsible* for managing his home. A part of that managing is delegating responsibility to others, including you. In order to help you understand your and your husband's God-intended roles, we need to begin with...

a. The Model of Christ and the Church

The wife is to model ("act out") the church being submissive to and glorifying Christ.

> *Wives, be subject to your own husbands, as to the Lord...But as the church is subject to Christ, so also the wives ought to be to their husbands in everything...This mystery is great; but I am speaking with reference to Christ and the church.*
>
> Ephesians 5:22, 24, 32

The church refers to the "body of Christ." It is made up of all people who became or will become Christians from the time of Christ until He returns. This group of people is also called the "Bride" of Christ. Undeniably, Christians are to submit to Jesus' authority and utilize their energies to glorify Him. Well, the wife's role is a model of the church's relationship to Christ. Therefore, you should submit to your husband's authority and use your energies to glorify him.

On the other hand, the husband is to model ("act out") Christ's response to the church.

> *This mystery is great but I am speaking with reference to Christ and the church.*
>
> *Ephesians 5:32*

b. Christ's Response to the Church

1. Christ died for the church, a *sacrifice* of self.

> *Husbands, love your wives, just as Christ also loved the church and gave Himself up for her...*
>
> *Ephesians 5:25*

2. Christ *loves, nourishes,* and *cherishes* the church.

> *So husbands ought also to love their own wives as their own bodies. He who loves his own wife loves himself; for no one ever hated his own flesh, but nourishes and cherishes it, just as Christ also does the church...Nevertheless let each individual among you also love his own wife even as himself...*
>
> *Ephesians 5:28, 29, 33*

It may be easier for you to understand the husband and wife roles through studying the following model. In this model, you will see how the two relationships come together. Christ/the husband cherishes, sacrifices for, nourishes, and loves the church/wife. On the other hand, the church/wife is to submit to and glorify her Christ/husband.

Model of Christ and the Church
The Husband and Wife Roles

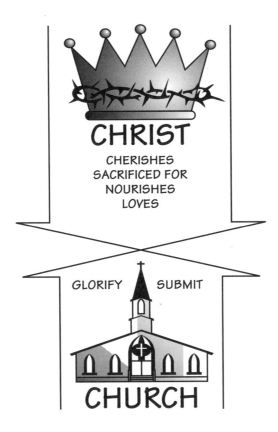

It is only in fulfilling and living out these roles as God intended, that you and your husband will have close unity and harmony in your marriage. In Christ, the closeness that was lost at the fall of man can be regained.

Basically, we have said that the wife's role is to glorify and submit to her husband. She was created to fulfill her role as "helper" for her husband. It's easy to see Eve's role, but what about you? How, practically, can you carry out your God-given role?

Eighteen Ways a Wife May be the Glory of Her Husband

1. Ask your husband, "What are your goals for the week?"

2. Ask your husband, "How can I help you to accomplish these goals?"

3. Ask your husband, "Is there anything that I can do differently that would make it easier for you?"

4. Be organized with cleaning, grocery shopping, laundry, and cooking. As you fulfill your God-given responsibilities, your husband is then free to do his work.

5. Save some of your energy every day for him.

6. Put him *first* over the children, your parents, friends, job, ladies' Bible studies, etc.

7. Willingly and cheerfully rearrange your schedule for him when necessary.

8. Talk about him in a positive light to others. Do *not* slander him at all, even if what you are saying is true.

9. Do whatever you can to make him look good, to accomplish his goals. Some examples are offer to run errands for him, organize your day to be available to help him with his projects, pray for him and make good suggestions. Give him the freedom not to use your suggestion, and do not be offended if he does not follow it.

10. Consider his work (job, goals, hobbies, work for the Lord) as more important than your own.

11. Think of specific ways that you can help him accomplish his goals. Examples are get up early in the mornings to help him get off to work having had a good breakfast, take care in recording telephone messages for him, anticipate any needs he may have in order to attain a specific goal, and keep careful records of money spent to keep up with the budget.

12. Consider the things that you are involved in. How do they glorify your husband? Ask his guidance.

13. Be warm and gracious to his family and friends. Make your commitment to him obvious to them.

14. Do and say things that build him up instead of tear him down.

15. Dress and apply your makeup in an attractive manner that is pleasing *to your husband*.

16. When your husband sins, reprove him privately and gently, always giving him hope and pointing him to the Lord.

17. Encourage him to use his spiritual gifts in ministry.

18. Realize that just as God is glorified when man obeys Him, your husband is glorified when you obey your husband.

The question always comes up, what if your husband is not a Christian? What if he is not glorifying the Lord? I'm reminded of a story that my grandmother told me once about her parents. They were born around the time of the Civil War. Apparently, her mother was a Christian and her father was not. Reflecting back, my grandmother told how her mother always wanted to please him. In order to please her husband, she was gentle and kind, and cooperated in all of the many relocation moves they made. Her usual answer when he requested something was, "Yes, Dad." She did not complain or grumble. She seemed to go gladly along with him in his plans. Even when she differed, she still respectfully supported him. I asked my grandmother, "How did your father treat your mother?" and she said, "He *adored* her." Well, my great-grandfather may not have glorified Christ but my great-grandmother did by magnifying her husband, by living out the role that God intended for her. A special blessing for her was how her husband treated her and loved her. You see, a Christian woman can do the right thing and fulfill her God-given role regardless of whether her husband fulfills his or not.

Part Two

A Wife's Responsibility

Faithful Commitments
of the Excellent Wife

Chapter Seven

Christ

The Wife's Heart

Recently I heard someone say, "God has given me a heart to pastor a church." What he meant was he had a desire to become a pastor. Certainly, to pastor a church is a good desire. As I walked away, I prayed that someday God will grant him the **"desire of his heart"** (Psalms 37:4). However, his desire to pastor is only as good as his willingness to wait on God's timing. In the meantime, he must continue to serve the Lord Jesus Christ whether he ever becomes a pastor or not. If he is not content to wait on God, if he is miserable and sins as a result, then his heart's desire is not set on the glory of the Lord Jesus Christ. Instead, his desire has become an idol (Ezekiel 14:1-11) or a lust (1 John 2:15-17; 5:21).

Idols/lusts in the heart are rampant. We all set our hearts on attaining things that God does not want us to have or to have right now. Some people only have idols/lusts in their heart. They are unbelievers, thus they have no capacity to worship Christ. On the other hand, believers do have a God-given capacity to worship the Lord Jesus Christ. In fact, one of the foundational truths we saw earlier was God's provision for sin through the Lord Jesus Christ. This chapter builds on that previous foundation by addressing the wife's day to day heart's devotion to Christ. Unfortunately, her devotion and longing is not always purely to the Lord Jesus. You see, Christians can have idols in their hearts, too.

"An idol can be anything. It may even be a good thing. But if we want it so badly that we sin if we don't get it or sin to attain it, then we are worshipping an idol rather than Christ."[9] Each of us is worshipping something or someone within our heart every waking moment of each day. Pastor Stuart Scott says that we worship what we "serve, speak about, sacrifice for, seek after, spend time and money on, and trust in." (See Psalm 115 and 135). In other words, who or what you worship is "what's on your mind," "what you long for — wish for," "what is really important to you," and "what you have your *heart* set on."

The word "heart" is used 830 times in the Scriptures. It includes such non-material things as your thoughts, motives, and choices.

> *Let the words of my mouth and the meditation of my heart be acceptable in Thy sight, O LORD, my rock and my Redeemer.*
>
> *Psalm 19:14*

Believers have a God-given capacity to have a pure devotion to and worship of the Lord Jesus Christ, but they frequently struggle with other "gods"/ lusts/cravings competing for their affections. These "desires" are not necessarily bad. For example, going fishing is fun and certainly not sinful. However, idolatry comes into play at the point that the fisherman does not get to go on a planned trip and he sins. The problem is his affections are set on fishing, not on the Lord Jesus. Fishing could possibly have become an idol. A person whose heart is set on fishing may become angry, frustrated, feel self-pitying, anxious, manipulative, or bitter. Fishing is not sinful, but what a person thinks about it may be.

Like the frustrated fisherman, wives may have idolatrous affections. For example, how her husband behaves or treats her can easily become an idol even to the point of displacing the Lord Jesus Christ as her deepest affection and longing. The following is a list of common idols/lusts with which Christian wives struggle. Before you read the list, ask God to show you your idols/ lusts (Psalm 139:23-24). Circle the ones of which you are guilty.

List of Common Idols ("False Gods") Wives May Have Their Heart Set On

1. Good health.
2. Physical appearance.
3. Having a Christian marriage.
4. Being treated fairly.
5. Having a hurt free/pain free life.
6. Worldly pleasures (drugs, alcohol, sex).
7. A child or children.

8. Another person (man or woman).

9. A material thing.

10. An ideal ("pro-life movement," "peace movement").

11. Money.

12. Success.

13. Others' approval.

14. Being in control.

15. Having your "needs" met.

As long as things are going well in the areas you have your heart set on, you will feel all right. When they do not turn out as you may desire, frustration and perhaps anxiety begin to build even to the point of desperation. You become willing to do anything, including sin, to have your "idol." In addition to the frustration and possible anxiety, God also frustrates your idol worship because He wants your pure devotion to Him (Matthew 22:37-38). As a result, the painful emotions become seemingly unbearable. Pastor Stuart Scott diagrams what is happening this way:

Pastor Scott's diagram includes a heart which is symbolic of your thoughts, motives, and choices - the "control center" of one's being. The small icons represent what or whom you are worshipping. Your worship is going on every waking moment of every day. You may be worshipping the Lord Jesus Christ or something or someone else.

The small icons represent competing "gods" in our heart. When something is so important to us that we sin to get it or we sin when it doesn't go well, it can be an idol in our heart.

As idolatrous sin abounds, painful emotions increase, and the pressure builds. It is like a steam engine with no safety or relief valve. If you do not repent and turn to God for a refuge (comfort and relief on His terms), you will be forced to seek relief, comfort, and escape somewhere else. What this amounts to is what David Powlison, from the Christian Counseling and Education Foundation East, calls a "false savior." As you read the following list of "false saviors," think about yourself and circle the ones you have sought for comfort and relief.

List of False Saviors / Refuges

1. Unbiblical view of God ("genie in a bottle obligated to grant your wishes").
2. Sex (immorality, pornography, masturbation).
3. Sleep.
4. Work.
5. Television.
6. Reading.
7. Food.
8. Withdrawing, running away.
9. Clinging to people for comfort.
10. Shopping sprees.
11. Sports.
12. Exercise.
13. Recreation.
14. Hobbies.
15. Ministry as an escape.
16. Being busy at church or volunteer activities.
17. Drugs.
18. Alcohol.

David Powlison
Christian Counseling + Education
Foundation East

Pastor Scott diagrams the release of the emotional pressure in the following way:

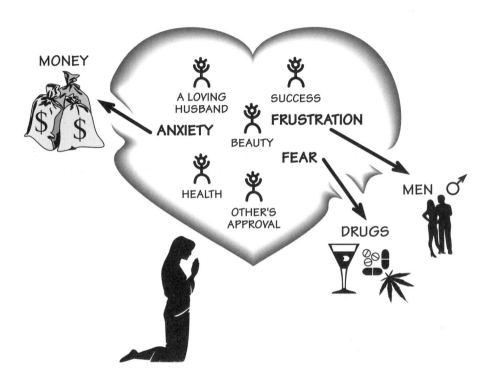

MONEY

A LOVING HUSBAND

ANXIETY

SUCCESS

FRUSTRATION

BEAUTY

FEAR

HEALTH

OTHER'S APPROVAL

DRUGS

MEN

Pursuing a "false savior" only compounds sin and makes matters worse. What may start out as a temporary relief measure may end up enslaving the person and could very well become an idol/lust. Also, there are obvious consequences to seeking such things as food, drugs, or alcohol for relief. Instead of compounding sin, the God of the Bible wants the undivided worship and devotion of your heart. He wants your thoughts, motives, and choices to be focused on glorifying Him. He should be your greatest longing and desire and refuge. Your thoughts, motives, and choices should be set on glorifying Him, not on your idolatrous heart's desire.

Allison's Story

Allison begins to tell her story as big tears well up in her eyes. She says that her husband is the problem as he is "not affectionate, he uses me for sex, and he never tells me that he loves me. He doesn't talk much, and he watches TV all the time. He'll do things for me if I ask him, but *he* should be taking initiative. When I try to talk to him about this, he gets aggravated with me so I just drop the subject. He's a good man, but I don't want to live the rest of my life with a husband who doesn't love me. He doesn't really care. I don't know what to do. I'm miserable."

Allison's story is a common one. Her husband is not a mean, wicked person, but he is reserved and somewhat selfish. He's satisfied with the status quo. Allison is not. She wants to be talked to, cherished, and made to feel special. In Allison's heart-of-hearts she wants romance and sweetness in their marriage relationship. Is that a bad thing? No, not at all. The problem with Allison is that she has *set* her heart on romance and special feelings instead of setting her heart on serving and worshipping the Lord Jesus Christ. As a result, she is frequently disappointed, frustrated, and bitter. The problem is...

Allison's Desire Has Become An Idol / Lust

Allison's deepest heart's desire is for her husband to make her *feel* a certain way. Her desires are not necessarily bad. The problem, however, is when they become more important to her than a pure devotion to the Lord Jesus Christ. Whenever a wife sets her heart on her husband behaving a certain way, she will likely end up disappointed, frustrated, and hurt. A primary clue to recognize that a heart's desire has become an idol (something more important to her than delighting in and serving God), is that the wife is willing to sin in order to attain that desire. Instead of setting her heart on her husband, Allison's deepest desires should be the same as those of the Psalmist in Psalm 119. He *desired*, *sought after*, and *longed after* God with all his heart.

The Psalmist's Heart's Desire
Psalm 119

How blessed are those who...<u>seek</u> Him with all their heart.
(Verse 2, emphasis added)

With *all my heart I have sought Thee*...
(Verse 10, emphasis added)

I shall *delight* in Thy statutes...
(Verse 16, emphasis added)

My soul is crushed with *longing* after Thine ordinances at all times.
(Verse 20, emphasis added)

✸ Thy testimonies also are *my delight*; they are my counselors.
(Verse 24, emphasis added)

Make me walk in the path of Thy commandments, for *I delight* in it.
(Verse 35, emphasis added)

✸ *Incline my heart* to Thy testimonies, and not to dishonest gain (covetousness).
(Verse 36, emphasis added)

Behold *I long for* Thy precepts; revive me through Thy righteousness.
(Verse 40, emphasis added)

And I shall delight in Thy commandments, *which I love*.
(Verse 47, emphasis added)

...*with all my heart* I will observe Thy precepts.
(Verse 69, emphasis added)

...I *delight* in Thy Law.
(Verse 70, emphasis added)

...for Thy Law is *my delight*.
(Verse 77, emphasis added)

If Thy Law had not been *my delight* then I would have perished in my affliction.
(Verse 9, emphasis added)

I am Thine, save me; for _I have sought_ Thy precepts.
(Verse 94, emphasis added)

O how I love Thy Law! It is _my meditation_ both day and night.
(Verse 97, emphasis added)

I have inherited Thy testimonies forever, for they are the _joy of my heart_.
(Verse 111, emphasis added)

My eyes fail _with longing_ for Thy salvation, and for Thy righteous word.
(Verse 123, emphasis added)

Therefore _I love Thy commandments_ above gold, yes, above fine gold.
(Verse 127, emphasis added)

I opened my mouth wide and panted, for _I longed for Thy commandments_.
(Verse 131, emphasis added)

Trouble and anguish have come upon me; yet _Thy commandments are my delight_.
(Verse 143, emphasis added)

I cried with all my heart; answer me, O LORD! I will observe Thy statutes.
(Verse 145, emphasis added)

I rejoice at Thy word, as one who finds great spoil.
(Verse 162, emphasis added)

Those who _love Thy Law_ have great peace, and nothing causes them to stumble.
(Verse 165, emphasis added)

My soul keeps Thy testimonies, and _I love them exceedingly_.
(Verse 167, emphasis added)

<u>I long for Thy salvation</u>, O LORD, and Thy law is my delight.

(Verse 174, emphasis added)

The Psalmist had a deep passionate heart's longing after God — to know Him, to know His Word, and to obey His Word. He also had delight in God's Word calling it " Thy Law," "Thy Precepts," "Thy Statutes," and "Thy Testimonies." What was most important to him was God. The Psalmist wanted what God wanted, no matter what. Likewise, the Christian wife can have that same passionate heart's desire and continual delight in her Lord as she focuses her thoughts on what God is like (especially His goodness) and how He is working in her life to glorify Himself.

God - Honoring Heart's Desires

Where does such a heart come from? It is a grace gift from God to the believer (Jeremiah 31:33; Ezekiel 36:26). Scripture says, **"Delight yourself in the Lord, and He will give you the desires of your heart"** (Psalm 37:4). This means God will put the desires in her heart that He wants to be there. In other words, God places that kind of passion within the deepest longings of a person. The wife's responsibility is to ask God for that passion and then diligently to seek God through His written Word. She also has a responsibility to cultivate a grateful attitude and thankfulness to God regardless of her circumstances (1 Thessalonians 5:18). To cultivate a grateful attitude, she will have to deliberately think grateful thoughts to God even though she may not feel like it. God will do the rest, because it is consistent with His character that He answer such a prayer. **"And this is the confidence which we have before Him, that, if we ask anything according to His will, He hears us. And if we know that He hears us in whatever we ask, we know that we have the requests which we have asked from Him"** (1 John 5:14,15).

How should her desires change? Of what should the new desires consist? What a wife desires is what she spends time thinking about, daydreaming about, planning for, and longing after. She may have her heart *set on...*

Wrong Desires
(If Idolatrous / Lustful)

1. That my husband will be affectionate.

2. That he will anticipate my needs without my asking.
3. That he will give me compliments.
4. That he will make me feel special.
5. That he will not hurt my feelings.
6. That he will talk to me and share his thoughts and feelings.
7. That he will put me first.

On the other hand, a wife should have her heart *set on ...*

Right Desires

1. That I may know God's Word and obey it.
2. That I may delight in Him.
3. That I may seek Him with all my heart.
4. That I may be pleasing to Him regardless of my circumstances.
5. That I may cultivate an attitude of joy and gratitude in what God is doing in my life no matter what my husband does or does not do.
6. That I may have joy in God deciding how my life and circumstances can glorify Him the most, that He can use me for His glory.

What is your heart set on? What is really important to you? What you have your heart set on will make all the difference in the world in your fulfillment and your joy. Ask God to give you new heart's desires. Then proceed to seek after God with the same passion and energy that you are currently expending on idolatrous desires (1 John 2:15-17).

> *If then you have been raised up with Christ, keep seeking the things above, where Christ is, seated at the right hand of God. Set your mind on the things above, not on the things that are on earth. For you have died and your life is hidden with Christ in God. When Christ who is our life, is revealed, then you also will be revealed with Him in glory.*
>
> *Colossians 3:1-4, emphasis added*

Some of the several ways to **"set your mind on the things above"** are as follows:

1. Think about and deliberately delight in the Lord — His works (creation, salvation, personal pruning in your life).

2. Build *contentment* in your life. Frequently thank Him for your circumstances. Think about today and the future in a positive way, look forward to what God is going to do in your life and how He is going to be glorified through you.

3. Pray and ask God to give you new motives for **"it is God who is at work in you, both to will and to work for His good pleasure"** (Philippians 2:13). If you delight in Him, He will give you new desires and motives in your heart. **"Delight yourself in the Lord, and He will give you the desires of your heart"** (Psalm 37:4). This means He will replace your idolatrous desires with the desires He wants you to have.

4. Invest more of your spare time in Scripture, meditate on Scripture, memorize Scripture, and think about Scripture.

5. Make your goal to please the Lord, not personal happiness.

6. Be alert to sinful anger (you'll feel frustrated) and/or anxiety as an indicator that your motive is likely not righteous. As soon as you are aware that you are sinning, confess it to God. Take the time and effort to think a God-honoring thought in place of the idolatrous thought.

Allison was miserable because she was sinning. It was not her circumstances that caused her to sin, it was her idolatrous heart. After counseling, Allison repented. Now it is more likely that her husband will begin to be drawn to her sweetness and he, too, may repent. Even if he does not, Allison will still be serving and worshipping the Lord Jesus Christ, the King on *her* throne, with all her heart.

Chapter Eight

Home
The Wife's Domain

Part One
A Worker at Home

Tracy and Stacy are young wives and mothers. They are both Christians. They are, however, different in some regards. Tracy loves to go places and be busy. She cannot say no. It seems that almost every minute of every day she is committed to being somewhere or doing something. A lot of her time is taken up with church activities. When she is not preparing the Wednesday night supper, she is teaching Sunday School and singing in the choir. She regularly attends two ladies Bible study classes each week. She is a room mother for both of her children's classes, and she volunteers one day a week at the school. There is not one single day that she is at home. Her husband has asked her to slow down, but she contends that, "Everything I'm doing is good and they need help. I'll be selfish if I don't do everything I can."

Stacy, on the other hand, is lazy. She does stay home, but she watches television a lot. She sleeps late and lets the children fend for themselves and catch the school bus. At night, she's not sleepy so she stays up late reading or watching television. She loves to talk on the phone, is always coming up with some sort of project to do but rarely, if ever, follows through. Her husband has asked her to do her work, to get up with the children, and to take care of the family.

Both Tracy and Stacy are Christians and have a desire to please the Lord. Both, however, need to reassess their lifestyles and their biblical responsibilities in the home. A godly wife is organized and works hard to operate her home with the least possible chaos. She also creates an optimistic, joyful atmosphere for her family. God has always intended for the home to be the wife's domain. Unfortunately, this is not a popular topic in our culture, but

God did and still does intend for the wife to be a **"worker at home"** (Titus 2:5). Consider the excellent wife in Proverbs 31:11-13 and observe how many verses pertain to the home.

> *She looks for wool and flax, and works with her hands in delight... She rises also while it is still night, and gives food to her household, and portions to her maidens... She considers a field and buys it, from her earnings she plants a vineyard... her lamp does not go out at night... She stretches out her hands to the distaff, and her hands grasp the spindle... ...all her household are clothed with scarlet... She makes coverings for herself; her clothing is fine linen and purple... She makes linen garments and sells them, and supplies belts to the tradesmen... She looks well to the ways of her house, and does not eat the bread of idleness.*
>
> *Proverbs 31:13, 15-16, 18-19, 21-22, 24, 27*

Out of twenty-two verses, nine refer directly to her work in the home. Her world revolved around her home, and apparently she experienced satisfaction in a job well done. The excellent wife's home-based ministry does not apply just to King Solomon's day, but to our day, as well. The Apostle Paul wrote to Titus about this very issue.

> *Older women (are to) teach what is good...that they may encourage the young women to love their husbands, to love their children, to be sensible, pure, workers at home, kind, being subject to their own husbands...*
>
> *Titus 2:3-5, emphasis added*

What exactly is a "worker at home?" In the Greek, "worker at home" is one word, *oikourgos* which comes from two root words. *Oikos*, which means "a dwelling, a home, or a household" and *ergon* which means "to work or be employed."[10] So, a "worker at home" is someone who guards the dwelling or is a keeper of the household. Common sense would dictate that the younger women, for the most part, would have to be at home to accomplish this objective well.

There is a similar expression to the "worker or keeper at home" in 1 Timothy 5:14. There the instruction is to the younger widows.

> *Therefore, I want the younger widows to get married, bear*
> *children, <u>keep house</u>, and give the enemy no occasion for*
> *reproach; for some have already turned aside to follow*
> *Satan.*
>
> *1 Timothy 5:14-15, emphasis added*

The Greek word for "keep house" is *oikodespoteo*. It means literally to "rule or guide the house."[11] Here the intent of the passage is to keep the widow out of trouble and to preserve her reputation. So, instead of getting into trouble, her job is to run her household in a way that is pleasing to God.

The biblical concept of a "worker at home" is not a popular one today, but I do believe that God intended for the women, especially the younger women, to stay home and do a good job of caring for their homes and for their families. A wife who is gone with too many activities or work does not have the time nor energy to keep her home as it should be kept.

If a wife is working or is thinking of returning to work, she should examine her motives. What is it she really wants? What is her heart set on? Is it to avoid becoming a "non-person?" Is it more material things? Is it wanting to be out from under the demands of child care? Is it to relieve her husband from his responsibility to work? None of these motives are for the glory of God. They are self-serving and sinful. Godly motives would be "learning to be content" (Philippians 4:11), "gratitude to the Lord for what she does have"(1 Thessalonians 5:18), and "whatever you do in thought, word, and deed, do all for the glory of God"(1 Corinthians 10:31). Staying at home and organizing a clean, well run household is a major biblical emphasis in the God-given ministry of the wife.

You may be thinking, "That's all well and good, but what about the couple who is in debt?" A couple who is in so much debt that the wife may have to work should consider making sacrifices in order to live within their budget while systematically working towards debt reduction. In other words, they would work towards her quitting work and staying home. Many times, if a couple did an honest appraisal of the wife's income, and looked at how much they spent on transportation, child care, taxes, clothing, lunches out, dinners out, and increased grocery bills due to buying prepared foods, the couple would likely see that they are actually losing money. How much wiser might it be for her to stay home and care for her family! Even if it means her husband getting an additional temporary part-time job for paying off the debts, he still is likely to have more left over energy than he currently does because his wife would be home helping him by organizing the family's life, clothes, food, etc.

What if a husband instructs a wife to work? Is she to be submissive? Yes, unless the wife can show him that she would be sinning by working. It would be sinful for her to financially support her husband so that he could be irresponsible or lazy. Instead, she should take advantage of the biblical resources God has given to protect her. (See Chapter Fourteen.) It would be wise (although not necessarily a sin) for the wife not to work and place the children in child care if the children are susceptible to repeated illnesses from exposure to the other children in the day care center. Certainly, it is a sin if through surrogate childcare, the children are not being brought up in the **"discipline and instruction of the Lord"** (Ephesians 6:4).

One young mother that I counseled showed her husband that with what she could earn she would ultimately lose money by working. She did, however, come up with a creative alternative and worked two to three mornings a week cleaning houses while the children were at school. Later, she worked part-time for her husband out of their home as he started a new business. This option worked better because she could still run her home and take care of her children.

What if the husband becomes ill or dies? In some cases, I believe her church has a responsibility to help her be able to stay home with her children (see 1 Timothy 5:1-16). If the church will not, she may have to seek employment either from her home or outside of her home. Unless providentially hindered by God, it is the wife's responsibility to be a "worker at home" and maintain an orderly and organized home. It does not mean that her husband and children cannot help, but she sets the tone. Chaos and disorder create tension and contention. It drains her of the needed energy to work on her relationship with her husband and children. A wife should make it her business to find out how to keep an orderly and clean home and stay organized with her grocery shopping and meals. There are many good books on the market or in the library that are very helpful, and if this area in her life is out of control, she should seek the resources to change.

Often tips like "Don't leave the house in the mornings unless the house is straight, the kitchen clean, and the bathrooms given a good 'once over'" can revolutionize housekeeping. Coming home to a clean kitchen surely makes it easier to begin cooking supper! Thinking about supper right after breakfast provides a fighting chance to be organized that night. Perhaps meat may need to come out of the freezer or she may need to *be home* by a certain time to prepare what she has planned. A little bit of prior planning makes all the difference in the world!

A wife should be good and efficient at what she does, not waste time, and not be lazy. If she is lazy, she must repent. A lazy person may always be doing something, but it is frequently self-indulgent activities such as reading, watching television, lying in bed, etc. Any Christian can repent of their laziness and with God's help become self-disciplined. A wife can learn to be a hard worker by **"doing her work *heartily* as unto the Lord"** (Colossians 3:23, emphasis added). Consider the general truths from Proverbs about the lazy person versus the self-disciplined person:

LAZY PERSON	SELF-DISCIPLINED PERSON
How long will you lie down, O sluggard? When will you arise from your sleep? "A little sleep, a little slumber, a little folding of the hands to rest"— And your poverty will come in like a vagabond, and your need like an armed man. *Proverbs 6:9-11*	*Go to the ant, O sluggard, Observe her ways and be wise, which, having no chief, officer or ruler, prepares her food in the summer, and gathers her provision in the harvest.* *Proverbs 6:6-8*
But he who sleeps in harvest is a son who acts shamefully. *Proverbs 10:5b*	*He who gathers in summer is a son who acts wisely...* *Proverbs 10:5a*
A slothful man does not roast his prey... *Proverbs 12:27 a*	*...but the precious possession of a man is diligence.* *Proverbs 12:27b*
He also who is slack in his work is brother to him who destroys. *Proverbs 18:9*	*The ants are not a strong folk, but they prepare their food in the summer . . .* *Proverbs 30:25*
Laziness casts into a deep sleep, and an idle man will suffer hunger. *Proverbs 19:15*	*She rises also while it is still night, And gives food to her household, And portions to her maidens.* *Proverbs 31:15*

I passed by the field of the sluggard, and by the vineyard of the man lacking sense; and behold, it was completely overgrown with thistles, its surface was covered with nettles, and its stone wall was broken down. When I saw, I reflected upon it; I looked, and received instruction. "A little sleep, a little slumber, a little folding of the hands to rest," Then your poverty will come as a robber, and your want like an armed man. *Proverbs 24:30-34*	*She looks well to the ways of her household, and does not eat the bread of idleness.* *Proverbs 31:27*

One word of caution... some wives are perfectionists. As a consequence, they unnecessarily overwork themselves and make everyone else miserable in the process. While it is good to teach the children self-discipline, it is bad to be intolerant, harsh, or anxious if everything is not perfect. Even the best schedule is going to be providentially interrupted on occasion by sickness or a husband or child who just needs to talk. People are more important than clean houses! In this regard, a wife or mother should be **"easy to be entreated"** (James 3:17). A wife who has her *heart set* on having a perfect house probably has an idol in her heart. Instead, she must set her heart on glorifying the Lord Jesus Christ. He, then, will decide how and on what schedule He wants her to glorify Him.

If you are intent on keeping the perfect house or you are lazy and not fulfilling your responsibilities at home, you are sinning. Confess that sin to God and to your family. Ask their forgiveness. Begin to do all your work as **"unto the Lord."** The world makes fun of the "June Cleavers," that devoted television wife and mother from the 1950's. The world is deceived. You can, by God's grace, begin today to be the excellent wife in Proverbs 31:27 as you **"look well to the ways of your household and do not eat the bread of idleness."**

Part Two
Creating a Godly Atmosphere in the Home

"If Mama ain't happy, ain't nobody happy!" We smile as we read the wall plaque in the novelty store. But our smile quickly turns to a frown if truly "Mama ain't happy." This is because the wife and mother in a family often "sets the tone" in the home. The "tone" God wants her to set is one of joy, optimism, and a delight in the Lord and in her family.

The wife and mother who views life as a "cross to bear" influences the others in the home to think the same way. She easily robs everyone else of joy and like the yeast in the bread she bakes, her ungodly attitudes spread to everyone else. If your family were called upon to describe you, what would they say? Would they report that you are a godly, Christian woman who loves life and loves her Lord? Or would they report that you are an unhappy, complaining, bitter woman?

If you do not have the **"joy of the Lord"** (Nehemiah 8:10), you can begin now to cultivate a joyful attitude. Find Scriptures that point to the goodness and the works of God. For example:

> *On the glorious splendor of Thy majesty, and on Thy wonderful works, I will meditate. And men shall speak of the power of Thine awesome acts; and I will tell of Thy greatness. They shall eagerly utter the memory of Thine abundant goodness, and shall shout joyfully of Thy righteousness. The LORD is gracious and merciful; slow to anger and great in lovingkindness. The LORD is good to all, and His mercies are over all His works. All Thy works shall give thanks to Thee, O LORD, and Thy godly ones shall bless Thee.*
>
> *Psalm 145:5-10*

Meditate on them by reading them repeatedly. Think about what the Scriptures mean and how you could actually incorporate them into your life. Meditate on them so often that you commit them to memory. Actually **"sing with thankfulness in your heart to God"** as you go about your daily chores (Colossians 3:16). Memorize favorite hymns and praise songs that are based upon Scripture and sing them over in your mind or aloud. Smile and share with the other family members what wonderful things God has done for you and for them that very day. Get out of the bed in the morning thinking **"This is a day the Lord has made, let *me* rejoice and be glad in it"** (Psalm 118:24, emphasis added).

Don't brood and fret and exaggerate problems in your mind. When there is a problem, be realistic. Face reality, but be righteously optimistic. For example, "This is hard, but God will give me the grace to get through it."

Put your husband and your family and friends first even if it is time for your period. If you require extra rest at certain times of the month, plan it in your day and cheerfully explain what you are doing. However, don't use naps as an excuse to lie around and brood.

Express an interest in the other family members. Take advantage of special moments with your husband to give him an extra hug or a little kiss. As you are mopping the kitchen floor, take time out to hug your child and whisper in his ear, "I love you. You are such a joy to me. God gave you to us!"

Love the Lord your God with all your heart, and love your family almost as much. Be patient and kind and do not be selfish. Create such an atmosphere in your home that your husband as well as other family members will look forward to coming home. They will want to be around you instead of avoid you. If you find yourself struggling emotionally with self-pity, not being appreciated, or being used by your family, become aware of your thoughts. Biblically deal with your husband or children's sins and replace sinful thoughts with biblically optimistic thoughts. Express those to others.

In addition to delighting in the Lord, being biblically optimistic, and loving, don't give in to hysterical fears. The key to overcoming fear is love (1 John 4:18). Fear will certainly ruin a godly atmosphere in any home. If you are fearful, your responsibility is to repent. (For more information on overcoming fear, see Chapter Nineteen.)

A wife who has a gentle and meek spirit from the Lord provides a calming, soothing, and reassuring atmosphere in her home. She trusts God deeply and does not panic at difficult circumstances. She has a quiet confidence that God will **"work all things for good to those who love God..."** (Romans 8:28). Her confidence and faith in God grows daily as she studies the Scriptures because she is **"growing in the grace and knowledge of (her) Lord and Savior Jesus Christ"** (2 Peter 3:18, adaptation added). She has a calming effect on the family, not the effect of alarming and upsetting them. It is reassuring to be around her.

A wife and mother who is gentle and meek is the opposite of one who is harsh and legalistic. A harsh, legalistic wife is just plain mean. As she holds to her rigid standard (which, by the way, may change depending on her mood) she is impossible to be reasoned with and does and says things that are extremely hurtful to the others in the home. She is most likely guilty of pride, anger, and malice. She leaves her family with a bad taste in their mouth about Christianity. Her domain is not a refuge and a comfort, it is a "war zone" for whoever happens to be home. Her home is a gathering place for strife and contention and fear. Her family fears what kind of mood she may be in.

No doubt that the God who said, "**Love is patient, love is kind...**" (1 Corinthians 13:4) wants you, if you have not created a godly atmosphere in your home, to become a woman with a "**meek and quiet spirit**" (1 Peter 3:4). You can begin today to pray for repentance, to search the Scriptures and implement what you learn for yourself, and to joyfully delight in what The Lord Jesus Christ has done for you, is doing now, and will do in the future. The home is the wife's domain. What are you going to make of yours?

Chapter Nine

Love
The Wife's Choice

As a counselor to women I frequently hear wives say, "I don't love my husband any more. We were in love at one time, but all that has changed." After we talk for a while, most of the time what she really means is, "Those romantic feelings I used to have are gone, never to return. Now what I feel is hurt, resentment, frustration, fear, or love for someone else." A wife who no longer loves her husband creates a dilemma because Christians *are* to love others. Loving others is so important the Lord Jesus taught that the second greatest commandment is to **"love your neighbor"** (Matthew 22:39). Husbands are their wives closest neighbors! Thus, loving their husband is something that wives must choose to do!

Since most wives are "in love" with their husbands when they marry, what happens to that love? If you analyze each individual situation biblically, many would fall into one of three categories of sin that will destroy love: selfishness (1 Corinthians 13:5), bitterness (1 Corinthians 13:5), or fear (1 John 4:18). Often, it is a combination. However, no matter what has happened and what she is feeling, God can work in her life and her husband's life and He can give them a love for each other that they never dreamed possible. God's love is righteous and unselfish. When godly love is expressed between husband and wife, they will often experience tender feelings and a "sweetness" between the two of them. Their biblical love can draw them together in a more lasting intimate bond than all of the intensity of their early days of infatuation put together. The bond of love between a husband and wife is special because of the "one flesh" intimacy that God has given them (Genesis 2:24). And even if her husband does not respond in love, it is a choice the wife must make because of Christ's command. There are several ways God shows wives their responsibility to love their husbands.

The Love of a Wife for Her Husband: Biblical Principles

Principle #1
Wives <u>are</u> to love their husbands

In the Bible, all Christians are given a general command to love others.

> *A new commandment I give to you, that you love one another, even as I have loved you, that you also love one another. By this all men will know that you are My disciples, if you have love for one another.*
> *John 13:34-35*

The Greek noun for love here is *agape*, the verb is *agapao*. *Agape* love is an attitude of God towards His Son and the human race in general — it is sacrificial love, giving. Agape is God's will for believers concerning their attitude towards one another as well as an attitude towards all men.[12] In other words, it is a love that gives to others even if nothing is given back in return. The noun form (*agape*) is primarily an attitude. The verb form (*agapao*) is primarily a practical action. Either way, it is a *choice* and we are held responsible.

Just how much of a choice *agapao* love is can be seen in the example of a wife who becomes angry at her husband. As the intensity of her anger increases, she begins to scream and throw things. In the midst of all this mayhem, the doorbell rings. She goes to the door and opens it to find their pastor. She smiles at him and cheerfully says, "Hello." It is not likely that she *felt* kindly disposed. (Note: whether or not she was *truly* showing *agape* love would depend on her outward actions *and* her motives.) However, she (at least outwardly) chose to show love to her Pastor since **"love is kind, and love is not rude"** (1 Corinthians 13:4). The point is that this wife could have chosen to show love to her husband as she did her pastor whether she *felt* like it or not!

Christian love is on a higher plane than human love. It came down from the God of love to us. W. E. Vine describes *agape* love this way:

Christian love...is not an impulse from the feelings, it does not always run with natural inclinations, nor does it spend itself only upon those for whom some affinity is discovered...love seeks the opportunity to do good to all men... a practical love (one person to another).[13]

Wives are to love their husbands because all Christians are to love others. They are also told (indirectly) in Titus 2:3-4 to love their husbands. Here the **"older women... are to... teach what is good, that they may encourage the young women to *love their husbands*"** (Titus 2:3-4, emphasis added). The Greek word here for "love their husbands" is *philandros*. *Philandros* means literally "love of man." It comes from two Greek words *phileo* and *andros*. According to *Vine's Dictionary*,[14] *phileo* "more nearly represents tender affection...kindness." *Andros* is the word for "man or husband," but in this context it is rightly translated "love of husband."

A wife may practically express a "tender affection" to her husband in many ways which we will see later in this chapter. One particular incident that stands out to me personally happened after our daughter gave birth to twin baby girls. I was at Anna's home caring for her. The tiny babies were asleep in their cribs. Sanford, my husband, came by after work to help. The first thing he did was go into the babies room, lean over each crib and study each baby for a long while. I followed him and watched him watching the babies. I thought as tears came to my eyes, "He is so dear to me." Later, I told him what I had been thinking. Right then, I just cherished the moment that God had given us. That was *philandros* love because of the "tender affection" I thought and felt.

There is another (very special) way to describe the love between a husband and wife – they are to become "one flesh" (Genesis 2:24). Although the physical union is involved, it is primarily an emotional bond. "One flesh" love implies and grows out of the revealing of themselves one to the other. Before the fall, Adam and Eve experienced complete openness with each other as they were **"naked and not ashamed"** (Genesis 2:25). Since the fall, husbands and wives have the potential to regain through Christ the openness and oneness that Adam and Eve had before they sinned. Being "one flesh" is a gift from God and is extra special.

Wives are also to love their husbands as their closest neighbor. The Lord Jesus made it clear, **"You shall love your neighbor as yourself"** (Matthew 22:39). Compare how hard you work at showing love to your girl friends with how hard you work at showing love to your husband. He is your closest neighbor. He should come first.

VINE'S DICTIONARY

Not only are wives to love their husbands as their closest neighbor, but also as a manifestation of God's grace. God's grace, in this sense, is a Divine favor bestowed on believers to enable them to live the Christian life. Jerry Bridges further explains God's grace to believers as having:

> ...*two related and complementary meanings. The first is God's unmerited favor to us through Christ whereby salvation and all other blessings are freely given to us. The second is God's Divine assistance to us through the Holy Spirit. Obviously, the second meaning is encompassed in the first, because the aid of the Spirit is one of the "all other blessings" given to us through Christ.*[15]

Even under the most trying circumstances, you can show love to your husband because God's **"grace is sufficient for"** you (2 Corinthians 12:9). God will give you (if you are a Christian) supernatural power (grace) to show love to your husband, if you obey God by thinking loving thoughts and doing loving actions. Remember, at times, you will have to go directly against your feelings.

Godly love is not primarily a feeling, it is a choice. It will help you show love if you will think objectively (biblically), not subjectively (based on feelings). You do that by renewing your mind with Scripture as you study, meditate, memorize, and think Scripture. The Apostle Paul tells us that we are to **"...be transformed by the renewing of our mind"** and **"...to be renewed in the spirit of your mind"** (Romans 12:2 and Ephesians 4:23). This will not just passively happen to you. You must work at it. Here are some examples of unbiblical wrong thoughts compared with biblical right thoughts. One is sinful, the other is loving.

UNBIBLICAL WRONG THOUGHTS	BIBLICAL RIGHT THOUGHTS
"I don't love him any more."	*"I don't feel love right now, but God will change my feelings as I learn to think and act in a loving way."*
"I'm not going to live a lie and be a hypocrite — at least if I leave I'll be honest."	*"I am never being a hypocrite when I obey God in spite of my feelings."*

"He'll never change."	"Only God can know whether he'll ever change or not. I commit to love him whether I feel like it or not."

Wives are to love their husbands. In fact, it is so important that God approaches the subject from several angles: the older women are to teach and encourage the younger women to love their husbands, wives are to love their husbands through revealing themselves to their husband in an intimate, special "one flesh" physical and emotional bond, wives are to love their husbands as their closest neighbor, and love is a manifestation of God's grace. Unfortunately, there are many unbiblical responses that destroy love. One of them is selfishness.

Principle #2
Selfishness Hinders Love

All people are naturally selfish. They come into this world selfish. It does not take a long period of observation to realize that a baby is only concerned about himself. Toddlers look out for themselves as they fight over toys and their mother's attention. Teenagers are renowned for being self-absorbed and putting themselves first. Adults, unfortunately, are not much better. In fact, Americans as a rule yearn to have their needs met, to feel good about themselves, and to protect their rights.

In our hedonistic, narcissistic culture it is revolutionary to hear someone say, "Deny yourself." "Put others first." Yet, this is exactly what God tells us to do. It is a paradox. In other words, we have to do the opposite of what seems logical. Generally speaking, to have the happiness, joy, and fulfillment you desire, you must put yourself aside and place God and others first. In regards to earthly relationships, you must put your husband first. In regards to your relationship with God, set your heart on glorifying God whether you ever have your way or not.

> *Do nothing from selfishness or empty conceit, but with humility of mind let each of you regard one another as more important than himself; do not merely look out for your own personal interests, but also for the interests of others.*
>
> *Philippians 2:3-4*

> *Be devoted to one another in brotherly love; give prefer-*
> *ence to one another in honor...*
>
> *Romans 12:10*

Plainly and simply put, the wife is to show love to her husband by putting her husband first. She should think, **"Love does not seek its own (way)..."** (1 Corinthians 13:5). "I can show love to my husband by giving in to him on this point." As she prefers her husband and "puts on" love (see Principle # 5), she will be loving her husband instead of being selfish.

You may be gasping at this point and thinking, "If I do that, he'll take advantage of me! He's been incredibly selfish for years." You may have a valid concern, but Christians are to counteract evil with blessings and re-proof, not more evil and selfishness. God does want you to deal biblically with your husband's selfishness. (See Chapter Fourteen for the practical details.) However, you are to be unselfish even if he is always selfish. Remember that you do not have to *feel* "led" to be unselfish, you just have to do it.

When circumstances come up and your husband wants to do one thing and you really want to do something else, express your opinion. If he is still wanting very much to have his way, tell yourself, **"'Love does not seek its own way'** (1 Corinthians 13:5). I can show love to him by considering him to be more important than myself and letting him have his way."

As a counselor, I have worked with many women who were selfish. As I questioned them further, I discovered that they usually held some secular beliefs about love. Often those beliefs were "love is romance and feelings," "love is unconditional even to the point of accepting sinful behavior," or "love is having my needs met." Often the ladies I counseled admitted that they daydreamed frequently about other men being romantic towards them. Their beliefs about love were only serving to encourage the lusts of their flesh. Unfortunately, longings of this kind can never be satisfied since our flesh wants more and more and more. We must all be on guard against these thoughts especially since **"in the last days difficult times will come. For men will be lovers of self ... lovers of pleasure rather than lovers of God"** (2 Timothy 3:1-4).

Basing love on romance and feelings is immature at best. It is self-seeking and usually has more to do with physical lust than love. It is also another one of *the* consuming passions of the United States of America. "Feelings" are always somewhat disappointing. It reminds me of being a child and having unrealistic expectations of Christmas and then always being disappointed. Just as I never received the pony I longed for, most women are never recipients of the romance that they desire. It is much better to think, "How can I show love?" (love is patient, etc.) rather than, "How can I get love?" Perhaps you have been influenced by the world's way of thinking about love. If so, adopt the Scriptural view that love is giving and patient, kind, etc. As you change your thinking, your expectations will change.

Another wrong view about love is that love is unconditional. It is common for both husband and wife to believe that they are to be loved unconditionally. To love unconditionally usually means that even if their partner is sinning, they must accept that sinful behavior without trying to restore the sinner to a right relationship with God. It is never loving, however, to ignore recurring sin because **"Love rejoices in the truth, it does not rejoice in unrighteousness"** (1 Corinthians 13:6). (For more information, see Chapter Five.) (Note: Biblical love *is* unconditional in the sense that love constrains them, usually, to stay married and continue to show love even if the other person never changes.) Remember, if you have had wrong thoughts about what real love is, you are responsible before God to change your thinking (Romans 12:2, 2 Corinthians 10:5).

Any time someone has a philosophy of life that is based on "my needs" (self), they are likely to fall into the trap of being unloving, selfish, vain, or proud. Consider the Apostle Paul or the Lord Jesus Christ. Neither one had their "needs" to be loved by everyone met, yet they continued to show love to God and to others. Their focus was on what God wanted them to do. That was their joy and hence their satisfaction. We, on the other hand, are naturally lovers of ourselves. If you are struggling with being unloving and having a wrong view of love, perhaps you are longing for the wrong kind of love. Hence, there is an idol in your heart.

Other typical idols are self-rule, being treated fairly, having your husband's approval and agreement, romance and excitement, and having a Christian husband or a Christian family life. Since we have already covered Idols in the Heart in Chapter 7, I will not recover that material. But if your heart is *set* on the wrong thing, you are guaranteed to be disappointed. Begin by repenting of the idol in your heart.

It will make it easier for you to repent if you stay away from **"provisions of the flesh"** (Romans 13:14). Fleshly provisions are those pleasures in your life that will stir up your sensual self-seeking desires and reinforce an unbiblical world view of love. Provisions of the flesh include soap operas, romance books, masturbation, and daydreaming. You must stop making provision for your flesh if you are going to love your husband instead of yourself.

Selfishness is not the only impediment to biblical love, bitterness also hinders love.

Principle #3
Bitterness Hinders Love

Many of the wives I have counseled have told me they were not bitter, they were, however, "hurt." Gently, I explain to them that the emotions of feeling "hurt" and "resentful" are usually how you feel when you are bitter. There are several common signs of bitterness. As you read through the following list, ask yourself if you are manifesting any of these signs.

Common Signs of Bitterness

1. Gossip and Slander.

In the process of complaining, the wife gossips about him and slanders her husband, thereby defiling others. She has either nothing or very little that is good to say about him.

> *See to it that no one comes short of the grace of God; that no root of bitterness springing up causes trouble, and by it many be defiled ...*
>
> *Hebrews 12:15-17*

2. Ungrateful and Complaining.

The wife is not grateful to her husband. She murmurs to herself and complains to others about him.

> *Do all things without grumbling or disputing...*
>
> *Philippians 2:14*

3. Judges Motives.

Whatever he does is suspect in her eyes. Even if he does something nice, she thinks his motive must be off. For example, "He only did that to look good to his parents." "I know it seemed like a nice gesture, but he didn't really mean it."

> *Therefore do not go on passing judgment before the time, but wait until <u>the Lord comes who will</u> both bring to light the things hidden in the darkness and <u>disclose the motives of men's hearts;</u> and then each man's praise will come to him from God.*
>
> *1 Corinthians 4:5, emphasis added*

4. Self-Centered.

The wife spends a lot of time thinking about herself. She is very self-absorbed. Her focus is fixed on herself and the hurts done against her.

...do not merely look out for your own personal interests...
Philippians 2:4

5. Excessive Sorrow.

Grief and hurt has crowded out any joy, peace, or love that she used to have. It has, in fact, filled up her heart. It may, at times, overwhelm her.

But because I have said these things to you, sorrow has filled your heart.
John 16:6

6. Vengeful.

The wife looks for ways to avoid her husband. Perhaps she leaves when he is home, pouts, or gives him the cold shoulder. She is paying him back for what he has done to her.

Never pay back evil for evil to anyone...Never take your own personal revenge, beloved, but leave room for the wrath of God...
Romans 12:17, 19

7. Brooding.

The wife broods about what her husband has done. She thinks about it often and plays it over and over in her mind.

Love does not take into account a wrong suffered.
1 Corinthians 13:5

8. Loss of Joy.

Lately, the wife has little or no delight in her relationship with the Lord. Because of her sin, instead of God's peace and joy, she is experiencing intense emotional pain and misery.

And I shall delight in Thy commandments which I love.
Psalm 119:47

---

9. A Critical, Judgmental Attitude.

It is difficult for the wife to take her focus off what her husband has done wrong and focus instead on what she is doing wrong.

You hypocrit, first take the log out of your own eye, and then you will see clearly to take the speck out of your brother's eye.

Matthew 7:5

If your husband has hurt you, it will help if you take a moment and think about what percentage of the problems in your marriage are his responsibility and what are your fault. For example, suppose you believe that the problems in your marriage are 40 % your fault and 60% his responsibility. These percentages could be illustrated in the following manner:

GUILT

HIS 60%

YOUR 40%

God wants you to begin biblically dealing with your bitterness by taking 100% responsibility for your 40%.

GUILT

TAKE RESPONSIBILITY FOR YOUR 40%

HIS 60%

YOUR 40%

That's what the Lord Jesus meant when He said, **"Before you can see clearly to take the speck out of your brother's eye,** *first* **take the beam out of your own"** (Matthew 7:5, emphasis added). One way to help identify your sin is to do "The Put Off and Put On" Bible study included in the addendum of this book. Ask a mature Christian to hold you accountable and get to work today on your own sin. God will help you if you ask Him.

> *For we do not have a high priest who cannot sympathize with our weaknesses, but one who has been tempted in all things as we are, yet without sin. Therefore, let us draw near with confidence to the throne of grace, that we may receive mercy and may find grace to help in time of need.*
> *Hebrews 4:15-16, emphasis added*

I would also recommend that you read Psalm 139:23-24 and pray the prayer that is contained therein.

> *Search me, O God, and know my heart; Try me and know*
> *my anxious thoughts; And see if there be any hurtful way*
> *in me, And lead me in the everlasting way.*
> **Psalm 139:23-24**

Taking the "beam out of your eye" is the starting point for repenting of bitterness. The next step is to study the doctrine of bitterness and to respond righteously.

The Doctrine of Bitterness

Bitterness grows when you **"take into account a wrong suffered"** (1 Corinthians 13:5). In other words, as you think about the bad, hurtful things your husband has done, you are feeding bitterness. You may be like so many women who sit and brood over what has happened or lie awake at night replaying it over and over in their minds. God is usually nowhere in the scenario unless you are blaming God or angry at God.

If you dwell on what your husband has done, your emotional pain will greatly intensify, becoming seemingly unbearable at times. You will begin to feel like the prophet Jeremiah. Listen to how Jeremiah expressed his bitterness.

> *And my soul has been rejected from peace; I have forgot-*
> *ten happiness. So I say, "My strength has perished, And*
> *so has my hope from the LORD."*
> **Lamentations 3:17-18**

It is a terribly sad state to have no strength left, no happiness, no peace, and no hope. At this point, your emotional pain intensifies and your sin will likely begin to multiply.

In addition to the bitterness you may begin to think sinful thoughts as well as express anger, wrath, clamor, slander, and possibly malice (Ephesians 4:31). At this point, your husband will be unable to do anything right in your eyes even if he is trying. The author of Hebrews expressed it this way, **"See to it that no one comes short of the grace of God that no root of bitterness springing up causes trouble, and by it many be defiled..."** (Hebrews 12:15). To be sure, if you do not repent your sin will spread to others.

Your bitterness will hurt your children, to say nothing of the sin against God. Instead of hurting others and sinning against God, you can repent. You repent by asking God's forgiveness and your husband's forgiveness (1 John 1:9). God is faithful and He will forgive you and cleanse you from your unrighteousness. As you ask your husband's forgiveness, keep in mind that you are concentrating on taking 100% responsibility for your 40%. We will see later how to respond biblically to his 60%.

Your bitter feelings will improve as you clear your conscience and then begin to make second mile investments. A second mile investment is doing something extra special nice for your husband. It is going above and beyond the call of duty. The Lord Jesus put it this way, **"And whoever shall force you to go one mile, go with him two"** (Matthew 5:41).

Your husband may not deserve a "second mile investment," but you do it anyway. Do something that he would really like, such as prepare his favorite meal or rub his back or buy him a gift and wrap it up in pretty paper. Think about what you would like for him to do for you and then do it for him. Put into practice the exhortation from the Lord Jesus that **"...however you want people to treat you, so treat them"** (Matthew 7:12). It is never easy to go against your feelings and go the "second mile," but it is a necessary step towards overcoming bitter feelings. God will help you as you respond righteously to difficult circumstances.

As you make second mile investments, keep in mind that you are **"not returning evil for evil, but giving a blessing instead"** (1 Peter 3:9). You also are **"not becoming overcome by evil, but overcoming evil with good"** (Romans 12:21). God does want you to fight back, but with "good" and not evil. Do this in a practical way. The more intense your hurt, the greater the need for you to give him **"blessings instead."** Eventually, your emotional pain will abate and in the meantime you will be glorifying God immensely if your motive is to obey and please God.

Confessing bitterness, clearing your conscience, and giving blessings will go a long way, but in addition you must put off the bitterness by putting on kind, tender-hearted, and forgiving thoughts. Carefully read and consider Ephesians 4:31-32.

Let all bitterness and wrath and anger and clamor and slander be put away from you, along with all malice. And be <u>kind to one another, tender-hearted, forgiving each other, just as God</u> in Christ also has forgiven you.
Ephesians 4:31-32, emphasis added

How does a person become kind, tender-hearted, and forgiving? It begins with what they think. Carefully study the following examples:

Bitter Thoughts	Kind, Tender-Hearted, and Forgiving Thoughts
(1) "He doesn't love me. He only loves himself."	(1) "He does not show love as he should but his capacity to love can grow." 〈Colossians 3:14〉
(2) "How dare he come in from work in a bad mood and take it out on me!"	(2) "Perhaps he feels under pressure from work." Ephesians 4:31-32
(3) "I do so much for him and look what I get in return!"	(3) "I wonder if I could do something differently to make it easier for him." Philippians 2:3-4
(4) "He's only thinking of himself."	(4) "Maybe he doesn't feel well today." Colossians 3:12
(5) "He's stupid, see if I ever try to talk to him again!"	(5) "Maybe he misunderstood what I was trying to say." Ephesians 4:1-3
(6) "I can't believe what he decided. How ridiculous!"	(6) "Maybe he has information that I don't have." 1 Corinthians 4:5
(7) "I can't believe what he has done to me!"	(7) "What he has done is difficult but God will give me the grace to get through it." 1 Corinthians 10:13

(8) "I will never forgive him."	*(8) "After all that the Lord has forgiven me, this is the least that I can do."* *Matthew 18:32-33*
(9) "He'll never change."	*(9) "By God's grace, he can change."* *1 Corinthians 6:11*
(10) "This is more than I can bear. There is no hope."	*(10) "There is nothing that has happened that God cannot forgive, that I cannot forgive, and that we can't work through."* *1 John 1:9*
(11) "He did that on purpose to hurt me."	*(11) "Only God can know why he did what he did. It's my responsibility to believe the best."* *1 Corinthians 13:7*
(12) "He should have known better."	*(12) "How could he possibly know? I've never told him. He can't read my mind."* *Ephesians 4:15*
(13) "I'll show him what it's like."	*(13) "I'll give him a blessing instead."* *1 Peter 3:9*
(14) "We never should have gotten married in the first place."	*(14) "He is my husband and I am committed to him no matter what."* *Matthew 19:6*
(15) "God understands that I can't take this."	*(15) "God will give me the wisdom and grace to hang in there."* *James 1:5*

(16) "I prayed about it and have 'peace' about pursuing the divorce."	(16) "It would be nice to have this settled but I am committed to proceeding in the way God has determined." *Colossians 3:2*
(17) "I wish he were dead."	(17) "I pray that God will have mercy on him and he will repent." *2 Peter 3:9*
(18) "I hate him."	(18) "I can show love to him whether I feel like it or not." *1 Corinthians 13:4-7*
(19) "He is repulsive to me. The thought of him touching me is nauseating."	(19) "My husband desiring to have sex with me is a good thing. I can show love to him by concentrating on pleasing him." *1 Corinthians 7:3-4*
(20) "How could God let him do this to me?"	(20) "God has a purpose in all that I am experiencing. He can and will use it for my good and for his Glory." *Romans 8:28-29*

Keep a brief log of your bitter thoughts. Each time you feel hurt or resentful, write down your thoughts word for word. Then take the time to go over each thought and convert it to a kind, tender-hearted, or forgiving thought. Know that you will be showing love to God and to your husband as you take **"each thought captive in obedience to Christ"** (2 Corinthians 10:5). (See also Romans 12:2 and Philippians 4:8). Lastly, destroy your bitter thoughts list so that no one else could possibly be hurt by your wrong thoughts if they happened upon the list.

It is important that you see your bitterness from God's perspective. Often the wives that I counsel are bitter. Each one's bitterness may very well be a more wicked sin than what her husband has done, *especially* if he is repentant and she will not forgive. I often tell my ladies, *"There is nothing that your husband has done that God cannot forgive and you cannot forgive!"* Let me repeat for emphasis, if you are bitter and will not forgive then you are being wicked. We are to forgive as we have been forgiven. Even the most difficult circumstances can be reconciled. Keep in mind that the church members in Corinth were a group of former drunkards, adulterers, homosexuals, fornicators, revilers, etc., yet Paul wrote of them **"such *were* some of you"** (1 Corinthians 6:9-11, emphasis added).

In order to understand how important it is to God that we forgive, consider Matthew 18:22-35. In Matthew 18 Jesus tells the story of the slave who owed so much he could never have repaid his debt. He begged for mercy and received it from his master. The slave, in turn, was owed a small amount of money by a fellow slave. The fellow slave begged for mercy and more time and promised to repay. The slave who was owed the money, however, was hard-hearted and unforgiving and had his fellow slave placed in prison. The master of the first slave found out what had happened and was angry. In Matthew 18: 32-33 he said to his slave, **"You *wicked* slave, I forgave you all that debt because you entreated me. Should you not also have had mercy on your fellow slave, even as I had mercy on you?"** The master then turned his slave over to the torturers. What follows is a solemn warning to us all, **"So shall My heavenly Father also do to you, if each of you does not forgive his brother from your heart" (Matthew 18:35).** If you are bitter, then you are unforgiving. You must repent.

You may be thinking, "How can I forgive him, he keeps on being unfaithful, irresponsible, deceptive, drunk, or out of control?" Realize that God has made many provisions to protect you if this is the case (See Chapter Fourteen). Also, realize that forgiveness and trust are not the same thing. There are some circumstances in which you would be naive to trust your husband. Be careful since **"the naive believes everything"** (Proverbs 14:15). However, you must still forgive and work towards reconciliation. Then as your husband is more and more faithful, your trust in him will increase.

For example, one wife I counseled had a husband who had a violent anger problem. He would go into rages, say mean, cruel things, and hit her. Afterwards, he always apologized. Because this was a recurring pattern of sin in his life, she told him, "I forgive you, but I do not trust you. Therefore, one of us will need to inform the leaders of the church about your problem with this sin of anger. Would you like to do it or shall I?" As he placed himself under the authority of the church, her trust in him gradually increased. It was his responsibility to re-earn her trust. It was her responsibility, though, to repent of her bitterness and to forgive. When a husband will not cooperate with reasonable accountability, then his wife should take advantage of the other avenues to protect her that are explained in chapter fourteen.

Let me summarize this section about bitterness with the following flow chart. Suppose you have been hurt by your husband. And suppose that what he has done is bad but is not biblical grounds for divorce. You may believe that you have done absolutely nothing wrong. The initial hurt that you feel is not necessarily sinful. Anyone would have been hurt by what you have just experienced. What you do next, however, is critical. You can choose to respond to the hurt in humility or in pride. See what happens when you respond humbly as opposed to responding in pride.

Two Different Responses to Being "Hurt"

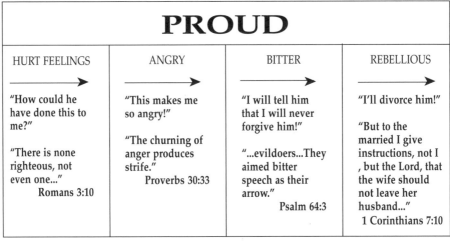

PROUD

HURT FEELINGS	ANGRY	BITTER	REBELLIOUS
"How could he have done this to me?"	"This makes me so angry!"	"I will tell him that I will never forgive him!"	"I'll divorce him!"
"There is none righteous, not even one..." Romans 3:10	"The churning of anger produces strife." Proverbs 30:33	"...evildoers...They aimed bitter speech as their arrow." Psalm 64:3	"But to the married I give instructions, not I , but the Lord, that the wife should not leave her husband..." 1 Corinthians 7:10

HUMBLE

HURT FEELINGS	KIND, TENDERHEARTED, FORGIVING	LOVING	FORGIVING
"Lord, what do You want me to do?"	"I feel badly for him as he is really struggling."	"I will show love to him by not dwelling on what he has done to me."	"I forgive him."
"Have this attitude in yourselves which was also in Christ Jesus... He humbled Himself." Philippians 2:5-8	"...be kind, tender-hearted, and forgiving just as God in Christ has forgiven you." Ephesians 4:31	"Love does not take into account a wrong suffered." 1 Corinthians 13:5	"If your brother sins, rebuke him; and if he repents, forgive him." Luke 17:3-4

Bitterness destroys love. It stirs up overwhelming "hurt" feelings. The sin of bitterness spreads and hurts other people. It is, foremost, a grievous sin against God. The key to repenting of bitterness is to "take every thought captive," replace those bitter thoughts with kind, tender-hearted, and forgiving thoughts, and go the "second mile." Truly, there is nothing that your husband has done that you cannot forgive. If your husband is not trustworthy, he can re-earn your trust. Regardless of whether your husband is a failure before God, you do not have to be. If your heart is hardened and bitter, won't you pray right now and begin the process of repenting? Plan out how you can go the "second mile." Write down your bitter thoughts and replace them with godly thoughts. If you are struggling with forgiving your husband, take a long time and think about all that the Lord has forgiven you. What is your prayer?

Principle #4
Fear Hinders Love

Fear is a common struggle for many wives. One may be afraid that she will not get her own way. Another may live in fear because her husband is angry or an alcoholic, etc. Either way, her feelings of fear will make it very difficult for her to love him. The biblical key to overcoming her fear is to trust God and love her husband. King David wrote a Psalm about trusting God when faced with frightening circumstances:

> *The LORD is my light and my salvation; whom shall I fear? The LORD is the defense of my life; whom shall I dread? When evildoers came upon me to devour my flesh, my adversaries and my enemies, they stumbled and fell. Though a host encamp against me, my heart will not fear; though war arise against me, in spite of this I shall be confident.*
>
> *Psalm 27:1-3*

In addition to trusting God, the wife is specifically told to **"do what is right without being frightened by any fear"** (1 Peter 3:6). As she does what is right, she will be showing love to God by obeying Him and also showing love to her husband. (See also Matthew 22:37-39). Whether your fear is that your husband will die, leave you, or abuse you in some horrible way, the key to overcoming your fear is trusting God and loving your husband. (For more information on overcoming fear see Chapter Nineteen.)

Principle #5
The Wife Is To "Put on" Love

And so, as those who have been chosen of God, holy and beloved, put on a heart of compassion, kindness, humility, gentleness and patience; bearing with one another, and forgiving each other, whoever has a complaint against anyone; just as the Lord forgave you, so also should you. and <u>beyond all these things put on love</u>, which is the perfect bond of unity.

Colossians 3:12-14, emphasis added

Some people seem to be more naturally loving than others. Whether you are one of these people or not, you are told repeatedly in Scripture to **"pursue love"** and **"walk in love."** You do that by being patient, kind, etc. Take a few moments and ponder each of the following practical suggestions about "putting on" love.

Putting on Love

1. "Love is patient."

It is common for a wife to get aggravated when things do not go her way, when something interferes with her plans, or when she does not feel well. However, by an act of her will, she can be patient whether she feels like it or not. It is an active, humble, dependent choice to obey God in this manner. If she does, the Holy Spirit will help her by pouring out a measure of God's grace. One good way to develop the character quality of patience is for her to memorize Scripture and quote it to herself as she begins to *feel* the irritation beginning to build up. For example, **"Be quick to listen, slow to speak, and slow to anger, for the anger of man does not achieve the righteousness of God"** (James 1:19,20). Another example is thanking God for specific irritants since Scripture commands us to **"Be thankful for all things for this is the will of God in Christ Jesus concerning you"** (1 Thessalonians 5:18). Often, simply saying to herself **"love is patient"** helps tremendously when tension is mounting. Feeling impatient or frustrated are the emotions a wife experiences as she thinks sinfully angry or selfish thoughts. She should confess this sin to God while it is at the mental attitude stage before it is outward sin.

2. "Love is kind."

Being kind is a key to creating the proper atmosphere in the home. Kindness is shown in a gentle tone of voice and in kind acts. Kindness draws people to us whereas criticism and harshness push them away. This should not be a surprise as **"it is the kindness of God that leads us to repentance"** (Romans 2:4). The wife should think of ways to express kindness to her husband. For example, her husband gets aggravated with a project he is trying to complete because the instructions are not clear. She could kindly say to him, "I'm sorry that this is so aggravating. Is there anything I can do to make it easier for you?" Speaking in a kind tone of voice and doing kind acts can be done by the grace of God.

3. "Love is not jealous."

Jealousy is fear of being displaced by another person or thing. It may be a valid concern or it may be a **"vain imagination"** (2 Corinthians 10:5, KJV). Either way, it is self-focused and self-concerned. Instead, a wife can show love by being glad for her husband that he can go fishing. Another example of showing love instead of jealousy is being glad for him when he has the opportunity to visit with his family, looking forward to his coming home, and then expressing that gladness to him. A wife who is not jealous shows love to her husband in that he need not dread coming home after working late. Instead of being jealous, she is pleased he is finally home. If she has legitimate concerns of being displaced, she responds in a biblical manner instead of in hysterical fear and jealousy.

4. "Love does not brag."

Love does not boast. The Greek word for "brag" means to "talk conceitedly." Conceit is an "excessive appreciation of one's own worth."[16] Many times wives "boast" about their husbands and their relationships. They try to make things look better than they are. They take their husbands for granted thinking they deserve all the nice things their husbands do for them. There may be an underlying belief that a wife deserves more. Instead, God wants her boasting to be done **"in the Lord"** (2 Corinthians 10:17). Then she will be gratefully giving God the credit instead of boasting about herself or her husband from a heart of pride.

5. "Love is not arrogant."

An arrogant heart is full of self-importance. You will find it difficult to tell an arrogant wife anything. She is opinionated and defensive when disagreed with, reproved, or corrected. Arrogant and "know it all" is how she acts when she is prideful. A wife who is prideful is likely to hurt her husband deeply. Instead of arrogance, a wife should be a humble servant to her husband and to others, listen carefully to his opinion, and consider the possibility that she may be wrong or misinformed. Such responses are one way a wife can show love to her husband.

6. "Love does not act unbecomingly."

A wife acts unbecomingly or rudely when she is disrespectful and not submissive to her husband. When she is disrespectful, she shames her husband. A loving wife acts properly and in a manner that is fitting. She does not respond based on her mood. She is consistent, and her husband can depend on her to respond in love. She has good manners.

7. "Love does not seek its own (way)..."

A lack of love is selfish. Selfishness is a common problem that pastors and marriage counselors encounter. A wife can show love to her husband by giving in to his wishes as long as he is not asking her to sin. She should be more concerned with what she does for him than what he does for her. A stubborn, selfish wife provokes her husband to frustration and discouragement. Instead, she should consider him to be more important than herself (Philippians 2:4) and not seek her own way (1 Corinthians 13:5).

8. "Love is not provoked."

Showing love means that a wife controls herself even under very difficult circumstances. The sad fact is that wives are sometimes irritated and provoked even when the circumstances are not especially difficult. A wife shows love by having the godly character quality of self-control. She realizes that **"no pressure has overtaken [her] but such as is common to man; and God is faithful, who will not allow [her] to be pressured beyond what [she] is able, but with the pressure will provide the way of escape also, that [she] may be able to endure it"** (1 Corinthians 10:13, parenthetical comment added.) Instead of becoming provoked, she responds with patience and kindness.

9. "Love does not take into account a wrong suffered."

A wife shows love by not holding onto her bitterness, by forgiving, by not bringing up the past to her husband, and by not replaying bitter thoughts to herself in her mind. Catching herself and correcting her thoughts are a tremendous way to show love. Rehearsing the offense suffered is unloving as it is **"taking into account a wrong suffered."**

10. "Love does not rejoice in unrighteousness but rejoices in the truth."

A loving wife is one who not only deals properly with the sin in her life, but also does not entice, influence, or provoke her husband to sin. She tells him the truth. One of the by-products of being righteous is that she is, at the same time, showing love. Another way she can show love to her husband is by **"stimulating him to love and good deeds"** through encouraging him and supporting him to be godly and to do godly deeds (Hebrews 10:24).

11. "Love bears all things."

"Bearing all things" includes times when her husband is being selfish or when he is having a tough time at work. She is committed to him, and he knows it. Loving involves sacrifice of self, and it is important to remember that if she must suffer, it should be for **"doing what is right"** (1 Peter 3:17).

12. "Love believes all things."

Biblical love paints the other person in the best possible light. In other words, the wife shows love to her husband by believing the best instead of assuming the worst about what he says or does and his motives. When, at times, the "worst" is a fact, then a wife is to order her life and her goals by faith and not by sight. In other words, no matter what her husband has done, a godly, loving wife trusts in God's sovereign care over her marriage. She knows that God has a purpose in the circumstances for her. She believes, without a doubt, that He *can* **"work all things together for good to those that love Him"** (Romans 8:28).

13. "Love hopes all things."

Every Christian wife's hope is based on Jesus Christ and **"In Him [she] will not be disappointed"** (Romans 10:11). Her hope is a confident expectation, not just wishful thinking. Her hope is rooted in the Eternal King of Glory, the all-powerful Creator of the Universe who will eventually **"bring it to pass"** (1 Thessalonians 5:24). An outgrowth of her hope in God is hope that her husband will become more and more godly if he is a Christian and perhaps be saved if he is not. "All things" (that love hopes) encompasses every aspect of her marriage and her relationship with her husband. She should tell herself things like, "My husband has disappointed me, but God never will. God can use what has happened to put pressure on my husband to repent."

14. "Love endures all things."

This wife sees trials and pressures as coming into her life for a special opportunity to become more like the Lord Jesus. She does not usually enjoy those difficult times, but she does *endure* them with God's help. She shows love like Jesus did when He **"endured the cross, despising the shame"** (Hebrews 12:2). Why did He do it? **"...for the joy that was set before Him"** (Hebrews 12:2). Likewise, a wife can choose to show love to God and to her husband as she righteously endures trials and pressures in her marriage. She can tell herself, "This is especially difficult, but with God's grace I can endure."

Putting on love begins with biblical thoughts and motives then progresses to your actions. Feeling love and warmth towards your husband begins only after you have been thinking and doing the loving actions for a while. Carefully consider the following examples of loving thoughts.

Loving Thoughts

1. "He may not be in a good mood, but I am not going to avoid him because **'love is not rude.'**"

1 Corinthians 13:5

2. "I *can* show love to him by listening in a patient manner because **'love is patient.'**"

1 Corinthians 13:4

3. "Every day that I righteously endure this difficult time, I am showing love to my husband because **'love endures all things.'**"

1 Corinthians 13:7

4. "I am not going to keep thinking about what he did because **'love does not take into account a wrong suffered.'**"

1 Corinthians 13:5

5. "Since I can't prove otherwise, I am going to show love to him by **'believing the best.'**"

1 Corinthians 13:7

6. "I am going to show love to my husband by being glad for him that he is going fishing because **'love is not jealous'** and **'love does not seek its own (way)...'**"

1 Corinthians 13:4-5

Next, I would strongly suggest that you memorize 1 Corinthians 13:4-7. Write out each aspect of love within those Scriptures and think of and write down specific, concrete ways that you can express love to your husband through either your thoughts or your actions. If there is an older, more spiritually mature woman in your church, you might consider asking her to help you with this project. Work on it diligently. Putting on love does not happen automatically. It is the greatest commandment. It should be the character quality on which you work the hardest. Just reading this book will not make you a more loving person. Putting on love will.

Chapter Ten

Respect
The Wife's Reverence

One Sunday morning several years ago my husband walked out of the bathroom ready to go to church. Right away I noticed that his tie and shirt did not match. So I said sarcastically, "You're not going to wear that tie are you?" What followed was a difficult moment because obviously he *was* going to wear it. Finally he replied in a slightly irritated tone, "Yes, what's wrong with it?" So, I proceeded to tell him. Later as I thought about the incident, I realized that my question must have made him feel foolish. If he had answered, "No, I'm not going to wear it," he would have been lying because he already had it on. If he had answered, "Yes, I am going to wear it," it was apparent that I thought he looked ridiculous. There was no gracious way for him to change his tie without looking foolish. As I thought about how I made him feel, I also thought about the Scripture that admonishes a wife to **"see to it that she respect her husband"** (Ephesians 5:33). I know as his **"helper suitable"** (Genesis 2:20) that he needed help, not my sarcastic "put-down." My first responsibility before God in this situation was to be respectful and my second was to make helpful suggestions. This chapter challenges the excellent wife with her biblical responsibility to "reverence" her husband. It includes biblical principles and practical "how to's."

Disrespect to husbands is not something that I originated. It has been a problem since Sister Eve sinned. Scripture contains numerous examples of disrespectful wives including Job's wife and David's wife. Job's wife committed an appalling act of disrespect. Instead of being glad that **"in all of this [tribulation] Job did not sin"** (Job 1:22), Job's wife shook her fist at God and Job when she told Job to **"curse God and die!"** (Job 2:9). About five hundred years later, King David's Wife, Michal, stole from David his joy over the return of the ark of the covenant to Jerusalem. David was thrilled and danced for joy because now God's Temple could be built. Michal saw what he was doing and sarcastically scolded him saying, **"How the King of Israel uncovered himself today...as one of the foolish ones shamelessly**

uncovers himself!" (2 Samuel 6:5, 13-20; Note—David was not naked, but he had removed his royal robes and put on a simple linen ephod which is a priest's garment.)

Scripture not only contains many negative examples of disrespectful women, but fortunately it also contains positive examples of respectful women. For example, Bathsheba showed respect to David when she **"bowed with her face to the ground, and prostrated herself before the king and said, 'May my lord King David live forever'"** (1 Kings 1:31). Queen Esther also approached her husband, King Ahasuerus, in a respectful manner saying, **"...if it please the king...my petition and my request is if I have found favor in the King's sight..."** (Esther 5:4). Christian women today are exhorted by Peter to be like **"the holy women... who hoped in God..."** Peter used as his example Sarah, who later in her life **"obeyed Abraham, calling him lord, ..."** (1 Peter 3:6). Women today would be thought odd if they called their husband "lord," but they can show the same respect and deference through more modern vocabulary and a respectful tone of voice.

Regardless of the era, God says, **"...let the wife see to it that she respect her husband"** (Ephesians 5:33). In order to understand respect better, I have arranged this concept into five biblical principles that explain the wife's respect for her husband. Also I have ended this chapter with an assessment that you can complete for yourself to see just how respectful you really are to your husband.

Respecting Your Husband : Biblical Principles

1. The wife is to respect her husband. Ephesians 5:33

2. The wife is to respect his position. 1 Corinthians 11:3

3. The wife is to act in a respectful manner. Proverbs 31:23

4. The wife is to reprove her husband respectfully. Colossians 4:6

5. The wife who is disrespectful may experience severe consequences. Galatians 6:1

Principle #1
The Wife Is To Respect Her Husband

Respecting your husband is not an option for you if you are going to be in God's will. Ephesians 5:33 straightforwardly states, **"...let the wife see to it that she respect her husband."** The Greek word for respect is *phobeo* which comes from a word that means "to be frightened or to be alarmed." It means "to be in awe of, to revere, to reverence, or to treat as someone special."[17] The Amplified Bible gives us further insight into the meaning of the verse: **"...let the wife see that she respects and reverences her husband — that she notices him, regards him, honors him, prefers him, venerates and esteems him, and that she defers to him, praises him, and loves and admires him exceedingly."** The verb "respect" is in the present tense, middle voice, and subjunctive mood. (Note: A.T. Robertson says the use of the subjunctive here is a "practical imperative" without a principle verb.[18] In other words, for all practical purposes, it is an imperative, a command.) This means that the wife is to continuously choose to respect her husband. But, what if you feel (and possibly rightly so) that your husband's personality (character, talents, abilities, etc.) doesn't deserve your respect? You may ask, "Am I released from God's command?" No, because of...

Principle #2
The Wife Is To Respect His Position

Husbands have been given authority over their families by God. The wife is to respond respectfully to her husband because of his God-given position. The Scriptures make it clear that **"Christ is the head of every man, and the man is the head of a woman, and God is the head of Christ"** (1 Corinthians 11:3). God has appointed positions of authority in the home, church, and state that always require respect from the one under authority (1 Peter 2:17; Hebrews 13:17; Ephesians 5:23). This respect is not only an outward show, but also an inward heart's attitude of obedience to God. The attitude of treating the person with respect applies whether the authority is God over His creatures, parent over child, master over slave, elders over the church, or husband over wife (1 Corinthians 11:3).

You may be smarter, wiser, or more gifted than your husband, but you are still to respect the position God has given him. You are like the soldier who stands at attention, salutes, and says, "Yes, Sir!" to his superior officer.

That high ranking officer may, in fact, be inferior to the soldier in intelligence, professionalism, commitment, character, wisdom, talents, or physical looks, but the soldier is to salute the uniform. The respect is to the position, not necessarily to the personality. It will also help you to remember that you yourself do not have even one favorable attribute or talent that God did not give you.

> *For who regards you as superior? And what do you have*
> *that you did not receive? But if you did receive it, why do*
> *you boast as if you had not received it?*
> *1 Corinthians 4:7*

A godly wife will not only show respect to her husband's position during the difficult times such as his sin or his failure (see principle # 4), but she will also show respect on a daily basis when he is just an everyday, ordinary person. If your husband is in this category (as are most husbands), God wants you to be grateful for him and his ordinary job, looks, not-so-eloquent speaking ability, etc. In fact, God wants you to be **"thankful in all things..."** (1 Thessalonians 5:18). In our soap-opera, TV sitcom world, it's difficult to be satisfied with an everyday, ordinary husband. But if you will set your mind on the things of the Spirit (the things that God desires), you will be grateful for what you have instead of what you do not have (Romans 8:5). When you believe yourself to be deserving of better, you are likely **"...thinking more highly of yourself than you ought to think"** (Romans 12:3) and may be judging your husband by the world's standards instead of God's (1 Samuel 16:7).

Perhaps of all the times when a wife is to respect her husband, the most difficult may be if he is an unbeliever. If your husband is not a Christian, he is still to be respected because of his position. He is your husband and possibly the father of your children, not some "cross you must bear." God wants you to set about evangelizing your husband, but not in the way you might think. Your responsibility is to possibly **"...win him without a word by [your] behavior [as his wife], as (he) observes your chaste and** *respectful behavior"* (adaptation and emphasis added, 1 Peter 3:1-2). He is lost and under the condemnation of God. I cannot think of anything more important than influencing him for Jesus Christ. However, remember that it must be done God's way, not yours. Don't preach to him, instead pray for him, enjoy him, love him, and show him respect. Take care in how you talk to him and about him. God is at work in the world to save sinners. It's critical that you follow God's commands and wait on His perfect timing. (For more information on being married to an unbeliever see Chapter Thirteen, Principle #3 and Chapter Fourteen, Principle #4.)

Principle #3
The Wife Is To Behave In A Respectful Manner

Wives are disrespectful when they make fun of their husbands, cut them down, are sarcastic, impatient, short, or irritated. Disrespect can come in the form of hurtful words or "looks that kill." Most forms of disrespect are sin no matter to whom you are speaking, but as a wife you have a special mandate from God to act in a respectful manner to your husband.

It will help if you remember that acting in a respectful way is one way to show love to your husband since **"love does not act unbecomingly"** (1 Corinthians 13:5). It will also help if you become convinced that you can obey God whether you *feel* like it or not. Hormones, weariness, and even illness are not justification before God to be disrespectful or to sin in any other way. God will never **"...allow you to be tempted beyond what you are able..."** (1 Corinthians 10:13). You can, by the grace of God, get through those difficult times without sinning.

Be especially cautious of your words, tone of voice, and countenance as you speak to your husband. Your words should be wholesome and edifying (see Ephesians 4:29). Your tone of voice should be gentle and calm (see Galatians 5:23). Your countenance (a smile or pleasant expression) should show respect even when you disagree with him or he is obviously sinning. God will help you if you turn to Him. He is the **"help of your countenance, and your God"** (Psalm 42:11).

Probably the most helpful thing you can do is ask your husband to hold you accountable for showing respect to him. If he agrees, he would, then, point out your disrespectful words, tone, or countenance. If your natural tendency is to rebel and perhaps get "out of hand," ask him (before the next incident) that as it occurs to instruct you to take the time to think about how you are acting and pray about it. When you are calmer, then come back and he will discuss it with you. A fool will not listen and might "blow up" at this point. (Proverbs 12:15-16). However, you can choose to be wise and righteous. **"The heart of the righteous ponders how to answer, but the mouth of the wicked pours out evil things"** (Proverbs 15:28). How willing you are to let your husband help you in this way will reflect your level of maturity and commitment to the Lord Jesus Christ. Submitting to accountability may occasionally be embarrassing or even humiliating. But, do not forget that God gives grace to the humble!

Let me conclude this principle with an example. Suppose it is almost time for a wife's period. She's feeling very tense and nervous. It is Saturday morning. They are having company that evening and she is cleaning the house. She would like help with cleaning the house, but her husband is happily watching a golf match on television. She snaps at him in an angry, ugly tone, "*Why* don't you help me instead of just sitting there watching TV? It must be nice to do whatever you want! I can't believe you're not more thoughtful than this!" She has just been rude, unloving, and blatantly disrespectful. She has sinned against God and her husband. Instead, she could have calmly and gently said, "Honey, I'm having a hard time this morning because it is almost time for my period and I have so much to do to get ready for our company. I know that you are enjoying the golf game, but would you help me finish cleaning up? You may want to video tape the game and watch it later." It is easy to see how **"sweetness of speech increases persuasiveness"** (Proverbs 16:21). He will be much more likely to graciously help her if she asks him in a respectful tone and with respectful words. If he refuses to help her, she may perceive that he is being selfish or lazy. Then, perhaps, a respectful biblical reproof is in order.

Principle #4
The Wife Is To Reprove Her Husband Respectfully

Every Christian is to take *great care* while administering a reproof. A reproof is when you tell someone what he is doing wrong. Your motive should be to restore him to a right relationship with God. Reproofs are to be gentle, done while **"looking to yourself lest you too be tempted,"** and done privately if possible. (See Galatians 6:1 and Matthew 18:15.) If that much care is to be taken from one Christian to another, how much more care should be taken from a wife to her husband! If your husband is sinning, think about how you could show love to him by reproving him (Proverbs 27:5). After all, **"Love is not provoked, does not take into account a wrong suffered, (and) does not rejoice in unrighteousness, but rejoices with the truth..."** (1 Corinthians 13:5-6).

In addition to showing love, your respectful reproof is a way to **"...overcome evil with good"** (Romans 12:21). You will be retaliating with good instead of evil. God promises that He will use your "good" response to **"heap burning coals upon his head"** (Romans 12:20). In other words, God will likely put additional pressure on your husband to repent because of your righteous, respectful reproof.

Your husband will be much more likely to receive and at least consider your reproof if it is done respectfully. If you are disrespectful, he will almost certainly react to your attitude rather than the real issue. In order to give a respectful reproof, it is important that you think objectively about what has happened instead of subjectively. That means instead of self-focused thinking such as, "How could he do this to me?" think, "How does God want me to respond to help my husband change?" That way your emotions will not overwhelm you as you look at your husband's sin objectively as sin against God instead of dwelling on the personal hurts. (Note: if you would like more detailed information on giving reproofs see Chapter Five.)

As a wife, you are to respect your husband even when he sins and even when he is a failure. If your husband loses his job, is demoted or passed over for promotion, his business fails, or he is a failure in some other way, he may deserve your wise reproof. As important as a biblical reproof may be, your compassion and kindness are more important. Put yourself in his place and imagine how he must feel. If you become hysterical, lash out at him, and say cruel things, it will hurt him deeply and not be honoring to God. Instead, expressions like "I know this is hard, but somehow we'll get through it with the Lord's help," or "I'm sorry that you're having to go through this," or "we will recover financially and we can learn from this. God can use even this for our good" will go a long way towards helping him begin to repent and to humble himself, if necessary, before God and others. He may eventually need your gentle, biblical reproof, but your merciful and respectful heart will likely be the catalyst towards restoring him to a right relationship with God. Follow God's example:

> *But love your enemies, and do good, and lend, expecting nothing in return; and your reward will be great, and you will be sons of the Most High; for He Himself is kind to ungrateful and evil men. Be merciful, just as your Father is merciful.*
>
> *Luke 6:35, emphasis added*

> *The merciful man does himself good, But the cruel man does himself harm.*
>
> *Proverbs 11:17*

> *Blessed are the merciful, for they shall receive mercy.*
>
> *Matthew 5:7*

Speaking kind, edifying words in a gentle tone of voice is a righteous way to show respect and love to your husband if he has sinned or failed in some area. How wonderful that God can and will use your kindness to show Himself kind and glorify His holy name! If you are unkind and disrespectful, God can and will most likely put pressure on you to repent. If you do not, the consequences may be severe.

Principle #5
The Wife Who Is Disrespectful May Experience Severe Consequences

If you are disrespectful to your husband, the most likely consequence is that your husband may rebuke you. He, too, has a responsibility before God to reprove you when you are sinning (Galatians 6:1). In addition to reproving you, he may *feel* hurt, lose motivation to be your spiritual leader, allow himself to be paralyzed from taking responsibility as the leader of the family, and/or experience embarrassment and humiliation. Scripture describes how he feels when you are disrespectful: **"a wife who *shames* him is as rottenness to his bones"** (Proverbs 12:4, emphasis added).

In addition to feeling hurt, he may react sinfully by pouting, becoming embittered, angry, abusive, or defensive. What he would be doing is **"returning evil for evil"** (1 Peter 3:9). Even more grievous than receiving the brunt of his sin, your sin of disrespect tarnishes the reputation of the Lord Jesus Christ since you are to respond to your husband, **"...as is fitting in the Lord"** (Colossians 3:18). Anything other than a gentle and respectful attitude is not fitting or proper before God.

Wives are not the only ones instructed to respect their husbands. Children are told to honor their fathers (Ephesians 6:2-3). If you are disrespectful to your husband, your children will likely acquire the same attitude. It will be much more difficult for them to honor their father if you are belittling him and speaking to him in a harsh, sarcastic tone of voice. Your sin could very well make the children feel insecure or upset, think of their father in a disrespectful way, or even openly respond to him in the same manner as you have responded. If you do that, you are making it very hard for your children to honor their father as they should.

Now that we have covered the biblical principles of wives being respectful to their husbands, take a moment to make an assessment of how well you do in this regard. Take the following test and place a check mark beside the ways that you know you are guilty of disrespect. If there is any question, ask your husband what he thinks.

Respecting Your Husband...
A Self-Assessment

_____ *Not usually* 1. Do you speak to your husband in a condescending, "put down" manner?
    For example:
        "What's the matter with *you*?"
        "Anybody could have done better than you did."
        "My Dad would have never done that."
        "Can't you do anything right?"
        "I should have known better than to depend on you."
        "Don't be stupid."
        "What you just said is ridiculous."
        "You old fool!"
        "You're too slow, I'll do it myself."

It is better to live in a desert land, than with a contentious and vexing woman.

Proverbs 21:19

_____ *yes* 2. Do you treat your husband in private as respectfully as you do your pastor, your neighbor, or your friends in public?

Honor all men, love the brotherhood, fear God, honor the king.

1 Peter 2:17

(If "honor all men" is how you are to treat others, how much more should you show respect to your husband?)

_____ 3. Does your countenance show your disrespect by angry looks, looks of disgust, crossed arms, etc.?

Then the LORD said to Cain, "Why are you angry? And why has your countenance fallen? "If you do well, will not your countenance be lifted up? And if you do not do well, <u>sin is crouching at the door; and its desire is for you,</u> but you must master it."

Genesis 4:6-7

_____ 4. Do you talk for your husband or interrupt him?

Love is patient...does not act unbecomingly, it does not seek its own (way)...

1 Corinthians 13:4-5

_____ 5. Do you try to intimidate or bully your husband by making threats, verbally attacking him, crying, or in some other way manipulating him to have your way?

The wise woman builds her house, but the foolish tears it down with her own hands.

Proverbs 14:1

_____ 6. Do you bring up his shortcomings to others?

Her husband is known in the gates...

Proverbs 31:23

_____ 7. Do you inappropriately contradict him in front of others?

She does him good and not evil all the days of her life.

Proverbs 31:12

_____ 8. Do you compare him unfavorably with other men?

...for I have learned to be content in whatever circumstances I am.

Philippians 4:11

Not always

9. Do you listen carefully to your husband's opinion, trying to understand him?

Let everyone be quick to hear, slow to speak...
James 1:19

10. Do you respect his position in the home so much that he can depend on you to do as he asks even when he is not home?

The heart of her husband trusts in her, and he will have no lack of gain.
Proverbs 31:11

11. Do you respect his requests by trying to do as he asks, even if it doesn't seem important to you?

For in this way in former times the holy women also, who hoped in God, used to adorn themselves, being submissive to their own husbands.
1 Peter 3:5

12. Would your husband say that you have a meek and a quiet spirit? If you do, it will be apparent in how you treat him.

And let not your adornment be merely external braiding the hair, and wearing gold jewelry, or putting on dresses; but let it be the hidden person of the heart, with the imperishable quality of a gentle and quiet spirit, which is precious in the sight of God.
1 Peter 3:3-4

13. Are you obeying God by being respectful to your husband?

...let the wife see to it that she respect her husband.
Ephesians 5:33

If you have checked any of the above questions, then you are not as respectful to your husband as God would have you be. Confess it to God as sin, realizing He will be **"faithful and just to forgive..."** (1 John 1:9) and ask your husband's forgiveness. Be clear about what you have done wrong. Ask your husband to hold you accountable and to tell you when he perceives that you are being disrespectful.

Respecting authority is practically a lost art, but as a Christian wife, with God's enabling grace, you can cultivate a respectful attitude. Circumstances come and go, husbands succeed and fail, some merit respect and others do not, but whatever your situation, you can by an act of your will show biblical respect to your husband and show love to God in the process. It is important to God. Treating your husband with respect is not something that your husband must first earn, it is something that you choose to show him. It is an underlying heart's attitude that is to be prevalent regardless of your circumstances and in spite of your feelings. How hard are you willing to work at it?

Chapter Eleven

Intimacy
The Wife's Response

Two days before my daughter's wedding, one of her friends came over to our home to manicure Anna's fingernails. Her friend had been married for only a short time. As they talked and laughed and whispered together, Anna turned to me and said, "Mom, come talk to us." Sensing that something was "up," I stopped folding clothes and joined them. I said, "What do you want to talk about?" Neither one would tell me. Anna kept saying, "Oh, you know." At first, I didn't know, but I finally guessed. The subject was sex. So I asked, "What do you want to know?" They both said, "We want some tips." We talked and I gave them some "tips." Later as I reflected on the conversation, I thought how special that they came to me and we three Christians could sit there and have a conversation about sex that was honoring to the Lord.

The sexual bond between husband and wife is a gift from God for the enjoyment of physical intimacy and the procreation of life. All that God created is good, and physical intimacy between husband and wife is no exception. It is the world that has twisted and perverted what God intended to be holy and righteous. Christian husbands and wives possess the potential to have sexual relations and in the process remain pure in their thoughts, actions, and motives. To understand physical intimacy as God intended, we have to consider God's original intent.

God designed sex in marriage for physical intimacy and the procreation of life. "Procreation is the high privilege and responsibility God has given man to bring forth life. The conception of a child is a cooperative act between God and man to co-create and bring eternal beings into existence."[19] God said to Adam and Eve, **"Be fruitful and multiply, fill the earth and subdue it"** (Genesis 1:28). Again after the flood, **"...God blessed Noah and his sons and said to them, 'Be fruitful and multiply, and fill the earth....Populate the earth abundantly and multiply in it'"** (Genesis 9:1,7).

In addition to procreation, God gave man physical intimacy to enhance closeness and oneness within marriage. The Bible describes the union of man and woman in marriage as **"one flesh"** (Genesis 2:24). **"For this cause a man shall leave his father and his mother, and shall cleave to his wife; and they shall become one flesh"** (Genesis 2:24). "God gives the responsibility for the unity of marriage to the man. This command is repeated twice more in Matthew 19:5 and Ephesians 5:31. In both the Old Testament and the New Testament the words used for **'one flesh'** most commonly means the physical body of the man and woman (Hebrew *basar*, and Greek *sarx*.) **'Cleave'** in Hebrew is *dabaq*, and in Greek is *proskallao*. Both words mean 'to glue together, to stick to, to be closely joined.'"[20]

The physical union of husband and wife is designed by God to meet a God-given desire for companionship, to protect the husband and wife from temptation, and for the mutual giving and receiving of great pleasure and joy between the husband and the wife. Companionship is strengthened by the private, intimate, physical bond of a married couple. The Bible often speaks of the sexual union of a man and woman as "knowing" each other (see Genesis 4:1, Luke 1:34). Companionship through sexual intimacy is reserved for husband and wife and is designed to protect the husband and wife from temptation.

"A proper and healthy physical relationship between a man and woman in marriage protects either partner from the danger of temptation to adultery."[21]

> *But because of immoralities, let each man have his own wife, and let each woman have her own husband. Let the husband fulfill his duty to his wife, and likewise also the wife to her husband. The wife does not have authority over her own body, but the husband does; and likewise also the husband does not have authority over his own body, but the wife does. Stop depriving one another, except by agreement for a time that you may devote yourselves to prayer, and come together again lest Satan tempt you because of your lack of self-control. But if they do not have self-control, let them marry; for it is better to marry than to burn.*
>
> *1 Corinthians 7:2-5,9*

In addition to meeting a need for companionship and protecting the husband and wife from temptation, sexual intimacy is also designed for the mutual giving and receiving of great pleasure and joy between husband and wife. "There is great pleasure and joy in the act of each partner properly giving themselves to one another in a sexual relationship."[22] Solomon wrote, **"And rejoice in the wife of your youth...Be exhilarated always with her love"** (Proverbs 5:18-19). God intended for sex to be pleasurable, to enhance drawing the husband and wife into a deeply intimate bond, and for the procreation of children. God gave man these physical desires so that His plan could be carried out.

Men and women both have sexual desires. However, since the man's desires tend to be stronger, it may be difficult for men to think about anything other than sex when they experience physical longing. So, God instructed the wife to meet her husband's physical needs. Wives also experience physical longing. So God instructed the husband to meet his wife's physical needs. Otherwise, both husband and wife may be tempted to have immoral thoughts and actions. In fact, the husband should be *so* satisfied, that even if another woman entices him, he won't be tempted. Solomon expressed it to husbands this way:

> *Let your fountain be blessed, And rejoice in the wife of your youth. As a loving hind and a graceful doe, <u>Let her breasts satisfy you at all times</u>; Be exhilarated always with her love.*
> *Proverbs 5:18-19, emphasis added*

The word "satisfy" means to be "satiated." In other words, the husband is so satisfied with her love that no one else would even get a second glance from him. It would be like eating and eating and eating until you were stuffed. If someone then offered you your favorite dessert, you would not even be tempted. Likewise, the husband is to be "satiated" with his wife's love.

As I mentioned earlier, husbands and wives are to fulfill God's command to respond to each other's physical desires. In regard to the physical union with her husband, a wife does not have **"authority over her own body"**, but her husband does. In the same way, the husband does not have **"authority over his own body"**, but his wife does. **"Not having authority over their own bodies"** means that neither one have the option to refuse the other unless he or she is providentially hindered or the couple had agreed to temporarily refrain from sex because of devoting themselves to prayer.

Because responding to her husband physically is a command from God, when the wife obeys she is showing love to God as well as love to her husband by not defrauding him. What if her husband desires sex at a time that is inconvenient for her? If possible, the wife should arrange her schedule for them to have a time together so that he knows that fulfilling his desires is important to her. Sometimes, it may be possible to rearrange her schedule by putting off cleaning the house or by telling her friend she will call her back later.

If it is virtually impossible at that moment, the wife should give him a rain-check for a specific time in the future. Then, when she fulfills her promise, she should make it worth his wait! When a wife does not have sex with her husband and she knows that he has that desire, she must ask herself if she is being selfish and putting herself first. If so, she is defrauding him. "Well," you might ask, "what if she is not in 'the mood'?"

One of the best ways for a wife to get in "the mood" and enjoy having sex with her husband is for her to *concentrate on pleasing him.* To not have sex with her life partner makes it easier for him to think and feel as if she does not love him, or that she is not willing to meet his needs. He may end up physically frustrated, irritated, and tempted.

A wife should not only concentrate on pleasing her husband, but should also remember that her pleasure enhances his pleasure. As she concentrates on pleasing him, she is much more likely to become more and more interested in the process for herself. Therefore, it is important that the wife tell her husband what is pleasurable for her.

Some wives believe that their husbands know everything about sex, and they (the wives) should not have to tell them anything. That's not true. Only the wife can know for herself what is pleasurable for her. She should talk to him, be specific, and help him to be a good lover to her. She should lovingly take his hand and guide him to the parts of her body that she would like for him to caress. If he is too rough, she should guide his hand and gently show him what she would like. She should never assume that he automatically knows and is just uncaring or insensitive. Doctor Wayne Mack gives this illustration, "My wife has been scratching my back for years, and she has yet to hit the right spot the first time!" So it is with the act of sex. Even if a husband is sophisticated in the anatomy and physiology of a female, he will still need to be lovingly shown just the "right spot." It is her responsibility to teach him.

If the wife is not obtaining satisfactory sexual pleasure, then she and her husband should purchase or borrow one of the very fine Christian books on sex and become informed. One book that is especially well written and informative is Doctor Ed Wheat's book *Intended For Pleasure.*[23] This book is so practical that physician Dr. Bob Smith from Faith Baptist Counseling Ministries in Lafayette, Indiana, recommends to newly-weds they carry the book with them on their honeymoon. (Dr. Smith has written a review of *Intended for Pleasure* in *The Journal of Pastoral Practice.*)[24] During the honeymoon, they are to take turns reading it out loud to each other and experimenting and exploring each other's body. That way, the couple will become accustomed to talking with each other about their sexual relationship and overcome any potential embarrassment. Doctor Smith's idea is also a good one for couples who are already married and would like to improve their physical intimacy. Sexual relations between a husband and wife should not be a chore, but a pleasure that is enjoyed by both and anticipated by both.

Scripture teaches much on the subject of sexual relations. Consider each of the following biblical principles. They have been adapted for use in this book from Doctor Jay Adams' material in *The Christian Counselors Manual*.[25]

Principle #1
Sex Within Marriage Is Holy And Good

Let the marriage be held in honor among all, and let the marriage bed be undefiled...

Hebrews 13:4

And God saw all that He had made, and behold, it was very good.

Genesis 1:31

An "undefiled marriage bed" means the couple has sexual relations and neither one is unfaithful to the other nor impure in their thoughts or actions. A wife having undefiled sex with her husband is in no way sinful or dirty. She should have a godly attitude realizing that physical intimacy with her husband is not an unholy or less holy act than praying or singing in the choir. As long as her thoughts and motives and actions are pure, she is pleasing to God and God views what she is doing as good.

Principle #2
Pleasure Is Assured And Is Not Sinful

I am my beloved's, and his desire is for me. 'Come, my beloved, let us go out into the country, let us spend the night in the villages. Let us rise early and go to the vine-

yards; let us see whether the vine has budded and its blossoms have opened, and whether the pomegranates have bloomed. There I will give you my love.'
                                                    Song of Solomon 7:10-12

Pleasure resulting from physical intimacy between husband and wife is assumed by Scripture. It should be fun. There will, of course, be times when for various reasons, the sex act may not be at the same level of intensity as other times. However, it should still be pleasurable and a sweet time between each married couple. I know of one husband who prays with his wife before they "make love." They ask God to bless their time together, and they say that God always does. Generally both husband and wife should come to a climax, but if one or the other is too tired or is providentially hindered in some way (such as the wife's period or pregnancy) they can still express love to the other if not through vaginal intercourse through manual stimulation.

Principle #3
The Wife Should Be "Other-Oriented" And Not "Self-Oriented"

I was asleep, but my heart was awake. A voice! My beloved was knocking: 'Open to me, my sister, my darling, my dove, my perfect one! For my head is drenched with dew, my locks with the damp of the night.' "I have taken off my dress, how can I put it on again? I have washed my feet, how can I dirty them again? "My beloved extended his hand through the opening, and my feelings were aroused for him. I arose to open to my beloved...
                                                    Song of Solomon 5:2-5

If a wife is thinking, "How can I give pleasure to my husband?" she will be showing love. In the process of giving pleasure to her husband, the wife is likely to begin to experience more pleasure than she originally thought possible. This is normal as it generally takes a woman longer to become sexually aroused. In being "other-oriented," a wife should think about her husband and his attributes that draw her to him. She should compliment him freely on qualities she admires. Unfortunately, in our society it is often easy for wives to overlook this principle simply due to exhaustion.

Sometimes it is difficult for young mothers with small children to have any energy left over at the end of the day. Still, the busy mother should plan ahead in her day or week for a special time with her husband. She may be busy with the children, but she can *think* about her husband and anticipate being with him. She will also need to tell him so he can plan, too. Saving time and energy for him will be well worth the effort. This tip is a primary way that even a busy mother can be "other oriented."

Another way a wife can be "other-oriented" is to seek her husband to satisfy her sexual desires rather than seeking sexual release through masturbation which is sinful and selfish. Remember that he does not have authority over his body to refuse her! Sometimes a wife is hesitant to approach her husband and she is hurt because he does not seem to be interested in her. Rather than assume that he is trying to hurt her or does not love her or is not attracted to her physically, she should openly talk with him and make overtures to him. Then if he does not respond, he may be sinning. (See Chapter Fourteen for how to deal with a husband's sin.) If he does respond to her overtures even though he would rather be doing something else, he will have the joy of knowing that he is **"suffering for righteousness sake"**! The Bible is clear that both husband and wife are to be "other-oriented" and not "self-oriented."

Principle #4
Sexual Relations Should Be Regular And Continuous

Let her breasts satisfy you at all times...

Proverbs 5:19

There are no certain number of times per week, but it should be often enough that neither one is experiencing frustration and temptation. Sometimes couples fall into a habit of not having sex or of rarely having sex. They stay busy and tired and end up living together more like brother and sister than husband and wife. Sexual intimacy, however, should be a regular and continuous part of their relationship.

Principle #5
The Wife Should Never Bargain With Her Husband In Return For Her Favors

Do nothing from selfishness or empty conceit, but with humility of mind let each of you regard one another as more important than himself; do not merely look out for your own personal interests, but also for the interests of others.

Philippians 2:3-4

Bargaining with her husband in return for her "favors" is selfish. Such a wife has an unrighteous motive. Instead of self serving she should be "husband serving." A wife is being very selfish when she bargains with her favors and is treating him more like a child than a husband by trying to manipulate him. The wife's motive *should not* be what she can get from her husband. It *should* be for the glory of God.

Principle #6
Sex Relations Are To Be Equal And Reciprocal

Let the husband fulfill his duty to his wife, and likewise also the wife to her husband. The wife does not have authority over her own body, but the husband does; and likewise also the husband does not have authority over his own body, but the wife does. Stop depriving one another, except by agreement for a time that you may devote yourselves to prayer, and come together again lest Satan tempt you because of your lack of self-control.

1 Corinthians 7:3-5

Equal and reciprocal sex relations means either the wife or the husband may and should initiate sex. Either should feel free to do so as long as they are being reasonable and considerate of the other person. Anything goes as long as it is mutually agreeable, pleasurable, and not offensive to the partner. Exceptions to this would include anything that is sinful such as, sodomy (anal penetration), watching pornography, and sharing sexual fantasies about other people (Galatians 5:19). Having sex is proper any time of day or night and does not have to be restricted to just bedtime. It is perfectly acceptable and sometimes preferable for the husband or the wife to bring their partner to sexual climax by manual stimulation and/or penetration. Their sexual relations are to be equal and reciprocal.

To summarize this chapter, remember the wife has several biblical obligations to her husband regarding their physical intimacy. She is to satisfy him completely if at all possible. She is to go to him to meet her own needs in this area, realizing that she has authority over his body. She is to initiate sex sometimes and plan ahead, anticipating their time together rather than dreading it. She is not to participate in any sinful practices such as masturbation, pornography, anal sex, or sexual fantasies about other men. She is to have a pure motive before God and view sex as a good and holy act that God declares is **"good"**.

If you have not been thinking about sex or participating in sex with your husband in a God-honoring way, you must repent. Right now, you may bow your head and confess your sin to God. If you ask, God will be faithful to forgive and cleanse you from all unrighteousness. Then you must do what James suggested to show your faith by your works (James 2:18). Plan times for physical intimacy with your husband, give yourself to him, anticipate being with him, and look forward to the times when you can be together. Be a loving wife, warm and responsive. If you are not in the mood, concentrate on pleasing your husband. Your mood will likely improve. Don't just glorify God on Sunday morning, but also in the intimacy of your marriage bed.

In this chapter, I've just shared with you some of the same "tips" I told Anna and her friend. God is good and sex within marriage is good. Won't you view it His way and respond to your husband unselfishly in love?

Chapter Twelve

Submission
The Wife's Joy

A teacher of second and third graders in a suburban Atlanta church heard the girls talking excitedly among themselves as she entered the classroom. The teacher asked them, "Girls, what are you talking about?" One little girl, speaking for the group, stepped forward and said, "We can't wait until we're seventeen years old!" "Why?," their teacher asked, thinking the little girl would answer that they could date or wear make up. Instead, she announced, "Because when we are seventeen, no one will tell us what to do!" After sitting down and gathering them together, the teacher (holding back her amusement) explained, "I'm afraid I have some bad news for you. I'm almost forty years old and people are still telling me what to do!" She went on to explain that this is not really a bad thing, but a good thing. It is part of God's plan for every person. What those precious little girls had to learn is that God wants everyone to live under authority. What I want *you* to learn in this chapter is how God wants you to "walk with Him" in *joyful* biblical submission to your husband.

God's Orderly World

God has created an orderly world. To maintain that order, He has appointed three institutions with their own spheres of authority: the family, the church, and the state. God planned it this way so that people could live in harmony together and be protected. For example, God intends parents to protect their children (Ephesians 6:1-4), elders to protect church members (Hebrews 13:17), and the government to protect its citizens (Romans 13:1-2). Within the family, God has given the husband authority over the wife for her protection (Ephesians 5:28-29). In fact, submission to her husband is the *heart of God* for the Christian wife. It is so important to God that He made submission to her husband a manifestation of **"walking with the Lord," "being in the will of God,"** and **"being filled with the Holy Spirit"** (Ephesians 5:15-18).

> *Therefore, be careful <u>how you walk</u> ... understand what the <u>will of the Lord is</u>... <u>be filled with the Spirit</u>... speaking to one another in psalms and hymns and spiritual songs... always giving thanks for all things in the name of our Lord Jesus Christ... be subject to one another in the fear of Christ... wives be subject to your own husbands...*
> *Ephesians 5:15-22, emphasis added*

Many times a wife may fail to see clearly the importance of her submission because she is so focused on what her husband is doing wrong. Instead, she must learn to...

Focus On Her Responsibility

Because husbands are also sinners, they will, at times, be guilty of sinning against their wives. If a wife's primary concern is what her husband should do, she will likely miss what God wants her to understand and do. The wife must focus on her THREE MAIN GOD-GIVEN BASIC RESPONSIBILITIES towards her husband: to love him, to respect him, and to submit to him. Her "good works" are not dependent on what her husband does, but on her obedience to God in these three areas.

When a husband has hurt his wife deeply by sinning against her, she can easily get caught up in thinking thoughts that help her to overlook or justify her own sinful behavior such as:

"If only he would do what he is supposed to do."

"If only he weren't so selfish then I could be a better wife."

"I can never be what God wants me to be because my husband is not doing the right thing."

"He's the one who needs to change, not me."

"God does not expect me to submit to a tyrant like him."

"There's no point in my trying, he'll never change."

No doubt most if not all husbands need to make some changes in their lives. But Scripture never says that the wife's obedience to God depends on her husband's conduct. Any wife who finds herself thinking thoughts like these needs to turn her focus from what her husband is doing wrong and instead make it her priority to please God by first laying aside her own disobedience to God's Word. The Lord Jesus put it this way...

> *You hypocrite, <u>first</u> take the log out of your own eye, and then you will see clearly to take the speck out of your brother's eye.*
>
> *Matthew 7:5, emphasis added*

As a wife focuses on her God appointed responsibility to biblically submit to her husband, she will likely begin to see her circumstances more clearly and learn how to better deal with her husband's sin in a biblically appropriate way. In addition, as she studies what God's Word says about a godly wife's submission, any confusion she may have about submission should be cleared up.

It could be that a wife's understanding of true biblical submission has been greatly distorted. Distrust and hostility towards biblical submission in our society is rampant. And because of the lack of clear faithful teaching, that same distrust and hostility often exists within the Christian community itself. One common misunderstanding is that submission of a wife to her husband is a burden, a "cross that the wife must bear." However, this is counter to the Bible's true teaching. The submission of a godly wife is more than a duty, it should be her heart's delight. There are at least -

Four Biblical Principles Concerning A Wife's Submission and Joy

1. Joy results from trusting and obeying God's Word.
2. Joy results from knowing that God is working to accomplish His purpose even in difficult circumstances. *Need help here*
3. Joy results from following the example of the Lord Jesus in difficult times.
4. Joy results from a Spirit-filled life.

Principle #1:
Joy Results From Trusting and Obeying God's Word

...Thy testimonies... are the joy of my heart.

Psalm 119:111

God's testimonies, His Word, were a joy to the Psalmist. He did not have joy in *some* of God's testimonies, but *all* of them. For the Christian wife, biblical submission to her husband is one of God's testimonies and should therefore be a joy for her.

For this is the love of God, that we keep His commandments, and His commandments are not burdensome.

1 John 5:3

The godly Christian life should be one of joyful delight in God's commands, not one of resentment and struggle against them. God's commands are given for our good and our protection (Deuteronomy 10:13). Therefore, they should be your joy, not your burden. God's commands become a joy to you when you *resolve* to humbly submit to Him in advance of the actual opportunity. Then when tested at this point, you will have already made up your mind whom you are going to obey.

Principle #2:
Joy Can Result From Knowing That God Is Working To Accomplish His Purposes Even In Difficult Circumstances

Consider it all joy my brethren when you encounter various trials...

James 1:2

God is always working His purpose in a wife's circumstances. He wants to develop Christlike character within her and give her the special opportunity and privilege to glorify Him. God can even overcome what is evil or wicked for the wife's good as the character of Christ is developed within her. God's purpose will be accomplished no matter what! **"And we know that God causes all things to work together for good to those who love God, to those who are called according to** *His purpose"* **(Romans 8:28,29)** So, we are commanded to "consider it joy." You do that in the midst of a trial by thinking, "This is good for me and God has purpose in it or He would not permit it. This is not fun, but I do have joy in knowing that God is working in my life to accomplish His purposes."

Principle #3:
Joy Comes From Following The Example Of The Lord Jesus Especially In Difficult Times

... Jesus, ... who for the joy set before Him <u>*endured the cross, despising the shame*</u>*...*

[Hebrews 12:2, emphasis added

Like the Lord Jesus, a wife can have joy in knowing that she is pleasing to the Lord and that this (as Paul said) **"...momentary light affliction is producing for [her] an eternal weight of glory far beyond all comparison"** (2 Corinthians 4:17) adaptation added).

As you look to tomorrow, it should be with hope in the Lord Jesus Christ. Because of Him, you can **"smile at the future"** (Proverbs 31:25). You must train yourself to see all of life through God's providential care over you. In trials, tell yourself "'**Love endures all things'** (1 Corinthians 13:7). I *can* endure this one more day. I can have joy in pleasing the Lord and will have joy in eternity because I pleased Him now."

Principle #4:
Joy Results From A "Spirit-Filled" Life

There is joy from within a person who is Spirit-filled. Ephesians 5:18 commands Christians to be **"...filled with the Spirit..."** Being Spirit-filled means you are controlled by the Holy Spirit and by the Word of God

(Colossians 3:16). It is not an experience that you feel but is a biblical responsibility which involves, in part, a way to think about life and God that is described in Ephesians 5. As you read further in Ephesians 5, you see joy in a "Spirit-filled" person because he or she is...

> *...singing and making melody with (his or her) heart to the Lord; always giving thanks for all things...*

This joyful "Spirit-filled" person will also be **"subject to her own husband, as to the Lord... in everything"** (Ephesians 5:22-24). So, being filled with the Spirit encompasses both wifely submission *and* joy (**"singing and making melody in (her) heart to the Lord, always giving thanks in all things."**) In addition, there is another biblical connection with a person who is Spirit-filled as they will be manifesting the fruit of the Holy Spirit, one of which is joy (see Galatians 5:22).

If you are "Spirit-filled," you will be expressing gratitude to God in all circumstances daily. Gratefulness should often be in your thoughts as well as verbally expressed. "Lord, thank You for..." is a frequent thought of the person who is joyfully "filled with the Spirit."

In understanding the biblical relationship between submission and joy, remember that submitting will not always be fun, but there is always joy in glorifying the Lord Jesus Christ. You should therefore commit yourself to learning submission, not with a dread of what is to come but with an anticipation of how you can best glorify your Lord. This is God's ordained purpose for you. He has created an orderly world, and He alone has the sovereign right to determine how He wants you (as a part of *His* creation) to glorify Him. In the next two chapters, the biblical principles of submission and God's provisions for protection of a submissive wife are discussed. If you are struggling with submission, take a moment to pray and ask God to help you see the subject of wifely submission through His heart and eyes.

Part Three

A Wife's Submission

Fulfillment of the Excellent Wife

Chapter Thirteen

Biblical Submission
Basis of the Wife's Protection

Many women, even Christian ones, are confused and sometimes hostile about what it means for a wife to be submissive to her husband. The topic is much maligned and misunderstood both in the world and the church. Women are often made to feel like fools if they ascribe to such teaching. Feminists are vehement in their objection to this. They bring up questions such as, "Is the wife supposed to say nothing and let her husband beat her?" or "Her husband is a drunk and is irresponsible. She's been supporting him for years. Is she supposed to let him run over her like that?" These questions deserve an answer, a real biblical answer.

Some Christians teach that a wife must be totally submissive to her husband even when he is sinning against her (eg. threatening her or actually harming her with physical or verbal abuse). Does the Bible *really* teach what some call "doormat theology?" No, the Bible teaches that God has provided several ways to protect a wife whose husband is sinning and that it is the wife's responsibility to take advantage of His protection. Some even think a wife is more spiritual if she does nothing and that she is called to suffer passively for the Lord's sake. But what merit is there in failing to take advantage of the measures God has provided for her protection?

The Bible teaches that suffering unnecessarily is not "spirituality" but foolish **"self-made religion"** (see Col. 2:18-23). We would call it a form of asceticism. Asceticism is "practicing strict self-denial as a means of religious practice."[26] In other words, the more she suffers, the more spiritual she must be. But that's not what Peter says in 1 Peter 3:17. He says, **"If you *must* suffer, suffer for doing what is right"** (emphasis added).

As a reaction to the "doormat" or "I'm suffering for the Lord" view of submission, some churches have gone to the other extreme. They have embraced a feminist view of the wife's role. The "liberated woman" is tolerated, even taught in many churches. Pastors often avoid the issue of submission because the subject is so volatile . Those who do address it make it more palatable with a sugar coating of some sort such as emphasizing "mutual submission of the husband and wife" instead of clearly teaching the wife's responsibility. Unfortunately, this is confusing and misleading to the many Christian women who want to know and do God's will. Because of the frequent misperceptions and misrepresentations of the true biblical teaching, a wife needs to know what biblical submission really is and how God intends for it to glorify Him. The following FIVE PRINCIPLES will help her understand biblical submission.

Five Biblical Principles Concerning The Wife's Submission

1. A wife is to be submissive to her husband in *all things* unless her husband asks her to sin.
2. A submissive wife is not afraid to do the "right thing."
3. A wife is to be submissive even if her husband is not a Christian.
4. A submissive wife does not dishonor the Word of God.
5. A wise wife will seek training and counsel on submission from a godly older woman.

Principle #1
A Wife Is To Be Submissive To Her Husband In All Things Unless Her Husband Asks Her To Sin

> *Wives, be subject to your own husbands, as to the Lord. But as the church is subject to Christ, so also the wives ought to be to their husbands in everything.*
> *Ephesians 5:22, 24*

The verb "be subject to" in the Greek is the word *hupotasso,* a military term which means to be ranked under in military order. This ranking of the wife under the husband's authority was sovereignly chosen by God so that there will be order and harmony in the home. She has a different rank or POSITION, she is *not* an inferior PERSON. Christian wives need to see themselves as God sees them.

For there is no partiality with God.

Romans 2:11

...there is neither male nor female; for you are all one in Christ Jesus.

Galatians 3:28

God is not partial to males or females. Although equal in that regard, the wife should take the attitude of the Lord Jesus Christ, one of submissive servanthood, to carry out her God-intended role in the marriage.

> *Have this attitude in yourselves which was also in Christ Jesus, who, although He existed in the form of God, did not regard equality with God a thing to be grasped, but emptied Himself, taking the form of a bond-servant, and being made in the likeness of men. And being found in appearance as a man, He humbled Himself by becoming obedient to the point of death...*
>
> *Philippians 2:5-8*

Just as Christ is not inferior to the Father, the wife is not inferior to her husband. Christ subordinated Himself to the will of the Father in order to carry out the plan of redemption. So, too, the wife submits herself to her husband so that God's plan for the family can be carried out. She is not inferior but her role is different. The wife's role is one of a "helper suitable" to her husband. Certainly God knew that husbands need all the help they can get!

> *Then the Lord God said, "It is not good for the man to be alone; I will make a helper suitable for him."*
>
> *Genesis 2:18, emphasis added*

> *For indeed man was not created for the woman's sake, but woman for the man's sake.*
>
> *1 Corinthians 11:9*

In considering the scope of submission, **"in everything"** (Ephesians 5:24) means in all areas of life such as finances, decorating the house, the length of her hair, what to have for supper, and discipline of the children. For example, consider the case of an unsubmissive wife who was furious at her husband because he did not like the antique sofa she had purchased and he told her to take it back. Since he was not asking her to sin, she should have graciously submitted. The point is, a wife must obey her husband unless he asks her to sin. Even though a husband has God-given authority over his wife, only God has absolute authority over her. In other words, God's authority is higher. So, if her husband asks her to sin, she must **"obey God rather than man"** (Acts 5:29). Let's consider how a husband might ask her to sin.

Examples of How Husbands Ask Their Wives to Sin

THE HUSBAND'S COMMAND:

"I forbid you to go to church."

GOD'S COMMAND:

"...forsake not the assembling of yourselves together."
Hebrews 10:25

EXPLANATION:

If a husband is an unbeliever and does not want his wife to attend church, she must respectfully disobey. However, she should make sure that his resentment is not because she values her Christian friends at church more than she cares for him. If that is the case, the wife should make the concessions necessary to ensure that her husband knows that he is more important to her than her other friends. Therefore, if a husband occasionally desires his wife to go fishing or camping with him, then she should go and enjoy the time with him. God is more pleased with her desire to be faithful in all things than He would be with a rigid attitude about church attendance.

THE HUSBAND'S COMMAND:

"I forbid you to talk to the children about God."

GOD'S COMMAND:

"The fear of the LORD is the beginning of knowledge; fools despise wisdom and instruction. Hear, my son, your father's instruction and do not forsake your mother's teaching..."

Proverbs 1:7-8

EXPLANATION:

Again, the husband is asking his wife to go against God's command to Christian parents. The wife should respectfully and gently explain to her husband why she cannot submit to his command. What she can do, however, is plan devotional and teaching times when her husband is not home or it will not interfere with his schedule. Even when she must go ahead and reprove or correct her children, she can wait until she is alone with the child to explain the scriptural basis for her reproof. The wife should try very hard not to be offensive to her unbelieving husband (See Principle # Four), but she cannot agree to never talk to the children about the Lord.

THE HUSBAND'S COMMAND:

"I want you to participate in immorality/pornography."

GOD'S COMMAND:

"But do not let immorality or any impurity ... even be named among you, as is proper among saints..."

Ephesians 5:3

EXPLANATION:

When a husband has a problem with sexual lust, it is common for him to try to draw his wife into the same sin. A wife can develop a problem with lust if she allows herself to be exposed to pornography or sinful, perverted sexual acts. Instead of participating, the wife must refuse to participate. Depending on whether the husband is a Christian or not, she must use the appropriate provisions God has given her for protection. These will maximize her husband's opportunity to repent. (See Chapter Fourteen.)

THE HUSBAND'S COMMAND:

A Christian husband says, "I forbid you to reprove me."

GOD'S COMMAND:

"Brethren, even if a man is caught in any trespass, you who are spiritual, restore such a one in a spirit of gentleness, each one looking to yourself, lest you too be tempted."

Galatians 6:1

EXPLANATION:

Some wrongly believe that a Christian wife should never reprove her Christian husband. Such wrong belief is often based upon an erroneous interpretation of 1 Peter 3:1 which says that the husband is to be **"won without a word by the behavior of their wives..."** This passage refers specifically to a woman who is married to an unbeliever (see Chapter Fourteen, Resource #4). It cannot be rightly applied to marriage in which both husband and wife are believers. They are not only husband and wife but also brother and sister in the Lord. Christian marriage partners are to help each other become as much like the Lord Jesus Christ as possible since they are **"...fellow heirs of the grace of life"** (1 Peter 3:7).

Others believe that a wife should not reprove her husband because if she does, she is not loving him unconditionally. In other words, she is to love him and say nothing whether he ever changes or not. But godly love **"rejoices in the truth, it does not rejoice in unrighteousness"** (1 Corinthians 13:6). When a wife discerns a pattern of sinful behavior in her Christian husband, she needs to go to him privately, gently, and in a straight-forward manner and reprove him in love. If he forbids her to reprove him, then he is asking her to disobey the Lord. She must then choose to obey God instead of her husband.

THE HUSBAND'S COMMAND:

"Do not tell anyone about my sin. I want you to lie for me."

GOD'S COMMAND:

"Therefore, laying aside falsehood, SPEAK TRUTH, EACH ONE of you, WITH HIS NEIGHBOR, for we are members of one another."

Ephesians 4:25

EXPLANATION:

Whether her husband is a believer or an unbeliever, this is not a promise that she can rightly make. If she has already made that promise to him, she should go to him and explain that she has made an unbiblical promise that she cannot keep (Proverbs 6:2-3). Instead of covering up for him, she should put appropriate biblical pressure on him to repent. (For more details see Chapter Fourteen.)

The Scripture is clear that the wife is to be submissive to her husband in all things unless her husband asks her to sin. A word of caution is in order. If the wife refuses to submit because she believes he is asking her to sin, she must make sure that what he is asking is really a sin. For example, suppose a wife has a strong conviction against eating in a restaurant that serves alcohol and her husband wants her to go with him to that restaurant to eat. What should she do? She should search the Scriptures to see if her refusal is really a biblical mandate or her own personal standard. Since it is not a biblical mandate, then she should graciously go.

Here is another word of caution. Most Christian wives believe themselves to be submissive since they would never buy a house without their husband's permission or sell their car without his approval. However, if their husbands were asked if they are submissive, they would likely say, "No." Obviously, these are two differing perspectives. A wife's responsibility is to change her perspective and view submission through God's *and* her husband's eyes. The husband is the head of the home, and the wife is to submit to even very small and seemingly unimportant requests or directives from him because they are important to him. Unless she is providentially hindered, her failure to comply is not only insubordination to her husband but also disobedience to God.

One way a wife can humbly begin to make the changes she should make is to ask her husband, "What am I doing wrong in our marriage?" Even if he is an unbeliever, he can likely see character flaws or a lack of submission in his wife. Whether he is a Christian or not, she is to submit to him. She is to be submissive in all things unless he asks her to sin.

Principle #2
A Submissive Wife Is Not Afraid To Do The "Right Thing"

> *Thus Sarah obeyed Abraham calling him lord, and you have become her children if you do what is right without being frightened by any fear.*
>
> *1 Peter 3:6*

Wives sometimes face very frightening circumstances because of immorality, physical or verbal abuse, irresponsibility, threats of leaving, or use of alcohol/drugs by their husbands. Anyone might be frightened if their husband were behaving in any of these ways. What can a wife do to overcome her fear? One key to overcoming fear is simply **"doing what is right"** (1 Peter 3:6). For instance, it is right to show love to God and love to her husband. Loving God and others are the two greatest commandments (see Matthew 22:37-39). Most Christians know they are to show love to God by obeying His Word and love to others such as a wife to her husband, but how is this actually done?

Practical Examples of Showing Love

In general, a wife shows love to God by obeying Him whether she feels like it or not, even if it means suffering personal embarrassment or painful emotions (John 14:23). A wife may also show love to God by thinking true, right, and praiseworthy thoughts (Philippians 4:8). She also shows love to God by giving appropriate biblical reproofs (Galatians 6:1). A wife shows love to her husband by not reviewing what he has done wrong over and over in her mind (1 Corinthians 13:5). She also shows love to him by giving him a blessing even if he does "evil" against her (1 Peter 3:9). She shows love when she endures a difficult time (1 Corinthians 13:7). In addition, she shows love to her husband by responding to what he has done in an objective, hopeful way. She realizes that he can repent no matter how difficult their circumstances. Another way for her to show love is by speaking with him in a gentle, respectful, but truthful way (1 Corinthians 3:6; Ephesians 5:33). And of course a wife shows love for her husband when she prays for him (James 5:16). As a wife seeks to love God and her husband more, her fear will abate. If it doesn't go away completely, it will, at least, not overpower her. Showing love to God and her neighbor is a much more powerful force than her own fear of whatever her husband may do to her.

But what about a husband who repeatedly disappoints his wife by lying or deceiving her? She must learn to place greater trust in God, but not necessarily in her husband. She has to forgive him, but in some situations it would be foolish to trust him. He can, however, regain her trust by being faithful and honest over time. The wife should be like the **"holy women in former times, who** *hoped in God...*" (1 Peter 3:6, emphasis added). A key to not being afraid to do the right thing is for her to learn to think thoughts that are right, true, honorable, excellent, and worthy of praise (see Philippians 4:8). That same Scripture mandates **"Let your mind dwell on these kinds of things."**

Examples of Fear Producing and Love Producing Thoughts

Fear Producing Thoughts	Love Producing Thoughts
1. "If he gets angry and leaves me, I won't be able to take it." (This thought is wrong because it is self-focused.)	1. "If he gets angry and leaves me, he'll just have to get angry. I'm going to show love to God and my husband whether he leaves or not. God will give me the grace to get through my husband's anger *at that time*." (This thought is right because it points to God and gives Him the credit.)
2. "He's drinking again. What will happen if he loses his job?" (This thought is wrong because it is worry and is focused on the wrong issue.)	2. "It's more important for him to repent than for him to keep his job. Getting fired may be the extra pressure that it takes for God to get his attention. If he loses his job, it will be difficult, however, God will *at that time* give me the grace to get through it."

3. "What will others think if they find out what he has done?" (This thought is wrong because it is focused more on what others might think rather than on what God says.)	3. "It is the responsibility of others to see this as a sin that is 'common to man.' Hope lies in the fact that it is sin and he can repent of it and be forgiven."

A submissive wife is not afraid of doing the "right thing". She entrusts herself to God, knowing that in difficulty, God will give her the grace she needs to get through it at the very time she needs it. Not always, but most of the time, when a wife responds by standing up to her husband in the right way, it turns out better than she had anticipated. In the event that it does not turn out well, the wife can have the comfort of knowing that she was pleasing to her Lord and whatever suffering she undergoes will be **"for doing what is *right*"** 1 Peter 3:17 (emphasis added).

Principle #3
A Wife Is To Be Submissive Even If Her Husband Is Not A Christian

In the same way, you wives, be submissive to your own husbands so that even if any of them are disobedient to the word, they may be won without a word by the behavior of their wives, as they observe your chaste and respectful behavior.

1 Peter 3:1,2

As will be seen in Chapter Fourteen, a husband who is **"disobedient to the word"** is an unbeliever (See 1 Peter 2:7). When a Christian woman is married to an unbeliever, her responsibility is to live a godly life and respond to her husband with respect. Her attitude should be one of being *for* him and not *against* him. She should enjoy him and love him, thinking of him as her husband and the father of her children, not her enemy. She should not expect him to think or act like a Christian nor should she be devastated if he has no interest in church or Bible studies. She can enjoy her husband and their relationship and still be all that God intends for her to be.

Sometimes, a wife with an unsaved husband is miserable and frustrated because she may have an idolatrous view of what she thinks her marriage should be like. She might say to herself, "I'll *never* be happy unless he becomes a Christian." Her frustration may be the result of not getting what she wants. Instead of being frustrated, her heart's devotion should turn from her idol of wanting a Christian marriage to devotion to the Lord Jesus Christ in worshipping and serving Him. He alone knows if, when, and how her husband will become a Christian.

As the wife of an unsaved man devotes herself to the Lord, she will respond to her husband with **"chaste and respectful behavior."** It is very likely that her godliness and respect to him will soften his heart towards her. If it does not and his heart becomes hardened, she may be put in a position where she must **"let the unbeliever depart"** (1 Corinthians 7:15). If he does leave her, it should be because of her submissive, respectful attitude and appropriate refusal to sin, not because she nagged and was disrespectful and rebellious.

Several years ago, I knew a Christian woman who was in a very stormy marriage to an unbeliever. Probably just as much of the problem was her fault as his. When she stopped contending with God because of her husband's attitudes and submitted to God in this area of her life, her husband began to treat her a little better. Later, they discovered that she had terminal cancer. As they went through her illness together, he saw her draw tremendous strength and comfort from God and His Word. One day, he came to her with tears in his eyes and asked her forgiveness and expressed an interest in becoming a Christian. She lovingly gave him the gospel, and they knelt together by their bed, where she led him to her Lord. She is with the Lord now and I think about her often. I am so glad for her that she had that joy before she died. She obeyed her Lord and was **"ready always to give an account of the hope that was in her"** (1 Peter 3:15).

In addition to being ready to share her faith if her husband asks her, the wife of an unbeliever should graciously go places with him and his friends, but draw the line at personal sins such as getting drunk, lying, sexual sin, etc. If she must decline, she should do it graciously by saying, for example, "Thank you for including me but that's not something I can participate in. Perhaps we could... (go bowling or out to eat)." That way she is letting them know she would like to be with them. Also, if she prepares ahead of time some interesting topics to discuss, then the conversation could, at times, be discreetly moved away from unrighteous topics without her appearing to be self-righteous and making him uncomfortable. She can prepare conversation topics ahead of time by reading and remembering the essence of magazine articles and newspaper articles that are interesting and not offensive to her husband and his friends. In addition to showing love to others, her efforts could make all the difference in whether she has a good time or not. Certainly, this would be a gracious way to show love to her husband and his friends.

Principle #4
A Submissive Wife Does Not Dishonor The Word Of God

...being subject to her own husband that the word of God may not be dishonored.

Titus 2:3-5

To dishonor is to "malign, slander, speak against, or speak of as evil."[27] When a wife is not submissive to her husband, she brings shame to God's Word because she is not living up to the standard God has clearly laid out for the godly wife. If she is outwardly expressing faith in Christ, but inwardly has not changed in her heart regarding submission to her husband, she is not submitting to the Lord in that area of her life. The Apostle Paul expressed it another way: **"Wives, be subject to your husbands, as is *fitting* in the Lord"** (Colossians 3:18, emphasis added). Anything other than godly submission is not fitting or proper for a Christian wife since it dishonors God and His Word.

A Submissive Wife Honors the Word of God When:

1. Obeying God is more important to her than having her own way. When she obeys rather than contends for her own way, she is being a **"living sacrifice" (Romans 12:1-2)**. She sacrifices what she wants for what the Lord wants for her.

2. She has an appropriate reverential fear of the Lord. She knows that God is a holy, Almighty God that she is here to serve. God is not some "genie in the bottle" here to serve her. The Psalmist put it this way, **"Worship the Lord with reverence, and rejoice with trembling" (Psalm 2:11)**. King Solomon warned, **"Do not be wise in your own eyes. Fear the Lord and turn away from evil" (Proverbs 3:7)**. Indeed, it is evil when a wife rebels against God's Word and her husband. An appropriate fear of the Lord puts all things into proper perspective: **"...and do not fear those who kill the body, but are unable to kill the soul; but rather fear Him who is able to destroy both soul and body in hell (Matthew 10:28)."**

3. She lets the Word of Christ direct her life. **Colossians 3:16** says we are to let the **"Word of Christ richly dwell within (us)"**. Evidence that the Word of Christ (the Scriptures) is dwelling within her and directing her life is shown by a wife's responding in *grateful* submission to God as well as *gracious* submission to her husband. As she does, the word of Christ will be **"richly dwelling within"** her (Colossians 3:16) and God's Word will **"not be dishonored"** (Titus 2:5).

4. Her life is not an affront to the pattern for marriage given in Ephesians Chapter Five, of the Church and its submissive relationship to Christ. **"But as the church is subject to Christ, so also the wives *ought to be* to their husbands in everything" (Ephesians 5:24)**. The church's relationship to Christ is a beautiful picture of marriage! As a wife submits to her husband she lives out the pattern God has appointed for her (see Chapter Six). Even if her husband does not respond properly, a submissive wife will truly be honoring to the Word of God and to the Lord Jesus Christ.

5. She is submissive whether she *feels* like it or not. The best biblical illustration of someone who went against his feelings and was submissive anyway is the example of the Lord Jesus Christ. In **Hebrews 12:1-2**, we learn that He **"endured the cross, despising the shame..."** The suffering and humiliation He underwent were not fun or enjoyable but He did it in order to carry out the Father's plan of redemption. He did it **"for the joy that was set before Him."** Likewise, a wife will certainly not *always* feel like being submissive but she *can* always with the grace of God be submissive with a godly motive and for the glory of the Lord Jesus.

When faced with a situation in which the wife should be submissive but does not want to be, she can overcome her feelings if she thinks biblical thoughts like: **"'Love does not seek its own way.'** I *can* show love to him by graciously giving in to his wishes" or **"'Love bears all things, endures all things.'** I *can* show love to him by enduring this and being submissive." A godly, submissive wife can, by God's grace as an act of her will, go against her feelings and do the right thing. If her husband is being selfish or unreasonable and his wife dwells on how he has hurt her, it will likely be very difficult for her to feel like being graciously submissive. She may outwardly do the right thing, but she will struggle with bitterness and will not feel like being submissive. Repentance from bitterness includes replacing her thoughts and actions with **"kind, tender-hearted, and forgiving"** thoughts and actions (Ephesians 4:31,32). How she channels her thinking and verbal responses will greatly affect her ability to *feel* like being submissive. God will help her through His grace.

And God is able to make all grace abound to you, that always having all sufficiency in everything, you may have an abundance for every good deed...

2 Corinthians 9:8

Principle #5
A Wise Wife Will Seek Training and Counsel On Submission From A Godly Older Woman

Older women likewise are to be reverent in their be-havior, not malicious gossips, nor enslaved to much wine, teaching what is good, that they may encourage the younger women to love their husbands...being sub-ject to their own husbands, that the Word of God may not be dishonored.

Titus 2:3-5

One of the best ways to find a godly older woman is through the recom-mendation of a faithful pastor or church leader. The pastor and other men in church leadership have responsibility to **"keep watch over your souls, as those who will give an account"** (Hebrews 13:17). It is important that the older woman be doctrinally sound, because it is so easy to be **"tossed here and there by waves, and carried about by every wind of doctrine, by the trickery of men" (Ephesians 4:14)**. Most of the time when an older woman disciples a younger woman, she will have a tremendous influence on the younger woman either for good or evil. Unfortunately, it is not uncommon for younger women to be drawn into mysticism, worldly philosophies, misperceptions of the character of God, a wrong view of the doctrine of sanc-tification, or even influenced to turn against their husbands. Because of those dangers, it would be wise for churches to develop a ministry to teach the older women how and what to teach the younger women. Part of this in-struction involves the older woman instructing the younger woman in what she is doing wrong biblically. If the younger woman is wise, she will listen to the **"life-giving reproof"** and eventually **"acquire wisdom"** (Proverbs 15:32, 33).

Ask yourself, "Am I being joyfully obedient? How should I pray?" As you consider just how pleasing to God you are in the area of submission to your husband, take a few moments to read over the following list of ways wives are not submissive and check the ones which apply to you.

Specific Ways Wives Are Not Submissive

These are typical of specific ways wives act in unsubmissive ways towards their husbands. In addition, you should develop your own list of ways that you have or might have been unsubmissive to your own husband.

1. She does things that are annoying or vexing to her husband.

   It is better to live in a desert land, than with a contentious and vexing woman.

   Proverbs 21:19

Note: a woman who is vexing is "irritating, annoying, puzzling, baffling, bothersome and will debate at length."[28]

2. She does not discipline the children as she should (even after her husband asks her to).

   The rod and reproof give wisdom, but a child who gets his own way brings shame to his mother.

   Proverbs 29:15

3. She is more loyal to others than to her husband.

   The heart of her husband trusts in her, he will have no lack of gain.

   Proverbs 31:11

4. She argues or pouts or gives him the cold shoulder when she does not get her own way.

   It is better to live in a corner of a roof, than in a house shared with a contentious woman.

   Proverbs 21:9

5. She does not stay within the limits of their budget.

   House and wealth are an inheritance from fathers, but a prudent wife is from the LORD.

   Proverbs 19:14

6. She corrects, interrupts, talks for her husband, and is too outspoken when others are around.

> *A constant dripping on a day of steady rain and a contentious woman are alike; He who restrains her restrains the wind, and grasps oil with his right hand.*
>
> *Proverbs 27:15,16*

7. She manipulates him to get her own way. She may manipulate by deceit, tears, begging, nagging, complaining, anger, or intimidation. Martha tried to manipulate Jesus when she said:

> *...Lord, do You not care that my sister has left me to do all the serving alone? Then tell her to help me:*
>
> *Luke 10:40*

8. She makes important decisions without consulting him.

> *But I want you to understand that Christ is the head of every man, and the man is the head of a woman, and God is the head of Christ.*
>
> *1 Corinthians 11:3*

Note: Occasionally, a husband will instruct his wife that in certain areas she is to make the decisions. In those cases, when authority is delegated to her she then has freedom to choose. Otherwise, he should be consulted in all matters (that are important to him) and she should submit to his headship.

9. She directly defies his wishes.

> *For rebellion is as the sin of divination, and insubordination is as iniquity and idolatry.*
>
> *1 Samuel 15:23*

10. She worries about the decisions he makes and takes matters into her own hands.

> *Be anxious for nothing, but in everything by prayer and supplication, with thanksgiving let your requests be made known to God. And the peace of God, which surpasses all comprehension, shall guard your hearts and your minds in Christ Jesus.*
>
> *Philippians 4:7,8*

11. She does not pay attention to what he says.

But let everyone be quick to hear, slow to speak and slow to anger...

James 1:19

In summary, submission is the way that all Christians should respond to God and the way the wife should respond to her husband. She can respond with tenderness, gentleness, and gracious obedience or she can respond with harshness or irritation. In the areas where you know you have failed, you should take a few minutes and confess your sins to the Lord (1 John 1:9). Then go to your husband and ask his forgiveness. It may be best for you to be specific and give examples. Your attitude should be humble, focusing at this time on what you have done wrong. You can begin today to be a gentle, godly, submissive wife to your husband. It is the *heart of God* for you.

Chapter Fourteen

God's Provision
Resources for the Wife's Protection

*(The material in this chapter has been adapted from
"Biblical Resources for a Wife's Protection" by Lou Priolo).*[29]

The last chapter explained five biblical principles concerning a godly wife's submission to her husband. This chapter explains eight biblical means by which God protects a submissive wife when her husband sins against her or others. These resources require a wife to take action as explained in God's Word and most are actions which can be taken whether or not the husband professes to be a Christian.

Since God Himself has provided these eight resources in His Word, a wife would be foolish not to take full advantage of them. In fact, when a Christian wife finds herself in a situation where her husband is sinning against her or others, as his **"helper suitable for him"** (Genesis 2:18), she has a biblical responsibility to use these resources. They are God's will for the wife, designed by God not only for her protection, but also to help her Christian husband live faithfully before God. If her husband is an unbeliever, they may be used by God to bring her husband to faith in Christ.

The eight resources are listed in the order a wife should usually implement them. They are not necessarily easy for a wife to do, especially in the middle of a conflict with her husband. However, if she commits herself to being obedient to God's Word in order to glorify Him, God *will* give her grace to do them. Initially, a wife might benefit from learning how to practice these things with the help of another spiritually mature woman. However, caution is necessary because many Christian women, even those who have been in the faith for a long time, may not be well grounded in how to biblically apply these measures. Some may have even been wrongly taught that Christian wives are to passively and silently endure their husband's sin. With that awareness in mind, here are the eight resources:

Eight Resources For the Wife's Protection

1. Learn to Communicate Biblically.
2. Learn to Overcome Evil with Good.
3. Learn to Make a Biblical Appeal.
4. Learn to Give a Biblical Reproof.
5. Learn to Biblically Respond to Foolish Demands.
6. Learn to Seek Godly Counsel.
7. Learn to Biblically Follow the Steps of Church Discipline.
8. Learn to Biblically Involve the Governing Authorities.

Resource #1
Communicate Biblically

The heart of the wise teaches his mouth and adds persuasiveness to his lips.

Proverbs 16:23

No skill will help a wife more in conflict with her husband than the ability to communicate biblically. Biblical communication is based on the principles of God's Word. God's desire for a wife is to train her tongue to respond properly in every situation. It can be done. Getting control of her tongue is one of the wife's first steps in biblically submitting herself to God and her husband.

This will take much practice and prayer. If a wife is frightened, frustrated, or angry, at first it may be difficult for her to think straight about what she should say or do. But, by God's grace, she can learn. A wife can learn how to biblically respond to her husband in a God-honoring way.

God-honoring responses are gentle, loving in tone, and edifying to the hearer. For example, instead of "snapping" at her husband in a harsh manner, a godly wife *thinks* about *what* she is going to say and *how* she is going to say it. Then, she responds with great care. That is God-honoring speech. (See Chapter Sixteen for further information on the principles of biblical communication.)

Failure to communicate biblically is sin — disobedience to God. A wife's own sin always makes her situation worse. But she can honor God with her obedience, by following the admonition of Ephesians 4:29, **"Let no unwholesome word proceed from your mouth, but only such a word as is good for edification according to the need of the moment, that it may give grace to those who hear."** Her tongue will become an instrument of God's grace. In this there is not only protection, but blessing.

Resource #2
Overcome Evil With Good

Do not be overcome with evil, but overcome evil with good.

Romans 12:21

When a husband sins against his wife, she must not only respond with the right words, she must learn to respond with the right actions and attitudes. Instead of returning evil for evil she must fight back with good. 1 Peter 3:9 adds, **"not returning evil for evil or insult for insult, but giving a blessing instead, for you were called for the very purpose that you might inherit a blessing."**

Romans 12:21, cited at the beginning of this section, is a command. The godly wife does not have an option. She must battle the sin of her husband with good and fight as long as it takes — until the Lord removes her or her husband from the conflict or the battle is won . Some battles last for a day, some for years. Some battles are extremely difficult but never overwhelming when fought God's way by His power and grace. The godly wife's responsibility is to fight evil with good — no matter how hard it is or how long it takes! God determines when the battle is over. In the meantime, while she is fighting back biblically, she can have the assurance of knowing her struggle will likely result in real peace with her husband; because , **"When a man's [or a wife's] ways please the Lord, He makes even his enemies to be at peace with him"** (Proverbs 16:7, parenthetical comment added).

How is evil overcome with good? When a husband sins, instead of dwelling on what he did and plotting a way to get back at him, a godly wife prayerfully considers a specific, practical act in which she can render a blessing to her husband. After she thinks of it — she *must* do it! 3 John 11 says, **"Beloved, do not imitate what is evil, but what is good. He who does good is of God, but he who does evil has not seen God." And Romans 12:14 says, "Bless those who persecute you, bless and do not curse."**

This is what the Lord Jesus meant when He said in Luke 6:31, **"And just as you want men to do to you, you also do to them likewise"** (See verses 27-29 for the context of this verse). Here are some examples of practical ways to fight evil with good. A wife should ask God for creativity and wisdom to think of other examples.

1. Pray for him daily.
2. Speak words of kindness, softly and gently to him.
3. Surprise him with a sweet note or card in his lunch.
4. Serve a special meal to him — his favorite food.
5. Give him an unexpected gift.
6. Fill up his car with gas.
7. Thank him for something good he has done.
8. Praise him for one of his good character qualities.
9. Be humble enough to confess your own failures to him.
10. Reaffirm your commitment to him.
11. Initiate a special time of love-making with him.
12. Spend time with him doing something he likes to do.
13. Ask him to take a walk (with you, of course).
14. Obey God and let your husband see Christ in you.

Giving her husband a "blessing instead" is not easy. It is especially difficult if a wife is struggling with bitter feelings such as hurt and resentment. She may even balk at the idea thinking bitterly, "But he doesn't *deserve* it!" That may seem true from a human perspective, but blessing him with kindness is one of God's most gracious and powerful ways to **"heap burning coals upon his head"** (Romans 12:19). The idea is that a wife can overcome her husband's evil by doing **"good"** (Romans 12:21).

God never intends for a godly wife to be a doormat in the way our society uses that word nor practice what is commonly known as "tough love." He intends for her to "stand firm" in the grace of the Lord (1 Peter 5:12) and the power of His might. A wife should learn to see the conflict in her marriage from the same perspective Jehosophat had when the Moabites and Ammonites came against Judah. Read Jehosophat's prayer in 2 Chronicles 20 especially noting (and perhaps memorizing) verse 15, **"...Thus says the Lord to you, 'Do not be afraid, nor dismayed because of this great multitude, for the battle is not yours, but God's.'"**

Godly wives do not take matters into their own hands (Proverbs 14:1). They never seek revenge against their husbands. When a wife does seek revenge, she violates God's command not to return evil for evil. God will not honor such a sinful tactic. Romans 12:19 says **"Never take your own revenge, beloved, but leave room for the wrath of God, for it is written, 'Vengeance is mine, I will repay,' says the Lord."** God wants her to be forbearing and patient when her husband sins against her. It is the responsibility of the wife to obey God and to trust God to execute His retributive justice for her husband's sin.

Giving her husband a "blessing instead" is like going a second mile. Matthew 5:41 says, **"And whoever compels you to go one mile, go with him two."** Having a second mile attitude will also help prevent a wife from becoming embittered. Hebrews 12:14 says, **"Pursue peace with all men, and holiness without which no one will see the Lord, looking diligently lest anyone fall short of the grace of God; lest any root of bitterness springing up cause trouble, and by this many become defiled."**

Often, the only thing that stands between obedience to the Lord and not being overcome by evil is endurance. The wife is to endure and continue overcoming evil with good; however, many wives give up too soon. **"For you have *need of endurance*, so that AFTER you have done the will of God, you may receive the promise"** (Hebrews 10:36, emphasis added). If a wife returns good for evil, she will receive a blessing if she endures.

✗ Resource #3
Make A Biblical Appeal

Sweetness of speech increases persuasiveness.
Proverbs 16:21

A biblical appeal is a request or plea to a person in authority for the purpose of asking them to reconsider or reevaluate a command, directive, or instruction. Daniel did this when he, **"purposed in his heart... therefore he requested..."** (Daniel 1:8). Daniel knew that a biblical authority should always be obeyed unless the one submissive to that authority is asked to sin. The bottom line is that a godly wife should always do what her husband wants her to do unless he asks her to sin.

However, when a wife believes she has a better or wiser idea, as her husband's helper, she should be ready to give her husband the benefit of her wise counsel and advice. A wise husband should always be ready to receive it. **"A wise man will hear and increase learning, and a man of understanding will attain wise counsel"** (Proverbs 1:5). Who knows a husband better than his wife and who has God placed next to him who is better able to give him wise counsel than the "helper suitable" for him?

A biblical appeal has several conditions. First, the appeal should be done for the purpose of achieving the husband's objective or desire (as long as the end that the husband has in mind is not a violation of God's Word). The second point is related to the first. The motive of the wife must not be manipulative. She should not use the appeal simply to get her own way. Third, the appeal should be made in a respectful manner and with a spirit of submission. Not with a condescending, harsh, or strident tone, but with a kind and gentle voice. Fourth, the appeal should be done at the proper time. A wise wife will plan a time when her husband is not rushed, tired or angry. This isn't always possible. Some appeals may have to be made on the spot because of pending serious consequences. Fifth, an appeal should be made only once. Serious circumstances may require a restatement of the appeal to ensure that it was understood. But, frequent or repeated appeals may give the appearance that a wife is nagging, contentious, and manipulative. This defeats the effectiveness of a biblical appeal. (A further appeal <u>must or can</u> be made when new information is available that the husband did not previously consider.) Sixth, an appeal should *always* be prefaced or concluded with a statement by the wife that she is willing to do whatever her husband decides (as long as he does not ask her to sin). She might say "Honey, I am committed to doing whatever you decide." Seventh, if her husband is asking her to sin, she should propose a viable alternative which seeks to accomplish the husband's intent. She might say something like, "Honey, I would really like to be able to do what you have asked, but that would require me to violate the Word of God. May I suggest this alternative ...? Would that be all right?"

When the appeal is made to a Christian husband it should be based on biblical principles to ensure that the appeal is made wisely. A wise wife will even use Scripture to strengthen her appeal. But, if the appeal is to an unbelieving husband, the use of Scripture or referring to God may only provoke him. **"The mind set on the flesh is hostile toward God, for it does not subject itself to the law of God , for it is not even able to do so"** (Romans 8:7). Instead, appeal to the unbelieving husband's conscience to do what is right. For example, "Honey, I would like to appeal to you to reconsider your decision not to take the course on managing a household budget. I know you are trying hard to provide for us, but your struggles in this area are really hurting us all. I would be willing to take the course with you so I could be a better help to you. It would mean a lot to me if you would take the course. I would appreciate it if you would consider it. Thank you for listening."

When a husband does not listen to or grant his wife's appeal, she must accept his decision as the will of God for her at that moment. (An exception would be if her husband is sinning. In that case, she may have to go immediately to the next steps for protection.) It might even be that God is preparing to chasten her husband for a foolish decision or a prideful heart. Unless the husband is sinning or asking his wife or others to sin, after an appeal is made, the wife must assume that his final decision is God's will for her at the moment — even if she must suffer for the sake of righteousness. Likewise, when she refuses to follow her husband's sinful and ungodly commands, it may mean that she must suffer consequences because of her obedience to God. But, in this case she should remember that 1 Peter 3:17 says, **"For it is better, if God should will it so, that you suffer for doing what is right rather than for doing what is wrong."** The godly wife should not forget that God has provided her other protective measures as well.

Resource #4
Give A Biblical Reproof

Be on your guard! If your brother sins, rebuke him; and if he repents, forgive him.

Luke 17:3

A biblical reproof is telling someone (not necessarily one in authority) that what they are doing is contrary to the Word of God. The purpose of a reproof is to restore the person to a right relationship with God. Since Christian husbands and wives are responsible for helping each other become as much like the Lord Jesus Christ as possible, either may reprove the other of sin. They are to **"... be subject to one another in the fear of Christ"** (Ephesians 5:21). (In Chapter 4, this process of "mutual sanctification" is more fully explained.)

Some wrongly teach that a Christian wife is not ever to reprove her Christian husband for his sin because 1 Peter 3:1 says **"... you wives, be submissive to your own husbands so that even if any of them are DISOBEDIENT TO THE WORD, they may be won without a word by the behavior of their wives"** (emphasis added). But, such a view misinterprets this verse by taking it out of context. Husbands who are "disobedient to the word" are husbands who are unbelievers. This is made clear in 1 Peter 2:7-8, where those who are **"disobedient to the word"** are said to be those who have rejected Christ. They are **"those who disbelieve."** They have rejected the **"Cornerstone"** (Christ) who is to them **"a stone of stumbling and a rock of offense."** The admonition in 1 Peter 3:1-2, then, is for Christian wives to win their *un*believing husbands to Christ by their **"chaste and respectful behavior"** without nagging them or using contentious words to badger them into believing.

Another wrong, but wide-spread teaching is that a Christian wife should never reprove her husband because she must love him unconditionally — she must accept him as he is. As this view goes, she must suffer in silence when her husband sins against her. Though there may be times when it **"...is a glory of a man to overlook a matter"** (Proverbs 19:11), this view is flawed because it misunderstands the true nature of biblical love. Proverbs 27:5 says, **"Open rebuke is better than secret love."** Certainly a wife must humbly, gently love her husband whether he ever changes or not. But, she also is given to him as his helper so that he might grow to maturity in Christ Jesus. A wife shows great love to her husband when she rightly encourages him to faithful Christian living. **"Love edifies"** (1 Corinthians 8:1). It builds up rather than tears down. A wife's reproof done in a biblical manner and with biblical motives is intended to build up her husband. This is the very purpose of the Word of God. **"All Scripture is inspired by God and profitable for TEACHING, for REPROOF, for CORRECTION, for TRAINING in righteousness, that the man of God may be adequately equipped for every good work"** (2 Timothy 3:16-17, emphasis added).

If a godly wife refrains from **"speaking the truth in love,"** her Christian husband will be deprived of one of God's greatest provisions for his own spiritual growth — the words of encouragement and exhortation of his own wife. True biblical love **"rejoices in the truth"** (1 Corinthians 13:6). A godly wife's biblical reproof is not only an act of love, but it will (if it is done properly and he humbly receives it) strengthen the love of the husband for his wife, **"...rebuke a wise man and he will love you"** (Proverbs 9:8). Surely, a godly wife will do this for the husband she loves. 1 Peter 4:8 adds, **"Above all keep fervent in your love for one another, because love covers a multitude of sins."** The idea here is that love will not broadcast a person's sins to others, but will "cover them" by dealing with the sins in a loving, biblical manner.

A Christian wife does not have the option of whether or not to reprove her Christian husband who continues in sin. She is commanded to reprove him because her husband is also a professing Christian brother in the Lord. Galatians 6:1 explains what a godly wife must do when her Christian husband sins against her, **"Brethren, even if a man is caught in any trespass,**

you who are spiritual, restore such a one ..." She must go privately and tell him in a straight-forward, clear manner how she believes he has sinned against her. This verse also cautions the one giving the reproof (in this case the wife) to do it **"in a spirit of gentleness; each one looking to yourself, lest you also be tempted."** The wife should examine her own motive first to ensure that when she goes to her husband she has a clear conscience, free of sin, and that she does not sin in how she speaks to her husband (e.g. in a disrespectful or argumentative way). Her motive should be to restore, not to expose, not to make things easier for herself, and not to get some other personal reward. She must also make sure that she follows Jesus' instructions in Matthew 7:5, **"...first remove the plank from your own eye, and then you will see clearly to remove the speck out of your brother's eye."**

A wise wife will choose a time when her husband is rested and can give her his attention. Also, she will plan out her words carefully. Proverbs 15:28 states, **"The heart of the righteous ponders how to answer."** She might want to even write the words out and practice saying them aloud several times. Her reproof should be spoken in love (Ephesians 4:15) and softened with some legitimate praise and encouragement. It is important that her tone of voice be gentle and that she be prepared to suggest a biblical solution.

A wife may state her reproof like this, "Sweetheart, there is something I want to tell you that is troubling me. You know that I love you and I know that you love me, but I have observed what I believe is a sinful pattern of behavior in your life which is harming your reputation and Christian witness. It seems that you are so easily frustrated and angry toward me and others when things don't go your way. For instance, you yelled at me and slammed your fist into the sofa when I interrupted you while you were watching the basketball game." A husband may acknowledge his sin and even repent at this point if he is a mature Christian man. If he does acknowledge that he has such a sin pattern and expresses a concern about it, the wife should encourage him by offering hope that he can change and overcome his anger problem by the grace of God.

If he disagrees about the extent of his sin problem or even denies he has a problem, it might be necessary for the wife to give several more specific examples of his behavior. In either case, the wife should continue, "Honey, James 1:20 says, '... the anger of man does not achieve the righteousness of God.' Would you prayerfully consider what I have said? If there is anything I can do to help let me know. We can work through this together."

After a reasonable length of time (possibly a week or less) if he still does not agree with her analysis, she should suggest that her husband speak to someone else about his sin problem. A good choice would be their pastor or a close, personal friend if that friend is a mature Christian. The wife might say "Because we see this differently, it would be helpful for another person to hear both sides. I would suggest our Pastor." If he refuses to see their Pastor either with her or by himself, then she should go alone, telling her husband beforehand that she is going and inviting him to come along. She might say to her husband, "I still really believe that what you are doing is sin. One of us needs to get the counsel of another mature believer such as the Pastor. I am willing to go with you to see him if you like. Would you like to go and ask our Pastor if he thinks it is a sin or shall I?" In any case, it is important to get another person involved because when two Christians cannot agree about what is and what is not a pattern of sinful behavior, the counsel of other believers is necessary to help bring the light of Scripture to bear on the difficult issue. The Apostle Paul wrote to Philippi urging the church to help two dear Christian ladies who could not get along with each other. He urged Euodia and Syntyche to **"live in harmony in the Lord"** (Philippians 4:2). Like the example of Euodia and Syntyche, it is important to get another person involved because accountability in changing sinful patterns of behavior is essential. In most cases, if the husband will seek the help he needs, this will provide additional protection for the wife against the husband's sin pattern. If the husband refuses to repent, denies the problem, or refuses to seek counsel from another mature Christian man, the wife is not left helpless. She has a further recourse. This is discussed later under church discipline.

But first let us consider whether or not a godly wife may reprove her unbelieving husband. The answer is "yes, unless he is a scoffer!" The basis of her reproof is for him to do what is right as a husband, father, friend, businessman, etc. Before the fall of man, Adam and Eve always did what was right and good. Only after the fall, did man begin to sin. Even if her husband is an unbeliever, the wife may appeal to her husband based on what is right. (As long as her standard for what is right is Scripture.)

As in making an appeal, a Christian wife will be wise not to quote Scripture or invoke the name of God in reproving her unbelieving husband because his mind is **"not subject to the law of God"** (Romans 8:7). However, she certainly can use the principles contained in Scripture to reprove her husband of sin as long as she does it in a respectful way that honors her husband and the Lord. If her husband scoffs (scorns, derides, or mocks) at her when she tries to reprove him, then she should not continue to try to reprove him since Scripture states, **"Do not correct a scoffer, lest he hate you; rebuke a wise man, and he will love you"** (Proverbs 9:8). Instead, the wife should then learn how to biblically respond to his manipulation and foolish demands (see Resource #5).

A husband, whether he is a believer or not, has a responsibility to receive his wife's reproof in a gracious manner. However, this does not always happen. Sometimes, a husband may refuse to receive a reproof from his wife or may even respond to it in a harsh, angry, blame-shifting, or threatening way. In that event, the wife must stand firm and focus on fulfilling her biblical responsibility. God will give her the grace at that time to respond to her husband's anger or intimidation. Her love for her Lord (**"Perfect love casts out fear"** 1 John 4:18) as she obeys His Word will overcome her fear of her husband's wrong response.

A loving, biblically appropriate, reproof is practically a lost art, but it needs to be regained both in the church and in the home. It is one of the resources that God has provided for the wife's protection.

Resource #5
Respond Biblically To Foolish Demands

Do not answer a fool according to his folly, lest you also be like him. Answer a fool as his folly deserves, lest he be wise in his own eyes.

Proverbs 26:4-5

Biblically, a foolish man is one who rejects the Word of God and does what is right in his own eyes (Proverbs 1:7; 12:15). Immature Christian husbands may act foolishly from time to time by making harsh or unreasonable demands or accusations against their wives. Likewise, a wife can be foolish in how she responds to her husband's foolish demands. Husbands may particularly act this way in pointing out their wives' failure to carry out responsibilities. This may be especially true if the husband has not yet learned how to lead his wife biblically. Instead of leading her in a loving way, he may sinfully resort to intimidation, manipulation, harsh criticism, or hostile teasing to accomplish his purposes. This abuse of his God-given authority often throws a Christian wife into total confusion. Such behavior is not only hurtful, but can be extremely provoking — even to a wife who is committed to biblical submission. How does a godly wife protect herself from the foolish, unreasonable demands of her husband, yet remain submissive to him?

As a first priority, she must understand what the Bible says about how to respond wisely to a foolish man. Proverbs 26:4 says, **"Do not answer a fool according to his folly lest you be like him."** The tendency for many wives is to respond to mistreatment by their husbands with sinful anger, fear, pouting, clamming up, yelling, going home to mother, crying, making brutal verbal attacks, or other defensive behavior. This, in short, is returning evil for evil — responding *to* a fool *like* a fool. A Godly wife must learn to respond to foolish behavior in a God honoring way. Proverbs 26:5 says, **"Give the fool the answer he deserves lest he be wise in his own eyes."**

In other words, the wife should respond to foolish behavior with the wisdom of Scripture. For example, suppose that a wife spends the whole day cleaning her house and cooking a special dinner for her husband, only to have him come home from work in a bad, critical mood. Instead of showing his appreciation for his wife's efforts, what if he angrily blasts her because she forgot to dust the mantle or burned the beans? In response to such unkind, insensitive, thoughtless behavior, she might briefly entertain murderous thoughts. More likely, she will either go on the offensive, or storm off to the bedroom. Later, she might even slander her husband to her friends for his mistreatment of her. And then, she might plan how to get her revenge. But, none of these foolish and vindictive responses are pleasing to God and none of them are appropriate for a godly wife.

When a Christian husband unreasonably and wrongly attacks his wife for her failure to carry out her responsibilities, the wife should first take note of the reproof even if it is given by her husband in a sinful way. If she has done wrong, she should first acknowledge her wrong. In demonstrating such humility, she sets a good example for her husband to respond similarly when she points out to him his own responsibility to act in a biblical manner.

Jesus used this method to respond to the manipulative acts of those who had authority over Him. In Luke 2:42-49, as a boy of twelve Jesus' parents once left Him in Jerusalem. When His parents finally found Him, they asked **"Son, why have You treated us this way?"** Instead of foolishly defending Himself or becoming sinfully angry, Jesus pointed out their responsibility by asking, **"Why is it that you were looking for Me? Did you not know that I had to be in My Father's house?"** Verse 51 makes it clear this was not a rebellious remark. Jesus never sinned, but **"continued in subjection"** to His parents. Much later at the end of His earthly life, when Caiaphas, the High Priest, questioned Jesus after His arrest about His teaching, Jesus answered him saying, **"Why do you question Me? Question those who have heard what I spoke to them, behold these know what I said"** (John 18:19-21). Jesus was always quick to discern when others were wrongly trying to use the authority of their position to manipulate Him and He usually answered them by pointing out their own responsibility.

A wife must do this with caution. She must recognize that she is not always without sin as Jesus was. It is best for her to acknowledge her responsibility and possible failure, before she points out the failure of her husband. For example, consider the ways that the wife could have responded to her husband in the earlier situation. First, the wife could have said, "Honey, if I have failed to clean the house to your satisfaction, would you please let me know by speaking to me in a loving manner? I know it is your responsibility to correct me when you think I have done something wrong, but could you please do it in a kind, tender-hearted way?" Also, if the husband was particularly abusive, the wife could gently say, "You are sinning in the way you are speaking to me. I will be glad to listen to what you have to say, but you must do it in loving manner."

Not answering back like a fool is easy to understand but hard to do in the heat of conflict. If confused, a wife does not have to immediately give her husband a direct answer since Proverbs 15:28 says, **"The heart of the righteous ponders how to answer..."** Likewise, a wife who is faced with harsh, unreasonable demands by her husband may ask him for time to consider her answer. She might say, "I need to think about how to answer you, and I will give you a response as soon as possible." If her husband has not fully considered all the facts or has not gathered the information necessary to make a wise decision, he may be making a rash judgment. A godly wife may respond to her husband's rash judgments concerning her by saying "Would you please wait until I can give you more information before you '...**answer a matter...**' (Proverbs 18:13)?"

Consider finally, the case of a man who is blaming his wife for his own sinful failures. Often, a husband will wrongly accuse his wife of provoking him to anger. When a husband makes this false charge, she can gently remind him that 1 Corinthians 13:5 says love **"is not *easily* provoked"** and that he is responsible for obeying Ephesians 4:26, **"Be angry and sin not."** Especially when a husband is making presumptuous unreasonable judgments, he may be reminded that Proverbs 13:10 says **"Through presumption comes nothing, but strife."** Many wives are reluctant to use Scripture in answering their Christian husband's foolish accusations, but they should remember that **"The Word of God is living and active and sharper than any two-edged sword, and piercing as far as the division of soul and spirit, of both joints and marrow, and able to judge the thoughts and intentions of the heart"** (Hebrews 4:12). The Word of God, is the most effective weapon that the Christian has. The wife should (in a gentle, quiet manner) use God's Word in a wise way to not respond like a fool and to give her husband the "answer that he deserves." (For more examples on "How to answer a fool", see addendum in the back of this book.)

Resource #6
Seek Godly Counsel

For by wise counsel you will wage your own war, and in a multitude of counselors there is safety.

Proverbs 24:6

Seeking godly counsel means seeking advice based on God's Word, the Bible. The only thing worse than not seeking or following godly counsel when it is needed is seeking, receiving, and following wrong counsel. Unfortunately, even within the church one can not always count on receiving biblical advice based on the Scriptures. Some in the church do not know what the Word of God says. Others may claim to receive special instruction directly from God apart from His Word. Still others rely on man's wisdom to give counsel. Godly counsel is advice that can be supported scripturally both in its major and minor points. So, it is important to make sure that you seek help from a faithful, godly person who knows the teaching of Scripture and is committed to living by Scripture. Such a person will believe that the Bible is true and is without error and that the Bible can not lead people astray if it is properly understood and obeyed. They will also believe that the Bible is given to man that he might know how to live a life pleasing to God. And finally, they will believe that the Bible contains practical guidance for all of life's circumstances. In other words, Scripture is sufficient for providing people the counsel they need. As explained in Psalm 19:7: God's Word, **"... is sure, making wise the simple."**

Here are additional guidelines for seeking counsel:

1. Counsel Should Be Objective.

Both sides must always be heard because **"The first to plead his case seems just until another comes and examines him"** (Proverbs 18:17). A biblically objective person is one who is more loyal to the truth of Scripture than to people. Sometimes a wife's mother, other family members, and close friends will be too willing to take sides against a husband to be of much help. In fact, receiving biased, unbiblical counsel will likely make a situation worse, not better.

2. Counsel Should Be Directed At Solving The Problem Biblically Using The Word Of God.

2 Timothy 3:16 says, **"All Scripture is inspired by God and profitable for teaching, for reproof, for correction, for training in righteousness..."** The Word of God handled accurately (used properly in its context) is useful in helping others in every facet of the Christian life. To begin with, the problem must be defined biblically. For example, what is the husband doing that is violating the Word of God? Is he sinning by displaying an angry temper, or lying, or cursing? Only after a problem is defined biblically, can a biblical solution be determined. The problem and solution should be described in biblical language using appropriate Scripture references. **"Now we have received, not the spirit of the world, but the Spirit who is from God, that we**

might know the things freely given to us by God, which things we also speak, *not in words taught by human wisdom*, but in those taught by the Spirit, combining spiritual thoughts with spiritual words" (1 Corinthians 2:12-13, emphasis added).

3. Counsel Should Be Directed Toward Restoration.

Restoring the wife's relationship with her husband and both of their relationships with God is critical and must be a priority. This means the counselor should help each one to identify their sin and seek and grant forgiveness from each other as well as God. If her husband refuses to participate in biblical counseling, the wife can go and work on her part in the failure of the marriage. Later, after the wife has made progress, she might be better able to encourage her husband to seek counsel with her.

4. The Wife Must Not Slander Or Speak Evil Of Her Husband When She Seeks Counsel From Another.

Proverbs 10:18 says, **"He who conceals hatred has lying lips and he who spreads slander is a fool."** It is one thing for a wife to seek advice on how to respond biblically to her husband's sin. It is another thing to run him down to others. If she appropriately conceals a matter, the only people who know should be those who are part of the solution.

5. The Wife Should Limit The Number Of People She Tells Of Her Husband's Problem.

Though the Bible does say, **"In a multitude of counsel there is safety"** (Proverbs 11:14), a wife who tells others of her husband's sin problems without making a serious effort to receive biblical counseling is often only engaging in sinful gossip.

6. The Wife Should Follow The Biblical Admonition That Older, More Mature Women Are To Teach Younger Women.

A godly older, more mature woman who meets the qualifications of Titus 2:2-3 is a good candidate to counsel a wife. Such a woman is instructed in Titus 2:4 to **"encourage the young women to love their husbands, to love their children, to be sensible, pure, workers at home, kind, being subject to their own husbands, that the Word of God may not be dishonored."** Since Scripture does **"... not allow a woman to teach or exercise authority over a man..."** (1 Timothy 2:12), the "older woman" should work only with the wife and not the husband.

7. Often Leaders Of A Church May Be The Best Source Of Biblical Counsel.

They have the biblical responsibility to provide such counsel. They are to **"...be ready in season and out of season; [to] reprove, rebuke, exhort, with great patience and instruction"** (2 Timothy 4:2). Should you desire to seek out a biblical counselor, determine if the counselor is certified by the National Association of Nouthetic Counselors (NANC).[30]

Resource #7
Church Discipline

And if he refuses to listen to them, tell it to the church.
Matthew 18:15

Church discipline is the process of the discipline and restoration of a sinning Christian. If a Christian husband continues to sin against his wife and she has faithfully exercised the other measures explained in this chapter, she should not hesitate to involve others as long as she does it biblically. A four step process for church discipline is provided in Matthew 18:15-17.

Step One:

"If your brother sins, go and reprove him in private, if he listens to you, you have won your brother" (Matthew 18:15). This step was discussed under Resource #4 - Make A Biblical Reproof. Unless a wife's or other person's physical safety is threatened (see the next section if there is a threat to physical safety), she should ensure that her husband has had time to think about what she has said in her reproof before moving to step two of church discipline. Sometimes a husband may put off making a decision as a device to manipulate his wife into leaving him alone. Therefore, it is generally a good idea for her to tell him something like, "I want to give you some time to think about what I said. So, I'll check back with you on Friday evening to see what you decided." If he continues to try to put her off, then she might say, "I have no choice but to take your lack of a decision as a 'no' answer. As a result, I am going to the next step in the church discipline process."

Step Two:

"But if he does not listen to you, take one or two more with you, so that by the mouth of two or three witnesses every fact may be confirmed" (Matthew 18:16). The wife must use care in approaching others in her church as witnesses against the sinful behavior of her husband. First, the wife's primary motive must be to restore her husband to a right relationship with God and his family. Second, she must approach those who are best able to help — usually these are spiritually mature men who are members of the church. Third, the wife must take care to not slander or speak evil of him. Fourth, a wife should usually tell her husband that she is going to seek help from others. This will show the husband the wife's intent is serious and may cause him to reconsider his sin and his unwillingness to seek help himself. However, under no circumstances may a husband rightly forbid his wife to pursue church discipline against him. That would be asking her to sin because the Scripture instructs her to continue in the process if he does not repent. So, a wife in such cases would have to obey God rather than her husband.

The wife should request that one or two of the men (preferably men who know her husband) or other qualified witnesses such as family or friends meet with her and her husband so that he may be confronted openly and directly concerning his sin. At the meeting, she should accurately report the facts of her husband's sin. She should not exaggerate the facts nor underplay them. Otherwise, she would be deceptive. Wives should realize that wise witnesses will always give the husband an opportunity to tell his side of the story in keeping with Proverbs 18:17. "The first to plead his case seems just, until another comes and examines him." They must fully hear both the wife's and husband's account, before they can take action. Proverbs 18:13 says, "He who gives an answer before he hears, it is a folly and shame to him."

Nevertheless, the wife and witnesses should discuss when the husband should be contacted and what should be said. Those who make up the team which speaks with the husband should be prepared to tell the husband in a clear, direct, but loving manner that he is sinning against God, if that is discovered to be the case. They should, of course, use Scripture to reprove the husband of his sin. Often at such a meeting the husband will repent. If he does not, his wife has a responsibility to move on to step three.

Step Three:

> *"And if he refuses to listen to them, tell it to the church..."*
> *Matthew 18:17.*

Sadly many churches will not practice church discipline. Regardless, the wife should still go to the church pastors or elders, accurately report the fact that her husband is unrepentant, and ask them to proceed with church discipline. If they will not, the wife will know she has done what she could.

Step Four:

"...and if he refuses to listen even to the church, let him be to you as a Gentile and tax gatherer" (Matthew 18:17). These steps require that the name of the husband and his sin be brought before the congregation. Then the entire congregation are to lovingly put pressure on him to repent. These are difficult steps and must not be done hastily. Many churches will not undertake steps three and four unless they have it written into their church constitution or doctrinal statement. However, these last steps are one of the most effective preventive measures that the church has for warning people against hardening their heart in continuing, unrepentant, willful sin. Just as in STEP TWO, these steps are undertaken for the purpose of keeping the church pure and of restoring a sinning brother to a right relationship with God, his church, and his wife. If he still refuses to repent, the church is to consider him to be an unbeliever (**"...a gentile and a tax gatherer"** Matthew 18:17). Jay Adams' book, *The Handbook of Church Discipline,* is an excellent resource for more details about church discipline.[31]

Resource #8
Involve the Governing Authorities

> *Let every man be in subjection to the governing authorities.*
> *Romans 13:1*

The governing authorities include the police, family and children's services, as well as local magistrates and courts. The involvement of these agencies are extreme measures and should only be used when there is danger to the wife or children or a serious criminal offense has been committed. However, the wife who is truly threatened with real harm should not hesitate to call the police.

If a husband threatens physical abuse or is sinning against his wife by verbally attacking her, she should not hesitate to involve her church's leadership to initiate the process of church discipline, or contact the governing authority (if appropriate). Letting her husband bear the consequences of his sinful behavior at the hand of either church or governmental authorities is an act of loving obedience to God since God Himself has appointed these authorities for her protection.

Any fear that the wife has that her husband might retaliate against her is understandable. However, a wife must obey God and take full advantage of these measures as His protective provision for her. Though no one can perfectly guarantee a wife's safety, neither can her safety be guaranteed if she continues to passively submit to physical abuse. If a wife takes advantage of God's protective resources and he harms her anyway, *then* she will be suffering for **"righteousness sake"** (1 Peter 2:21-23). In that case, the wife should follow the example of Christ, **"who committed no sin, nor was any deceit in His mouth and while being reviled, He did not revile in return, while suffering He uttered no threats, but kept entrusting Himself to Him who judges righteously."** Her love for God in obeying His Word and her love for her husband in wanting him to be restored to a right relationship with God can (if her motives are right) overcome her fear as **"perfect love casts out fear"** (1 John 4:18).

Conclusion

In summary, a Christian wife must take full advantage of all the biblical measures that God has provided her in His Word. This is the spiritually mature course. To do otherwise is foolish, and shows the wife's own unwillingness to obey or her ignorance of God's Word. A wife who desires to be godly must remember, the more she obeys God's Word, the more she can take advantage of the biblical resources God has given to protect her. Importantly, the more she submits to God and her husband in a biblical way, the more likely her husband is to repent and turn to God. Even if her husband does not repent, a godly wife will have the absolute assurance that her responses glorified God and were **"precious in God's sight"** (1 Peter 3:4).

Chapter Fifteen

Honoring Christ
Key to the Wife's Motivation

Wives respond to biblical teaching on submission in a wide variety of ways ranging from immediate acceptance to outright rejection. For example, some may respond in an objective matter-of-fact manner. Their attitude is, "OK Lord, now that I understand what you want me to do, it's settled!" They implement the principles of biblical submission in their lives, and they soon discover the joy that results. Others, perhaps because of bitterness or determination to have their own way, struggle terribly. Even if they outwardly obey, they are often resentful and rebellious in their hearts. Instead of experiencing the joy of biblical submission, they are miserable and spread their misery to others. Because accepting the biblical view of submission is so hard for some wives, this chapter explains the biblical motivation for a wife's submission.

Few wives naturally have the right heart's attitude to be submissive to their husbands. Even if a woman desires to please God by being submissive, she will not always *feel* like being submissive. Also in a conflict, when feelings are intense, it may be very difficult for her to submit. Regardless of her feelings, she should honor Christ by developing a mind-set or a resolve to do the right thing in the right way with the right motive whether she feels like it or not. In the process, her feelings will eventually improve.

Many wives are motivated solely or primarily by how they feel, and that makes their motivation at times selfish and sinful. There are many biblical principles that make it easier for the wife to change her motivation from "What can I get out of this?" to "How can the Lord Jesus Christ be honored in this?"

A Wife's Motivation To Be Submissive: Biblical Principles

1. A WIFE SHOULD BE GRATEFUL FOR WHAT GOD HAS DONE FOR HER.

It is overwhelming to think about what the Lord Jesus Christ has done for sinful mankind by His atoning work on the cross. No one deserves His forgiveness and grace. It is freely bestowed because of His love and mercy. Many things fall into proper perspective when a wife remembers what the Lord Jesus Christ has done for her. Everyone's redemption was purchased at a terrible price. Just thinking about all that the Lord underwent — scourged, mocked, despised, rejected, humiliated, and crucified — should evoke a deep gratitude from every believer. It would logically follow that Christians would want, out of a grateful heart, to show their gratitude for what God has done by their loving obedience to God. This should be a tremendously motivating factor in becoming biblically submissive to your husband.

> *...conduct yourselves in fear during the time of your stay upon the earth; knowing that you were not redeemed with perishable things like silver or gold from your futile way of life inherited from your forefathers, but with precious blood, as of a lamb unblemished and spotless, the blood of Christ.*
>
> *1 Peter 1:17-19*

2. A WIFE SHOULD LOOK TO THE EXAMPLE OF CHRIST'S SUBMISSION TO THE FATHER.

Even though the Lord Jesus Christ was equal to the Father in every regard, He chose to subordinate Himself to the Father in order to carry out their plan of redemption. He did not demand equal rights! Instead, He put Himself aside and obeyed the Father even to the **"point of death"** (Philippians 2:8). Following Christ's example is a compelling motivation for you to be submissive to your husband.

> *Have this attitude in yourselves which was also in Christ Jesus, who, although He existed in the form of God, did not regard equality with God a thing to be grasped, but emptied Himself, taking the form of a bond-servant, and*

being made in the likeness of men. And being found in appearance as a man, He humbled Himself by becoming obedient to the point of death, even death on a cross.

Philippians 2:5-8

3. A WIFE SHOULD REPENT OF ANY WRONG THINKING BY RENEWING HER MIND WITH SCRIPTURE.

Many wives have been taken captive by worldly philosophy. Women today commonly believe that they should aggressively pursue equality with or dominance over their husbands. In addition, some believe their husbands should always make them happy or cause them to feel "good about themselves." Her career and "having it all" become at least as important or possibly more important to her than her husband's career. If you think this way, your values and views are unbiblical. The solution is for you to bring your beliefs and values in line with Scripture. First, study the Scriptures and then if your values are wrong, *renew (change) your mind.* (And after all, changing your mind is certainly a woman's prerogative!)

> *See to it that no one takes you captive through philosophy and empty deception, according to the tradition of men, according to the elementary principles of the world, rather than according to Christ.*
>
> *Colossians 2:8*

> *...do not be conformed to this world but be transformed by the renewing of your mind.*
>
> *Romans 12:2*

4. A WIFE'S TRUE BEAUTY AND ADORNMENT COMES FROM BEING SUBMISSIVE TO HER HUSBAND.

Many wives strive for physical beauty, but Scripture says that **"beauty is vain"** (Proverbs 31:30). While it's alright for her to adorn herself with outward beauty, a godly wife's *first* concern is to adorn herself more with inward beauty. You do this by being submissive to your husband with the attitude of a **"meek and quiet spirit"** (1 Peter 2:3). You develop a **"meek and quiet spirit"** by humbly trusting God while being submissive to your husband. Your motivation comes from placing your hope and trust in God just like the **"holy women"** in **"former times"** (1 Peter 2:5).

> *And let not your adornment be merely external — braiding the hair, wearing gold jewelry, or putting on dresses; but let it be the hidden person of the heart with the <u>unfading quality of a gentle and quiet spirit which is precious in the sight of God. For</u> in this way in former times the holy women also, who hoped in God, used to adorn themselves, being submissive to their own husbands.*
>
> *1 Peter 2:3-5*

5. BIBLICAL SUBMISSION SHOWS LOVE TO GOD.

Biblical submission of a wife to her husband is a command from God to wives. Each time a wife is outwardly and inwardly submissive to her husband, she is showing love to God. Singing, "Oh, How I Love Jesus!" is meaningless unless she is <u>obedient to Jesus' commands.</u> Knowing that obedience in this area is a principal way that you can demonstrate love to God can provide extra motivation for being an excellent wife.

> *The Lord Jesus said, "If you love Me, you will keep my commandments."*
>
> *John 14:15*

> *For this is the love of God, that we keep His commands, and His commandments are not burdensome.*
>
> *1 John 5:3*

6. BIBLICAL SUBMISSION IS A WAY TO SHOW LOVE TO HER HUSBAND.

A wife who is more concerned about showing love to her husband than she is about having her own way will have a righteous sense of purpose. When faced with a specific circumstance and struggling with not wanting to be submissive, it will help you if you think thoughts like, **"Love doesn't seek its own (way)** (1 Corinthians 13:5). I *can* show love to my husband by being submissive to him." Thinking this in the midst of a struggle is tremendously freeing and powerfully motivating since...

> *Love does not act unbecomingly...*
> *Love does not seek its own (way)...*
> *Love rejoices in the truth, it does not rejoice in unrighteousness...*
> *Love endures all things.*
>
> *1 Corinthians 13:4-7*

7. BIBLICAL SUBMISSION SHOULD BE VIEWED THROUGH GOD'S SOVEREIGNTY AND GOODNESS.

Viewing life through God's sovereignty and goodness is seeing every tiny detail in life as arranged for you by God. There is no such thing as fate, luck, or chance. God has purpose in your *every* circumstance (including your husband's decisions). God channels the King's hearts, and He can certainly channel your husband's heart. God is in control whether you like it or not!

It will help motivate you when you think, "Lord, what do you have planned for me today? You are *good*, and You do all things well. Thank you for my husband's answer." As you view your life through God's sovereignty and goodness, you will be continuously aware of God's purpose and grace in your life. And you will become more motivated to want to please God.

> *...who has saved us, and called us with a holy calling, not according to our works, but according to His own purpose and grace which was granted us in Christ Jesus from all eternity.*
>
> **2 Timothy 1:9**

8. GOD USES OTHERS TO PUT PRESSURE ON A WIFE TO BE SUBMISSIVE.

God sometimes uses loving confrontation by your husband, friend, or an older woman to help motivate you to be biblically submissive. If you receive their reproofs humbly, God will use them to help mold you into His character. Your responsibility is to humbly receive these "wounds" as a good thing and admit when you are wrong. Then seek guidance and accountability until you do not struggle with submission any longer.

> *Husbands, love your wives, just as Christ also loved the church and gave Himself up for her; that He might sanctify her, having cleansed her by the washing of water with the word, that He might present to Himself the church in all her glory, having no spot or wrinkle or any such thing; but that she should be holy and blameless.*
>
> **Ephesians 5:25-27**

Faithful are the wounds of a friend.

Proverbs 27:6

Better is an open rebuke than love that is concealed.

Proverbs 27:5

*Older women...teaching what is good, that they may en-
courage the younger women to...be subject to their own
husbands.*

Titus 2:3-5

9. A WIFE SHOULD TRAIN HERSELF TO BE BIBLICALLY SUBMISSIVE.

The Greek word "train" in the Bible is *gymnazo* from which we get our English words gymnastics and gymnasium. *Gymnazo* implies doing something over and over until a person does it right. So, when you are not submissive in a godly way, you can train yourself biblically by thinking through what you *should* have thought and done instead of what you did. Next, ask God's forgiveness, then your husband's forgiveness. You might want to say something to the effect of, "When I said and did ... I was not submissive to you. If I had this to do over again, this is how I would respond — (give details of what you should have done). Will you forgive me?" This process takes work, but it will profit you not only in this life but the one to come. After all, practice does make perfect! Your motivation would be based on personal profit to you now as well as profit in eternity (see 2 Corinthians 5:10).

> *But have nothing to do with worldly fables fit only for
> old women. On the other hand, discipline [train] yourself
> for the purpose of godliness; for bodily discipline is only
> of little profit, but godliness is profitable for all things,
> since it holds promise for the present life and also for the
> life to come.*
>
> *1 Timothy 4:7-8, adaptation added*

10. A WIFE SHOULD LEARN THE BIBLICAL DYNAMICS OF AUTHORITY AND REBELLION.

God's Word is the final authority for the practice of your life. You may, in fact, be very active in your church and still not be doing what the Lord told you to do through His Word. You may be making a sacrifice but *not* the sacrifice that God intended. If so, you are likely taking matters into your own hands by doing what you *think* needs to be done instead of what God says He wants you to do. This is rebellion against God.

> *For rebellion is as the sin of divination and insubordination is as iniquity and idolatry... ...Behold, to obey is better than sacrifice and to heed than the fat of rams...*
> *1 Samuel 15:22,23*

Rebellion is a very serious sin. If you disobey your husband, you are indirectly shaking your fist at God. You are saying in your heart, "God, I don't care what You say. I'm going to do this *my way!*" When you rebel against your husband's authority, you are grievously sinning. It is a frightening thing. You may repent of your rebellion at any time by confessing your sin to God, clearing your conscience with your husband, and submitting to your husband's authority in all things unless he asks you to sin. When tempted to rebel, imagine shaking your fist at God and declaring, "No, I won't do it!" That will be a powerful motivation for you to be submissive.

11. A WIFE SHOULD SEEK TRULY BIBLICAL COUNSEL FROM SOMEONE WHO WILL EXHORT AND ADMONISH HER TO BE SUBMISSIVE.

All Christians are to exhort and admonish each other. However, God has gifted some Christians with the gift of exhortation. If someone has that gift and is appropriately knowledgeable about the subject of submission, they can energetically encourage and thereby motivate you to be submissive to your husband. Their attitude should be something like the Apostle Paul in Colossians 1:28,29:

And we proclaim Him, admonishing every man and teaching every man with all wisdom, that we may present every man complete in Christ. And for this purpose also I labor, striving according to His power, which mightily works within me.

Colossians 1:28,29

12. A WIFE SHOULD HUMBLY RECEIVE HER HUSBAND'S BIBLICAL CORRECTION AND REPROOF.

It is a very biblically loving act when a husband gently but firmly uses Scripture to correct his wife when she is sinning.

Husbands, love your wives, just as Christ also loved the church and gave Himself up for her...

Ephesians 5:25-27

If you are not submissive and your husband reproves you by using the Word of God, he is most likely trying to help you mature as a Christian and honor the Lord. You should view your husband's reproof as a wonderful gift from God to help motivate you to be submissive to him.

13. STUDY THE CHARACTER OF GOD.

You may have misperceptions about God's character. As a result, you may have wrong thinking about God and your appropriate response to Him. Bringing your misperceptions in line with the true God of the Bible will likely help you to be more motivated to be obedient by being submissive. Even if you do not have misperceptions about what God is like, studying God's character will help you to take the focus off of yourself and to focus instead on the Lord.

Thus says the LORD, "Let not a wise man boast of his wisdom, and let not the mighty man boast of his might, let not a rich man boast of his riches; but let him who boasts boast of this, that he understands and knows Me, that I am the LORD who exercises lovingkindness, justice, and righteousness on earth; for I delight in these things," declares the LORD.

Jeremiah 9:23,24

14. A WIFE WILL HONOR GOD'S WORD BY BEING SUBMISSIVE TO HER HUSBAND.

It is an honor to God and His Word when you do what God has instructed you to do. It shows a reverence for His Word and humility before God that what He wants you to do is more important to you than what you want. Desiring to honor God and His Word by being submissive is a very real motivation.

> *The older women are to ...encourage the younger women to... be subject to their own husbands, that the word of God may not be dishonored.*
>
> *Titus 2:3-5*

15. A WIFE CAN BE MOTIVATED TO BE SUBMISSIVE IN THE "BIG THINGS" BY BEING FAITHFUL IN THE "LITTLE THINGS."

Every tiny infraction matters to God, even if it is very small. Usually it is the **"little foxes that spoil the vine"** (Song of Solomon 2:15). Your true heart and character is shown with small, seemingly unimportant things that your husband asks you to do or to not do. It is with the little things that your husband will likely know if you are really being submissive or not. Others may never know, but your husband will, and God will. Realizing that your faithfulness in the seemingly small areas matters so much to God should help you be motivated to be even more faithful in the big things.

> *He who is faithful in a very little thing is faithful also in much; and he who is unrighteous in a very little thing is also unrighteous in much.*
>
> *Luke 16:10*

16. BIBLICAL SUBMISSION IS ONE WAY FOR A WIFE TO BE A "LIVING SACRIFICE" FOR THE LORD JESUS.

Any time you submit to your husband and it is not what you would have preferred, you are sacrificing self for obedience to God. If you do the right thing **"as unto the Lord,"** then you can delight in knowing that He is pleased with your sacrifice. Knowing that God is pleased is a powerful motivation to be submissive.

> *I urge you therefore, brethren, by the mercies of God, to present your bodies a living and holy sacrifice, acceptable to God, which is your spiritual service of worship.*
> *Romans 12:1*

17. A WIFE SHOULD REALIZE THAT BEING SUBMISSIVE IS A FRUIT OF HER SALVATION.

Godly fruit is the evidence that someone has become a Christian. They will have a desire and longing to please God and to obey Him. Each subsequent act of obedience to God's Word is part of the fruit Jesus said Christians would bear (John 15:8). Realizing that submission to your husband is one of the fruits of your salvation should be a motivating factor for you.

> *By this is My Father glorified, that you bear much fruit, and so prove to be my disciples.*
> *John 15:8*

18. A WIFE MAY BE MOTIVATED BY PERSONAL TESTIMONIES OF WOMEN WHO ARE ALREADY SUBMISSIVE TO THEIR HUSBANDS.

Testimonies of what God has taught faithful women in the area of submission can be very motivating and encouraging to you if you are struggling. In seeking these testimonies, be discerning about what the other person is telling you. Ask yourself, "Is this biblically correct?" If it is, then be encouraged. Scripture is replete with examples of wives who were submissive. Another good source may be biographies of Christian men and women which are selected with discernment.

> *For in this way in former times the holy women also, who hoped in God, used to adorn themselves, being submissive to their own husbands. Thus Sarah obeyed Abraham, calling him lord, and you have become her children if you do what is right without being frightened by any fear.*
> *1 Peter 3:5-6*

19. REALIZE THAT SOMETIMES SHE MAY BE "SUFFERING FOR RIGHTEOUSNESS."

Most of the time when a wife suffers, she is not suffering for the Lord but because of her own rebellious, willful heart. However, it is possible to suffer because of her righteous responses. For example, if your thinking and actions are pleasing to the Lord and your husband continues to be selfish, etc., then your suffering will have purpose — it will be for the Lord's sake. If you are suffering, make sure that it truly is for **doing what is right rather than for doing what is wrong** (1 Peter 3:17). Be motivated to endure in your righteous suffering by remembering.

> *...who is there to harm you if you prove zealous for what is good? But even if you should suffer for the sake of righteousness, you are blessed.*
> *1 Peter 3:13-14*

20. A WIFE SHOULD REMIND HERSELF OF THE POTENTIAL GRIEVOUS CONSEQUENCES OF NOT BEING SUBMISSIVE.

Some of these consequences are personal embarrassment, loss of reward at the judgment seat of Christ, Divine discipline, church discipline, and/or disqualification of her husband from the office of elder or deacon.

> *For those whom the Lord loves He disciplines, and He scourges every son whom He receives...He disciplines us for our good, that we may share His holiness. All discipline for the moment seems not to be joyful, but sorrowful; yet to those who have been trained by it, afterwards it yields the peaceful fruit of righteousness.*
> *Hebrews 12:6-11*

God will do what He has to do to turn you from your rebellion to humble submission to your husband. Many times, those consequences are painful, embarrassing, and very difficult to endure. If you repent, you will be able to say as did the Psalmist, **"Before I was afflicted I went astray, but now I keep Thy word. Thou art good and doest good; teach me Thy statutes"** (Psalms 119:67-68). Fear of consequences is a powerful motivation.

Summary

Biblical submission is not necessarily always what a wife would naturally choose to do, but her motivation should be greater than just her own selfish desires. There are different motivations with which God would be pleased, but her chief motive ought always to be the glory of God. Motivation is important! A wife will *never* be what the Lord wants her to be until she graciously and joyfully comes under the authority of her husband.

Chapter Sixteen

Communication
Control of the Wife's Tongue

Have you ever said something and immediately regretted it? All of us understand what James is talking about when he wrote, **"But no one can tame the tongue...from the same mouth come both blessing and cursing. My brethren, these things ought not to be this way"** (James 3:8-10). What we say and how we say it can hurt others. Words can crush and pierce people. Some wounds may never heal. In marriages, husbands and wives have the potential to hurt each other deeply by the words they say. Often, couples communicate in unbiblical, ungodly ways. Instead of love and kindness there is strife, anger, and malice. Instead of wisdom there is foolishness. Instead of careful words, there are careless words. Again let me express what is on my heart for all of us with what James said, **"My brethren, these things ought not to be this way"** (James 3:10).

This chapter is about communication — control of the wife's tongue. It is a necessary chapter because the Excellent Wife must communicate rightly to her husband if she is going to love, respect, and submit to him as God desires. In order to accomplish this purpose, I decided to address nine biblical principles regarding a wife's communication to her husband.

Communicating With Your Husband: Nine Biblical Principles

1. A WIFE'S WRONG WORDS BEGIN WITH WRONG THOUGHTS AND MOTIVES.

> *For out of the heart come <u>evil thoughts</u>, murders, adulter-*
> *ies, fornications, thefts, false witness, slanders. These are*
> *the things which defile the man; but to eat with unwashed*
> *hands does not defile the man.*
> > *Matthew 15:19-20, emphasis added*

"Heart" in Scripture includes a person's thoughts, choices, or motives. Your "heart" is not some emotional part of you that you have no control over. What you think about is a choice that you make. The Lord Jesus made the connection clear between what you think and what you speak. **"For the mouth speaks out of that which fills the heart"** (Matthew 12:34). Wrong words do begin with wrong thoughts. If you are saying wrong words, take the time to realize what you are thinking. The Lord Jesus' standard of holiness is not just outward conformity but inward transformation by what you think. Renew your mind with Scripture and change your heart.

You renew your mind with Scripture by meditating on Scripture appropriate to the areas of communication you need to improve. Biblical meditation includes reading the specific Scripture over and over and thinking of ways that you can personally apply it. For example, if you tend to be impatient towards your husband and "snap" at him, meditate on 1 Corinthians 13:4. **"Love is patient."** Think of ways that you could respond patiently given the same or similar circumstance. For instance, your husband takes a long time to tell you about an incident at work and you wish he would hurry up. Think **"Love is patient. I** *can* show love to him by patiently listening until he is finished." Then, express by your words an interest in his story. If you do, your *right* words will have begun with *right* thoughts.

2. A WIFE IS ACCOUNTABLE TO GOD FOR EVERY WORD SHE SPEAKS.

> *And I say to you, that every careless word that men shall*
> *speak, they shall render account for it in the day of judg-*
> *ment.*
> > *Matthew 12:36-37*

God is omniscient. He knows everything and will not forget anything. He desires for us to be holy all the time not just on Sunday mornings. This is a sobering thought when we consider how many **"careless"** words we probably do speak. Careless words are "idle, lazy, and useless."[32] They remind me of the old expression, "Some people talk just to hear themselves talk." As a Christian you are to take care with your words. As a wife you are to take extra special care if you are going to demonstrate love, respect, and submission to your husband as God desires. Realize that God is aware of what you say. Therefore, you are accountable to Him for your every word.

3. A WIFE IS TO SPEAK THE TRUTH TO HER HUSBAND, BUT SPEAK IT IN LOVE.

...but speaking the truth in love, we are to grow up in all aspects into Him, who is the head, even Christ...

Ephesians 4:15

Speaking the truth is not always easy. In fact, it may be agonizing. Sometimes you may have to tell your husband unpleasant truths. Sometimes it is easier to be deceptive or just avoid issues. However, in a patient, kind, and loving manner, you *can* tell your husband what he biblically needs to hear. For instance, imagine that you notice your husband being overly critical of someone else. It might be more pleasant to just discreetly change the subject, but Jesus said, **"If your brother sins, go and reprove him in private; if he listens to you, you have won your brother"** (Matthew 18:15). If you have been reluctant to tell your husband the truth – speak the truth, but do it in love.

4. A WIFE MUST "PUT OFF" ANY WRONG SPEECH.

But now you also, put them all aside: anger, wrath, malice, slander, and abusive speech from your mouth.

Colossians 3:8

Wrong speech is clearly defined in Colossians chapter three. Anger and wrath are varying kinds of anger. Anger can express itself in extremes from a slight edge in your voice to screaming, cursing, and full blown wrath. Malice is meanness, desiring ill towards the other person. Slander is painting another person in a bad light. Abusive speech refers to "obscene and derogatory speech intended to hurt and wound someone."[33]

Sometimes a wife is tempted to use angry, abusive, or even malicious words during emotional days just before her menstruation begins. Even though control is harder during that time, with God all things are possible (1 Corinthians 10:13). Work extra hard to think about what you are going to say and to say what is right in spite of how you feel. Any kind of wrong speech is sin. Begin by confessing to God each and every time you speak in a wrong way. End by replacing those wrong words with the truth spoken in love. Then you will have laid the wrong speech aside.

5. A WIFE MUST GIVE HER HUSBAND THE BENEFIT OF THE DOUBT WHEN IT COMES TO JUDGING HIS MOTIVES.

> *Therefore, do not go on passing judgment before the time, but wait until the <u>Lord comes who will both bring to light the things hidden in the darkness and disclose the motives of men's hearts;</u> and then each man's praise will come to him from God.*
>
> *1 Corinthians 4:5, emphasis added*

We are *not* to make judgments about the **"motives of men's hearts"** (1 Corinthians 4:5). No matter how well you think you know someone else, only God can judge their motives. It is presumption for one person to believe they know what another person is thinking or why they did what they did. Sometimes people who pride themselves on their "discernment" are in reality presumptuously judging motives. Often wives presumptuously judge their husbands and react based on what they think their husband is thinking.

Perhaps you can think of a time when you overreacted to something your husband said or did and he was consequently baffled by your reaction. You judged his motives if you said something like, "You did that deliberately to upset me!" or "You did that to get back at me for what your father did to you when you were a child!" Instead of judging his motive, give him the benefit of the doubt and place his action in the best possible light. For example, "He did not realize how important that was to me." or "Perhaps he knows something that I do not know about these circumstances." You will have to wait until the Lord comes back and then He will rightly judge your husband's motives.

6. A WIFE IS MORE LIKELY TO SIN IF HER WORDS ARE RASH.

> *There is one who speaks rashly like the thrusts of a sword, but the tongue of the wise brings healing.*
>
> *Proverbs 12:18*

Solomon likened rash speech to being like **"... the thrusts of a sword..."** (Proverbs 12:18). In other words, rash words deeply wound the person receiving them. They inflict pain. They hurt the other person.

If you speak in a way so as to hurt the other person, you may have a desire to be in control. A controlling person tends to communicate in vengeful ways. Often your threats and "lashing back" are full of more meanness than the original offense. Follow the example Peter wrote about of the Lord

Jesus Christ who **"while being reviled, He did not revile in return; while suffering, He uttered no threats, but kept entrusting Himself to Him who judges righteously ..."** (1 Peter 2:23). Our Lord entrusted Himself to God. He did not fight back with evil. Peter's point is that even while suffering an emotional battery from your husband, you are to look to the Lord Jesus Christ as your example. Instead of wounding your husband, use your tongue to bring healing (Proverbs 12:18).

7. A WIFE IS MORE LIKELY TO BE HEARD IF HER SPEECH IS FORBEARING AND SWEET.

> *By forbearance a ruler may be persuaded, and a soft tongue breaks the bone.*
>
> Proverbs 25:15

> *The wise in heart will be called discerning, And sweetness of speech increases persuasiveness. Proverbs 16:21*

Husbands are much more willing to consider their wives requests and even admonitions if they are given sweetly. This is not fake "sugar-sweetness," but genuine forbearance ("putting up with") and niceness. In fact, it is difficult for most husbands not to give in to their wives' requests when there is sweetness of speech. One word of caution, **"sweetness of speech"** is not to be used as a manipulative ploy for you to have your way, but it is a righteous way for you to persuade your husband to give you what you want. The test of your motive will be how you respond if you do not get your way. Indeed, God is glorified by your righteous speech whether you get your way or not!

8. AN EXCELLENT WIFE IS WISE AND KIND WHEN SHE TALKS TO HER HUSBAND.

> *She opens her mouth in wisdom, and the teaching of kindness is on her tongue.*
>
> Proverbs 31:26

A godly wife is wise and kind. When she opens her mouth to speak, wisdom and kindness flow out. Her wisdom comes from the Word of God and her kindness from the Holy Spirit. Her words are not rude, terse, harsh, or wounding, they are edifying and helpful. If you are to be wise and kind when you speak to your husband, speak your words in a soothing tone. Proverbs 15:4 says, **"a soothing tongue is a tree of life ..."**

Think about how you would like to be treated. What if you are wrong? What if you are sinning? Do you want kindness or harshness, foolishness or wisdom? Of course you want him to be kind and wise. So, treat your husband like you would like to be treated (Matthew 7:12).

Suppose your husband wanted to make a purchase that you consider to be foolish. First, think about what you are going to say. Next, say it in a soothing tone. For instance, (speak gently) "Honey, I know you would like to have a fishing boat. I would like for you to have your boat, but I think it would be wiser to save the money to purchase it instead of borrowing the money from the bank." No matter what the issue is, when you talk to your husband, be wise in your words and kind in your tone. That is how the Excellent Wife opens her mouth.

9. A WIFE SHOULD PURIFY HER SPEECH UNTIL IT IS MORE AND MORE FLAWLESS.

> *The tongue of the righteous is as choice silver. The heart of the wicked is worth little.*
>
> *Proverbs 10:20*

Silver is a rare, precious, treasured commodity. So is a righteous tongue. Just as the refiner purifies the silver time and time again to make it choice, a wife should purify her speech until it is more and more flawless. You can purify your speech by practicing over and over until you get it right (1 Timothy 4:7). Think through what you should say, then practice it out loud (alone). Concentrate on saying the words in a "soothing" tone of voice. You may feel silly at first, but if you want to be godly you must be trained! The value of your godly tongue would truly be like "choice silver," a precious commodity.

Conclusion

How you communicate is a reflection of your commitment to Christ. Certainly, these are skills that need to be fine tuned. Ask your husband to hold you accountable for how you speak and your tone of voice. When your husband points your failures out to you, immediately reconsider how you should have communicated. Tell him what you should have done and ask his forgiveness. How important is this?

An excellent wife, who can find? For her worth is far above jewels ... She opens her mouth in wisdom, And the teaching of kindness is on her tongue.

Proverbs 31:10,26

Chapter Seventeen

Conflict
Quietness of the Wife's Spirit

Communicating in a godly way is foundational to solving conflict in a manner that will glorify God. The Excellent Wife is one who **"opens her mouth in wisdom"** (Proverbs 31:26). She does not run and hide from conflict, but neither does she run over her husband like a bulldozer pushing over a mound of dirt. Christian husbands and wives are to live together in unity. Unity is difficult in the best of times because we all sin and we are all so very different.

So, it is important for you to learn how to biblically solve conflict with your husband. In this chapter, we will see thoughts that hinder as well as thoughts that enhance conflict solving. We will also explain the three causes (selfishness, differentness, and righteousness) of conflicts and their solutions. In addition to the causes and solutions, this chapter covers the four character qualities you will need in order to be able to solve conflict biblically and to be an Excellent Wife.

In his letter to the Church at Ephesus, the Apostle Paul strongly urged the members to have unity. He wrote urging them to be **"diligent to preserve the unity of the Spirit in the bond of peace"** (Ephesians 4:3).There cannot be unity in the church as God intends when there is marital discord. Others may take up an offense for one or the other of the quarreling couple and join in the conflict. Sin that is not contained will most certainly spread!

When marriages are in trouble, there are many self-serving justifications people tell themselves and others. Many times, these justifications include revenge for having been hurt. It is important to recognize unbiblical thinking, because it is only with correct thinking that couples can work through conflict in a godly manner. The following is a list of some of the unbiblical thoughts that wives tell themselves and thereby make it virtually impossible to solve conflict.

Unbiblical Thoughts That Hinder Conflict Solving

1. "I *will* have my way. I can't believe he wants to paint the house green!"
2. "Why try? He won't even listen."
3. "He makes me so mad. He only cares about himself."
4. "He'll never change."
5. "He is impossible."
6. "It's no use, the problems are too big to solve."
7. "Things will never get any better. Divorce is inevitable."
8. "I can't take the pressure."
9. "There's no hope."

Thoughts like these are self-serving and unbiblical justification for giving up and no longer trying to work through problems. When a wife is thinking like this, she will also be concurrently struggling with intense emotional pain. That could cause her to conclude that she cannot bear the turmoil any longer.

Instead of justifying an escape from the conflicts, a wife must be **"transformed by the renewing of her mind"** (Romans 12:2). In the process, her emotions will be more bearable, and she will be in a much better position to continue to work on the problems. Instead of the sinful thoughts, what should she be thinking? What thoughts would make it easier for her to work through conflict biblically?

Biblical Thoughts That Enhance Conflict Solving

1. "What is God trying to teach me in the midst of this conflict?"

> *Consider it all joy, my brethren, when you encounter various trials, knowing that the testing of your faith produces endurance. And let endurance have its perfect result, that you may be perfect and complete, lacking in nothing. But if any of you lacks wisdom, let him ask of God, who gives to all men generously and without reproach, and it will be given to him.*
>
> *James 1:2-5*

2. "I am a Christian. For me to initiate a divorce just because we are having a lot of conflict is not an option that I have."

> *But to the married I give instructions, not I, but the Lord, that the wife should not leave her husband...And a woman who has an unbelieving husband, and he consents to live with her, let her not send her husband away.*
>
> *1 Corinthians 7:10,13*

> *Therefore, what God has joined together, let not man separate.*
>
> *Matthew 19:6*

3. "God will help me to endure these conflicts."

> *No temptation has overtaken you but such as is common to man; and God is faithful, who will not allow you to be tempted beyond what you are able, but with the temptation will provide the way of escape also, that you may be able to endure it.*
>
> *1 Corinthians 10:13*

4. "If I must suffer through this conflict, I want it to be for doing what is right, not because I have sinned."

> *For it is better, if God should will it so, that you suffer for doing what is right rather than for doing what is wrong.*
> *1 Peter 3:17*

> *Therefore, let those also who suffer according to the will of God entrust their souls to a faithful Creator in doing what is right.*
> *1 Peter 4:19*

5. "God has a purpose in this conflict."

> *For we know that God causes all things to work together for good to those who love God, to those who are called according to <u>His purpose</u>.*
> *Romans 8:28, emphasis added*

(Joseph speaking to his brothers who had sold him as a slave years earlier.) "As for you, you meant evil against me, but God meant it for good in order to bring about this present result..."

Genesis 50:20

6. "What can *I* do differently to make it easier for us to solve this conflict?"

Do nothing from selfishness or empty conceit, but with humility of mind let each of you regard one another as more important than himself...

Philippians 2:3

It is important to realize how wrong thoughts powerfully influence your emotions and make it extremely difficult to resolve conflict in a rational, reasonable manner. Right thoughts, on the other hand, make it much easier to resolve conflict biblically. There are, basically, three kinds of conflict: differentness, selfishness/sinfulness, and righteousness.[34]

The first cause of conflict is conflict over differentness. Some examples are differentness over the time you go to bed and the time you get up in the mornings, holiday traditions, how clean to keep the house, foods you like to eat, where to squeeze the toothpaste tube, and whether to paint the living room blue or green. Differentness is not right or wrong. It is not sinful. It is all right for your husband to have a different opinion from yours. However, if differentness is not handled properly, it can culminate in sin.

The biblical guideline to overcome differentness is "forbearance" (Ephesians 4:3). In other words, putting up with the other person's traditions or idiosyncrasies. Neither partner should be a bully, insisting on having their own way, but if something is really important to your husband (and he is not asking you to sin), then you should willingly give in graciously for the sake of unity and for the sake of remaining under your husband's authority.

Another aspect to overcoming differentness is for the couple to "leave their parents and cleave to each other." (Genesis 2:24) As a couple, they need to develop their own, new traditions and ways of doing things. Parents do not always graciously agree, but the couple should decide their plans together, then defer to the parents when it is possible.

I remember the first Thanksgiving our daughter Anna spent away from us. It was her first year married and they chose to visit with her husband's parents. I graciously told her to "have a good time!" Then, I hung up the phone and cried. However, my grief was short-lived when Sanford, my husband, reminded me that we are to let her **"leave and cleave"** (Genesis 2:24). He was right. So, we decided to invite the whole church for Thanksgiving dinner and ended up with about thirty people. We had a wonderful time of celebration. It is difficult for parents to let go, but they will be fine if they respond righteously.

If parents do not respond righteously, the couple may need to lovingly confront them. For example, "Mom and Dad, we love you and would like to be with you this Thanksgiving but have decided to spend Thanksgiving with friends out of town. I know you are disappointed. Please be glad for us that we can be with our friends." If Mom and Dad do not respond graciously, a more direct reproof is in order. Gently respond with something like, "You have the freedom in the Lord to invite us and we appreciate that. However, we also have the freedom to make other plans. Your responsibility is to let us go graciously and be glad for us." Most parents will respond graciously. If not, implement the principle on "not answering a fool according to his folly" from Chapter Fourteen. (For more information on "leaving and cleaving," I suggest you obtain Dr. Wayne Mack's two excellent Bible study tapes. One is for the parent and the other for the child.)[35]

Whether the "differentness" conflicts are due to holiday traditions or the toothpaste tube, the key to overcoming them is forbearance. Differentness is certainly not a sin, but sometimes husbands or wives do respond sinfully. This takes us to the second cause of conflict which is selfishness.

The natural heart wants to have its own way. We do not like to be told what to do. We are naturally rebellious and selfish. As a result, when there is conflict, it may be because we are selfish. The conflict then results in angry outbursts, pouting, manipulating, nagging, or resentment.

When a wife is selfish, her husband will likely react more to her bad attitude than to what she actually wants. He is going to sense she is out of his control and may become embroiled in a conflict with her. If you realize that you have been selfish or rebellious and caused conflict, ask God's forgiveness as well as your husband's. Learn from your sin, and stop seeking your own way.

If your husband is being selfish, lovingly and gently confront him with his sin giving several clear examples. When conflict is due to selfishness, it will be resolved with repentance and "putting on" love since **"Love does not seek its own (way)"** (1 Corinthians 13:5). The sin of selfishness is the number one reason why people do not get along.

The third reason people have conflict is because of righteousness. A conflict over righteousness occurs when one partner believes the other is violating the moral will of God as revealed in Scripture. Righteous conflicts manifest themselves in a myriad of ways such as child rearing, movies, books, television, and more obvious areas such as truth telling, moral purity, and not profaning God's name. A wife needs to be careful to separate her own personal interpretation of God's Word from the level of God's absolute Law. For example, your husband might want you to go somewhere you might not be completely comfortable to go; however, it is not clearly a sin issue. In areas like these, a wife should be submissive to her husband unless he asks her to personally sin. In other words, she should come as close as she can to what her husband wants, but not step over the line of what would be a personal sin for her. She may, in the process, have to suffer for doing what is right, but she should never, ever, have to suffer because of her own sin.

The solution to conflicts over righteousness is for both partners to submit to the Word of God in the matter. If your husband will not, you should implement some or all of the appropriate biblical principles God has given to protect you (Chapter Fourteen).

Sometimes, conflicts do occur because of righteousness, but much more frequently conflicts occur because of selfishness and/or differentness. You must decide what is clearly a sin according to the Bible, and therefore, worth standing your ground. In the other areas, the Lord wants you to be flexible.

When conflict occurs, it is important how you respond. Regardless of the basis of the conflict, disagreement is not an excuse to sin. In his letter to the Ephesians, Paul reminded all believers of their obligation to get along. As you read the following Scriptures, note the attitudes that they were to have.

> *Therefore I, the prisoner of the Lord, implore you to walk in a manner worthy of the calling with which you have been called, with all <u>humility</u> and <u>gentleness</u>, with <u>patience</u>, <u>showing tolerance</u> for one another in love, being diligent to preserve the unity of the Spirit in the bond of peace.*
>
> *Ephesians 4:1-3, emphasis added*

As with all believers, couples need to have these attitudes in their personal lives so they can work through conflict without sinning.

Attitudes Needed to Solve Conflict

1. Humility.

Humility means "lowliness of mind."[36] In other words, a humble person views himself in proper perspective to God and others. They do not **"think more highly of (themselves) than they ought to think"** (Romans 12:3). We naturally think about ourselves first. God, however, commands the opposite (Philippians 2:3).

The humility necessary to solve conflict may best be described Scripturally as humility that **"let each of you regard one another as more important than himself..."** (Philippians 2:3). Humble yourself by putting your husband first over yourself. Consider his desire as more important than your own (unless he is asking you to sin). Resolve to continue to biblically work through the conflict as long as it takes (unless the Lord removes you from the battle). To the degree that you humble yourself and do not seek your own way, God will be glorified and any conflict you and your husband have had will be well on its way to being solved.

2. Gentleness.

Gentleness (meekness) is strength under control.[37] It is to be a part of the woman's adornment. It is also one of the characteristics that makes her **"precious in God's sight"** (1 Peter 3:4). This suggests that she is to have her emotions under control and not to overreact to conflict. Strongly expressed emotions are not, in and of themselves, sinful, but they can be used in a sinful way to manipulate to have her way in a conflict. Gentleness is part of the fruit of the Holy Spirit (Galatians 5:23). It is also something that we are to **"pursue"** (1 Timothy 6:11). Gentleness incorporates tenderness and compassion. It is not hard, harsh, or sarcastic. It is not hysterical and fearful. If you are gentle, you will be content in the circumstances God has given you. You do not have to try to manipulate circumstances to suit yourself. You will be calm while under pressure. You will also be careful and thoughtful in how you respond when you and your husband disagree. Your soothing tone of voice will be calming in the mist of conflict.

3. Patience.

Patience is manifesting forbearance under provocation or strain.[38] Paul prayed for the Colossians that they would be **"strengthened with all power, according to His glorious might, for the attaining of all steadfastness and patience" (Colossians 1:11)**. How is it that God teaches us patience? One way is through tribulation. (Romans 5:3) Another way is through testings (James 1:3). Tribulation and testings are both a common catalyst for conflict. Patience, like gentleness, is part of the fruit of the Holy Spirit (Galatians 5:23). So you are to patiently listen and respond to your husband *especially* when there is conflict.

4. Forbearance.

Forbearance involves self-restraint and putting up with one another.[39] God, in His forbearance, **"passed over the sins previously committed"** (Romans 3:25). Paul wrote that we are to **"bear with one another...whoever has a complaint against anyone..."** (Colossians 3:13). It is not through our sinful flesh that we forbear, but with God's enablement and in obedience to His Word. Forbearance means putting up with your husband. It goes a long way towards solving conflict and maintaining unity.

If there is conflict, look first to yourself to see if you are manifesting these four character qualities in your life. If not, identify specific instances of sin, confess them to God, and ask your husband's forgiveness. Think through how you should have responded. Next time, respond the biblical way.

Conclusion

If there is a conflict over differentness, put your husband first by considering his desire as more important than your own. Be loving, patient with him, and if necessary forbearing. If the conflict is one of selfishness, repent of your sin. If your husband is the one guilty of selfishness, gently and patiently reprove him. Finally, if the conflict is over an issue of righteousness, do not sin but go with your husband to the Bible to determine God's will.

If you are thinking, "There's no hope. He'll never change," you are not giving God the credit He deserves when He tells you that through His enabling Spirit and obedience to His Word, you can achieve and maintain **"unity of the Spirit in the bond of peace."** Regardless of the cause or even the outcome of the conflict, you can continue to be an *Excellent Wife* as you strive to solve conflict biblically.

Part Four

A Wife's
Special Concerns

Sin Problems
of the Excellent Wife

Chapter Eighteen

The Wife's Anger
Overcoming Impatience

I have had many women tell me how guilty they feel because of their anger. They are frustrated. Their anger may have been a major factor in the breakdown of their marriage or other relationships. One young woman would go into rages over the slightest incident that did not go her way. Afterwards, she was devastated over her sin, but it kept recurring. Others say, "I'm better than I used to be," justifying their anger so that it does not seem so bad any more. They are blind to the terrible effect their anger continues to have on others. One woman told me that she thinks her frustration and irritation is "what stress is." Anger and resentment are two powerful emotions you are likely to feel when you are frustrated or irritated. Getting it off your chest does not help the frustration, it only compounds the sin and guilt. Many wives use anger to manipulate in order to have their way. Many husbands will give in for the sake of peace. Sinful anger has ruined countless marriages. Since it is a common factor in most separations and divorces, this chapter explains what sinful anger is by giving biblical illustrations and principles to overcome anger. Scripture has much information regarding anger. So much, in fact, there are different Greek words for anger.

Greek Words for Anger

"Raging anger" is *Orge*.[40] It is a primary root word which means "violent passion, anger, indignation, or vengeance." It is one of the deeds of the flesh we are to put aside in Colossians 3:8. Deeds of the flesh are obvious sinful acts such as immorality, drunkenness, or raging anger.

An "outburst of anger" is one of the deeds of the flesh in Galatians chapter five. It is translated "wrath" in Colossians 3:8. It means "angry tempers, fierce, indignation, passion, rage, or wrath."[41]

"Irritation" is another form of anger. Ephesians 4:26 says **"do not let the sun go down on your anger *(parorgismos).*"** *Parorismos* most basically connotes to "provoke to anger."[42] These three words provide different slants to the one sin of anger. Now consider the following biblical examples.

Biblical Examples of Anger

King Saul became jealous and suspicious of David's success in battle. He became very *angry* as he heard the women singing, **"Saul has slain his thousands, and David his ten thousands"** (1 Samuel 18:7-8). From then on, Saul hardened his heart and sought to kill David. In addition to his sin against God, Saul's pathetic response to David is especially sad because David saw Saul as God's anointed. Hence David was still very loyal to him. So loyal in fact that David would have never done anything to hurt Saul. On the other hand (instead of being angry), Saul should have been glad for David for all the successes the Lord gave him.

Cain became angry at his brother Abel because God had regard for Abel's offering and not Cain's. Cain's anger began in his heart. God even warned Cain about his sin and told him, **"you must master it."** (Genesis 4:7) Cain continued to seethe. Later he murdered his brother.

The Pharisees were hard, angry men. In their hearts, they were proud and determined to control others. Like God warned Cain, Jesus warned the Pharisees.

> <u>Woe</u> to you, scribes and Pharisees, hypocrites, because you travel about on sea and land to make one proselyte; and when he becomes one, you make him twice as much a son of hell as yourselves.
> *Matthew 23:15, emphasis added*

To pronounce a "woe" is a curse. After one such warning in Luke eleven, the Scribes and the Pharisees **"began to be *very hostile* and to question Him closely on many subjects, plotting against Him, to catch Him in something He might say"** (Luke 11:53-54, emphasis added).

All of these examples of anger have a common thread. The anger began in their heart by what they wanted and subsequently thought. The intensity of the anger built and built until it culminated in heinous sin. King Saul tried to murder David. Cain did murder Abel. The Pharisees did incite the civil authorities to murder Jesus. Anger is a grievous sin. In order to overcome sinful anger, the best place to begin is with a study of the biblical principles on anger.

Biblical Principles Concerning Anger

1. God has righteous anger.

> *God is a righteous judge, And a God who has indignation every day.*
>
> *Psalm 7:11*

Even though God often **"restrain(s) His anger"** (Psalm 78:38), His anger will someday be completely released. Because God is holy, He has to punish sin. The Prophets spoke of God's wrath poured out, the day of the Lord's anger, and the fierce anger of the Lord. Unbelieving man is currently under God's wrath even though he may not realize it. However, man does not have to continue to stay under the pending wrath of God. If they are in Christ, Christ bore the wrath of God in their place. For those who know Christ, God's **"anger is for a moment, His favor for a lifetime"** (Psalm 30:5).

2. Man can have righteous anger also.

> *BE ANGRY, AND yet DO NOT SIN; do not let the sun go down on your anger.*
>
> *Ephesians 4:26, emphasis added*

Righteous anger is a rare occurrence. It is only right that other's heinous crimes make us angry. Certainly, it is only right that murdering unborn babies makes us angry. However, most of the time our anger is not righteous, it is sinful. Even biblically justifiable anger is often sinful coming from us. You can know your anger is righteous if in spite of provocation, you continue to think **"true... honorable... right... pure... lovely... good repute... excellent... and worthy of praise (to God)"** thoughts (Philippians 4:8). In addition, you must also **"not take into account a wrong suffered"** and **"not be provoked"** (1 Corinthians 13:5). Otherwise, your anger is not honoring to God. It is sinful.

3. Man's anger does not achieve God's righteous ends.

> *...for the anger of man does not achieve the righteousness of God.*
>
> *James 1:20*

I have had many wives tell me that if they did not get angry at their husbands, their husbands would never do anything for them around the house. Even if that were true, it would be better to live in a house that is in disrepair than to sin against God. It may seem that anger is the only way to prod some husbands into working around the house, but that's not true. God's way is to confront an erring husband with gentleness. Your anger will *never* achieve God's righteous ends. It would be better to be wronged by your husband's lack of concern for the home than to grieve God by your sin.

4. Man is to be slow to anger.

> *This you know, my beloved brethren. But let everyone be quick to hear, slow to speak and slow to anger;*
> *James 1:19*

How many times have you burned with anger when you did not have your way? Probably so many times that only God could really keep count. James warned us. First *listen*. Cultivate the art of listening. Be *slow to speak*. Think about what you are going to say. Choose words that are edifying instead of angry.

For example, your husband promises to wash the outside windows Saturday. You have a commitment and will be gone all day. It makes you happy just thinking about the windows being sparkling clean! When you arrive home, it is obvious that he did not wash any windows. Immediately, you begin to feel frustrated. By the time you find him, you are boiling on the inside. If you are wise, you remind yourself that you need to listen to his side of the story (**"quick to hear"**). He will most likely have a reasonable explanation. If not, say, "I need to think about what to say and I'll be back (**"slow to speak"**). Next, pray and think about what you want to say and how you want to say it. Finally, go back to your husband and talk with him, speaking in a gentle tone of voice. If you have done all of the above, you will be very **"slow to anger."**

5. Anger does not come alone, it brings its cohorts.

> *But now you also, put them all aside: anger, wrath, malice, slander, and abusive speech from your mouth.*
> *Colossians 3:8*

Many times, anger and wrath are accompanied by malicious (mean), slanderous (defamatory statements), and abusive speech (cruel, angry statements).

Often, this entire group of sin comes together bundled up in one big ugly vile package! You are to rid yourself of the entire "package" by laying these sins aside. You lay them aside by thinking right thoughts. Right thoughts are compassionate, kind, humble, gentle, patient, forbearing, forgiving, and loving (Colossians 3:12-14). Thoughts like, "He makes me so angry. He's so stupid just like his entire family!" have real potential to turn into abusive and malicious speech. Instead replace the thoughts with, "Love is patient and kind. I can show love to him by responding in a kind manner." Or, "Perhaps he misunderstood me because I did not explain this very well."

The sin of anger rarely surfaces alone. It is often like a snowball rolling down a hill picking up speed and force. You can easily stop the snowball at the top of the hill or you can run the risk of it wiping you out at the bottom of the hill! It is your choice.

6. Angry outbursts are deeds of the flesh.

> *Now the deeds of the flesh are evident...idolatry, sorcery, enmities, strife, jealousy, <u>outbursts of anger</u>, disputes, dissension's, factions,*
>
> Galatians 5:20, emphasis added

Many psychologists instruct their clients to vent their anger. Their counsel is wrong, because venting anger is sin. It is one of the deeds of the flesh. Like all sin, you must confess your angry outbursts to God by agreeing with Him that you have sinned (1 John 1:9). Become keenly aware that each and every time you have an outburst of unrighteous anger, your sinful flesh sets itself in direct opposition to the Holy Spirit (Galatians 5:17). Do not vent your anger. You will only compound your sin.

7. There is a biblical contrast between the man who stirs up anger and the man who subdues anger.

"Stirs Up Anger"	"Subdues Anger"
1. "Harsh words stir up anger." Proverbs 15:1	1. "A gentle answer turns away wrath." Proverbs 15:1

2. "A hot tempered man stirs up strife." Proverbs 15:18	2. "He that is slow to anger pacifies contention." Proverbs 15:18
3. "Do not associate with a man given to anger; or go with a hot-tempered man, lest you learn his ways and find a snare for yourself." Proverbs 22:24	3. "A gift in secret subdues anger." Proverbs 21:14
4. "When a wise man has controversy with a foolish man, the foolish man either rages or laughs, and there is no rest." Proverbs 29:9	4. "Scorners set a city aflame, but wise men turn away anger." Proverbs 29:8
5. "Wrath is fierce and anger is a flood." Proverbs 27:4	5. "He who restrains his lips is wise." Proverbs 10:19
6. "For the churning of milk produces butter, and pressing the nose brings forth blood, so the churning of anger produces strife." Proverbs 30:33	6. "Blessed are the peacemakers, for they shall be called sons of God." Matthew 5:9
7. "Anger resides in the bosom of fools." Ecclesiastes 7:9	7. "He who is slow to anger has great understanding..." Proverbs 14:29
8. "A fool's mouth spouts folly." Proverbs 15:2 "A fool's vexation is known at once." Proverbs 12:16	8. "The heart of the righteous ponders how to answer..." Proverbs 15:28

The contrast between one who stirs up anger and one who subdues anger is abundantly clear. One is a fool. The other is wise. One is harsh. The other is gentle. One produces strife. The other pacifies contention. One will spout folly. The other ponders carefully before he answers.

8. Pride frequently results in anger.

> *By pride comes nothing but strife, but with the well-advised is wisdom.*
>
> *Proverbs 13:10, NKJV*

The Hebrew word for pride means presumption or insolence. We can see how pride would produce strife when we hold onto our right to have life proceed the way we would like. Instead, we should gratefully submit to God's sovereign control over every detail of our lives. You have to decide who is going to be the boss. If God is, then you have to decide if you are going to agreeably let Him. Obviously the wisest course is for you to **"submit to God"** (James 4:7). If you graciously submit, you are responding in humility and God will give you grace.

We can see how pride would produce strife when we *presume* to know what another person is thinking. When we think negative, critical, and judgmental thoughts, they are often presumptuous. For example, your husband does something nice for you and you think, "He only did that to make himself look good." Instead, God wants you to assume the best about him, realizing that only God can read minds and judge the motives of men's hearts. If you do not assume the best, your presumption will likely result in strife. In addition to understanding biblical principles on anger, you are responsible to cooperate with God's training you not to be sinfully angry. The Bible tells us that **"All Scripture is inspired by God and profitable for** *teaching*, **for** *reproof*, **for** *correction*, **for** *training in righteousness...*" (2 Timothy 3:16, emphasis added). The purpose of this teaching, reproof, correction, and training is so that we will become righteous like Christ. In order to become righteous, God has to first teach us. In order to equip us, God has to use His Word to teach us. That is why we have already studied the biblical principles on anger. Next, God convicts us of what we are doing wrong (reproof). After the reproof, God corrects us. This entire process has to happen over and over. As it is repeated, God is training us so that we will be righteous. Since these four steps (teaching, reproof, correction, and training) are the general biblical pattern, let's cover each step and see your personal responsibility.

Biblical Steps to Change Character from Anger to Gentleness

1. Teaching

Teaching is the same as doctrine. Doctrine is simply what the Bible teaches about a particular subject. In this case, the subject is anger. This particular sin is so prevalent that I would suggest you take a lot of time and care to study back over the biblical principles on anger. Choose several Scriptures that seem especially relevant to you, meditate on them, and memorize them. I would suggest James 1:19-20, 1 Corinthians 13:4-7, Proverbs 16:32, and Proverbs 15:28. Study these principles so well that you could explain them to someone else. Go over the verses repeatedly until you can say them automatically without a great deal of thought. After you have thoroughly studied and retained the doctrine, go to the next step.

2. Reproof

A biblical reproof is telling someone what they are doing wrong based on Scripture. Ask others to hold you accountable and point it out to you when you seem to be angry or even slightly harsh. A suggestion is you may want to keep an anger journal for yourself.*⁸ Each time you *feel* irritated or frustrated, *write down* exactly what you are *thinking and what you said or did*. Write your thoughts and actions down as quickly as possible. Writing angry thoughts and actions down will help you to see more clearly where you are wrong. Do not stop here, move on to the "correction" stage.

3. Correction

Now that you know what you are doing wrong, it is time to correct it. Biblically analyze each thought you wrote down. Then write out a new, biblically corrected thought. Do the same for your angry words and actions. Remember to correct not only words, but also your tone of voice and your countenance. Practice out loud what you should have said. Ask yourself this question, "If I had this to do over again, what would I think and do?"

Next, confess each specific angry incident to God and to others if you have offended someone. Do this every time, even if it is a seemingly small incident. If you turn to God in your sin, He will help you. **"Hope in God, for I shall yet praise Him…** (Psalm 42:11).

Your words should be gentle and soft instead of harsh and angry. Consider the following examples of anger producing thoughts and gentle response producing thoughts.

Anger Producing Thoughts .	Gentle Response Producing Thoughts
1. "This makes me mad. I wish he would hurry up. I've got things to do!"	1. "Thank you Lord for the delay. I would like to finish my work on time, but I want you to be glorified whether I finish on time or not."
2. "How dare he 'snap' at me when he walks in the door from work? He's not the only one who has had a rough day." (note: angry people tend to be especially intolerant of others' sin.)	2. "He doesn't usually 'snap' at me like that. I wonder if he has had a difficult day at work or if he has a headache. What can I do to help him?"
3. "He's wrong about this teaching from the Bible. This burns me up and he won't even listen."	3. "He's wrong and I know it and so does God. However, God wants me to respond in gentleness since **'The Lord's bondservant is first of all gentle.'** 2 Timothy 2:24-26
4. "If I have to put up with his _____ one more time, I'll scream. I can't take it any more!"	4. **"I can do all things through Christ who strengthens me"** (Philippians 4:13). "If in the process of putting up with him, I have to feel uncomfortable I'll just have to feel uncomfortable. I am going to show love to him."

5. "He doesn't care about me. He only thinks of himself."	5. "I shouldn't judge his motives and thoughts. Instead, my responsibility is to consider him as more important than myself. So, how can I respond in the best way possible for him?"
6. "That really irritates me!"	6. **"Love is patient."** I can show love to him whether I feel like it or not."
7. "He's sinning and it makes me angry!"	7. **"...'the anger of man does not achieve the righteousness of God'** (James 1:20). How does God want me to respond?"

4. Training in Righteousness

The training phase involves plain old practice. Think and act according to the Word of God repeatedly until the gentle and loving responses are your first thoughts instead of afterthoughts. The results will be life-changing if you work long and hard on this training phase.

While you are working on changing, keep praying and asking God to change your heart and your character. Perhaps you have been an angry wife for years. Perhaps you have been angry as long as you can remember. In Christ, you can change, not just improve a little, but truly repent. If your character changes, you will be able to go through times of testing such as your menstrual period without sinning against God and offending others. Train yourself to **"...ponder how to answer"** (Proverbs 15:28). God will help you. You may be thinking, "It's not that simple." *Yes it is!* Humble yourself, cry out to God in prayer for help, roll up your sleeves, and get to work.

Chapter Nineteen

The Wife's Fear
Overcoming Anxiety

Fear is a common problem. Some fears are legitimate and some are groundless. Regardless of the basis, however, the result can be anguish for the person who is afraid. Not being afraid is an element of trusting God, of being a godly person, and of being a godly wife. In fact, being fearless is included in the description of the Excellent Wife in Proverbs 31. **"She is not afraid of the snow for her household...she smiles at the future"** (Proverbs 31:21,25).

Peter also exhorts wives not to fear as he admonishes them to **"do what is right without being frightened by any fear"** (1 Peter 3:5,6). So in His Word, God does acknowledge that fear may be a problem for some wives. Fear is a miserable emotion, but wives are to respond to their fears in a biblical manner.

Fear may result in a minor feeling of uneasiness or a full-blown panic attack. When a panic attack occurs, her body releases adrenaline, her heart pounds, and she feels short of breath and experiences a sensation of panic. Often the intensity of her fear does not correlate with the actual circumstances. In other words, she overreacts. But whether her fear is minor or full blown, what might cause a Christian wife to be afraid?

It is common for a wife to worry that her husband will die or become disabled and unable to support their family. Others worry their husband will find another woman and reject them. Some become consumed with the fear of failure as a wife or mother. Many are fearful of their husband's anger or his too controlling manner. Others are anxious about their husband's lack of spiritual leadership. For some, money is their greatest concern. There are those whose fear is groundless, yet they are convinced that "something terrible is going to happen!" Regardless of the specific reason for their fear, God has very definite instructions in Scripture on how to cope with fear. Carefully consider the following biblical principles regarding fear.

Biblical Principles Concerning Fear

1. Fear may keep us from fulfilling our God-given responsibilities.

> *And the one also who had received the one talent came up and said, "Master, I knew you to be a hard man, reaping where you did not sow, and gathering where you scattered no seed. And I <u>was afraid, and went away and hid your talent</u> in the ground; see, you have what is yours." But his master answered and said to him, "You wicked, lazy slave, you knew that I reap where I did not sow, and gather where I scattered no seed."*
> *Matthew 25:25-26, emphasis added*

Regardless of the underlying basis for your fear, fear can cripple you from fulfilling your responsibilities. For example, a wife might spend the day sitting in her room with the shades drawn in a panic for fear that if she gets in the car to go to the grocery store she might be killed in a wreck. As a consequence, none of her God-given responsibilities would be completed for that day.

Another wife might lie awake at night worrying about what would happen to her and the children if her husband loses his job or dies. Somehow, everything bad seems exaggerated in the middle of the night. By morning, she is so overcome with her fear that she cries her heart out and begs her husband to stay home from work to be with her for the day. She is so distraught that nothing gets done for the entire day. In addition to being anxious all day, she experiences guilt and increased fear because of not fulfilling her responsibilities.

2. Fear may motivate a person to commit other sins.

> *When the men of the place asked about his wife, he said, "She is my sister," <u>for he was afraid to say,</u> "my wife," thinking, "the men of the place might kill me on account of Rebekah, for she is beautiful."*
> *Genesis 26:7, emphasis added*

Untold numbers of lies have been justified because of fear. Wives have covered up for their husband's sin because they were afraid of his anger. When a wife feels anxious, she is much more likely to be impatient or harsh

with the children or with her husband. Fear operates like a flood gate opening and letting all the other sins loose. It is very difficult, if not impossible,
not to compound sin while experiencing sinful fear.

3. Fear may motivate a person to deny the Lord Jesus and His
   Word.

> *Now Peter was sitting outside in the courtyard, and a*
> *certain servant-girl came to him and said, "You too were*
> *with Jesus the Galilean." <u>But he denied it</u> before them all,*
> *saying, "I do not know what you are talking about."*
> *Matthew 26:69-70, emphasis added*

> *Then Saul said to Samuel, "I have sinned; I have indeed*
> *transgressed the command of the LORD and your words,*
> *because I feared the people and listened to their voice.*
> *1 Samuel 15:24*

How sad for Peter the day He denied the Lord Jesus Christ. We can all
understand his fear and would likely be tempted to lie if put in his position.
Peter openly denied the Lord, but it is also possible to deny the Lord or His
Word by just saying nothing. However, you do not have to sin in order to
cope with a frightening situation. Instead of denying God or His Word, remind yourself that God was and still is sovereign over every circumstance.
He chooses how you may best serve and glorify Him. God will give you the
grace to make it through any trial. There are a myriad of Christian martyrs
who would gladly attest to what I am saying.

4. Fear may be of other men.

> *The <u>fear of man</u> brings a snare, But he who trusts in the*
> *LORD will be exalted.*
> *Proverbs 29:25, emphasis added*

> *... so that we confidently say, "THE LORD IS MY*
> *HELPER, I WILL NOT BE AFRAID. <u>WHAT SHALL MAN</u>*
> *<u>DO TO ME?</u>"*
> *Hebrews 13:6, emphasis added*

> *Thus Sarah obeyed Abraham, calling him lord, and you*
> *have become her children if you do what is right without*
> *being <u>frightened by any fear</u>.*
> *1 Peter 3:6, emphasis added*

When I was a child, I remember thinking about the possible death of my parents or myself and becoming almost terrified. It was such a frightening thought that I decided I just would not think about death any more. So, I didn't. I felt better, but not thinking about death did not change the fact that death loomed somewhere in the future for me. Whether it is death, or the weather, or war, or man, people are often afraid. Even "doing what is right" is cause for alarm sometimes. In fact, depending on the circumstances, "doing what is right" can be almost as frightening as facing death or war. Regretfully, fear is a fact of life in a fallen world. How we respond to our fears depends on our relationship with the Lord Jesus Christ. In Christ there are tangible solutions to fear.

Nine Solutions to Fear

1. Do not be a man pleaser.

    > *For prior to the coming of certain men from James, he (Peter) used to eat with the Gentiles; but when they came, he began to withdraw and hold himself aloof, fearing the party of the circumcision.*
    > *Galatians 2:12*

    Peter had been saying one thing, but when the Jewish Christians showed up, Peter did another. He was being a man pleaser. His desire to please men placed him in the position of having to fear he would be found out. A man pleaser is one who seeks the approval of man rather than God. Instead of seeking man's approval, seek God's by having strong, clear biblical convictions and living them out. If you do, you need not be afraid to respond in a biblical manner because what God thinks about you will be more important to you than what others think.

2. Remind yourself of God's Word.

    > *I have remembered Thine ordinances from of old, O LORD, and comfort myself.*

Thou art my hiding place and my shield; I wait for Thy word.
Trouble and anguish have come upon me; Yet Thy commandments are my delight.
Those who love Thy law have great peace, and nothing causes them to stumble.

Psalm 119:52, 114, 143, 165

The promises in the Word of God are tried and true. Promises that apply to you will especially fortify you. There is no substitute for Scripture memory and meditation. For example, God used His word to help Jacob get through the terror of facing Esau and Esau's 400 men. Jacob reminded himself of what God had promised him as he prayed, **"O God... who didst say to me 'Return to your country and to your relatives, and I will prosper you'"** (Genesis 32:7,9). I doubt Jacob's fear abated completely, but he did calm down enough to continue towards home. Like Jacob, if you continuously remind yourself of God's Word, your fear will either ebb away or perhaps even dramatically disappear!

3. Make wise decisions.

My son, let them not depart from your sight; Keep sound wisdom and discretion, so they will be life to your soul, and adornment to your neck. Then you will walk in your way securely, and your foot will not stumble. When you lie down, you will not be afraid; When you lie down, your sleep will be sweet. Do not be afraid of sudden fear, nor of the onslaught of the wicked when it comes; for the LORD will be your confidence, and will keep your foot from being caught.

Proverbs 3:21-26

Wisdom is the ability to relate truth (God's Word) to life situations. For example, if you are wise you will know how to answer a fool and a scoffer. You will also make biblical decisions. As a result, your life will be much easier. You will sleep better and not be afraid. The Lord will be your confidence. Even in extreme circumstances such as the **"onslaught of the wicked,"** you will not be overcome with fear. On the other hand, if you are not wise, you are likely to set up many unnecessary snares for yourself.

4. Realize the power of God working within you.

For God has not given us a spirit of timidity, but of power and love and discipline.

2 Timothy 1:7

The power of God is unlimited. With His power, God can create a world and He can sustain it. He can raise someone from the dead. He can even enable Christians not to succumb to fear. You may wonder, "If God has given me enabling power so that I won't be so afraid, why am I afraid?" God was encouraging Timothy because of the impending persecution. Paul exhorted Timothy by reminding him that the Holy Spirit was not producing fear in him but was producing power. You, possibly like Timothy, become fearful because of what you *think* about particular circumstances, not because of the circumstances themselves. As a result, your focus becomes more and more inward. You become more and more frightened. Typically, you think, "What's going to happen to me?" An inward focus is a selfish focus, and the fear that results from selfish thinking is not from God. It is a consequence of your own sin. So, realize the enabling power of God that is working within you (if you are a Christian). Such thoughts will comfort you and you will not be overwhelmed with fear.

5. Fear the Lord and delight in His commands.

Praise the LORD! How blessed is the man who fears the LORD, Who greatly delights in His commandments.

Psalm 112:1

How foolish when we fear sickness or death, but do not fear God or His commandments. Jesus warned us to get it straight, **"...do not fear those who kill the body, but are unable to kill the soul; but rather fear Him who is able to destroy both soul and body in hell"** (Matthew 10:28). There are many things I have not done or have not continued to do because I am afraid of God's reaction and the subsequent consequences. This kind of fear is wise. It is the **"beginning of wisdom"** (Proverbs 1:7). God's commandments should be your delight. Read them, think about them, and enjoy following them. Take great delight in pleasing the Lord. If you do, you will have an appropriate fear of the Lord.

6. Realize God is ever-present with you.

> *Even though I walk through the valley of the shadow of death, I fear no evil; for Thou art with me; Thy rod and Thy staff, they comfort me.*
>
> *Psalm 23:4*

Remind yourself and trust that God is always with you. If you are a Christian, you are as sure to someday be in heaven with the Lord Jesus as you are reading this sentence right now. Your future with the Lord is as good as having already been accomplished. This fact is reality whether you feel like it or not. Recently, I attended the funeral of a young Christian wife and mother who was suddenly, tragically killed in an automobile accident. The church was packed. Practically everyone cried, but the grief was not overwhelming. Her family and fellow Christians have a real hope. We know where Carol is. She is with our Lord. Even if she had known her death was imminent, she had nothing to fear. If you are a Christian, remind yourself of God's promise to **"walk through the valley of the shadow of death"** with you. You will not be alone. You do not have to be afraid.

7. Trust God to keep His Word.

> *In God, whose word I praise, In God I have put my trust; I shall not be afraid. What can mere man do to me?*
>
> *Psalm 56:4*

You have to decide who or what you are going to trust to keep you safe and secure. Is it your own strength? Is it your ability to look out for yourself? Is it the gun you keep hidden in the bedside drawer? Is it your super-safe automobile with its dual air bags and anti-lock brakes? It is probably not difficult for you to see the folly in wholeheartedly trusting anything or anyone except God. You can trust God because He has sovereign control over all men. No matter what happens, you can trust that God holds you in His infinitely strong hand. How do you know? Because God promises you in His Word. God has bound Himself by His Word, and He cannot break a promise. How sure is God to keep His Word? The Lord Jesus Christ answered this way, **"Heaven and earth will pass away, but My Words shall not pass away"** (Matthew 24:35). Therefore, you can trust God to keep His Word.

8. Seek after the Lord when you are afraid.

> *I sought the LORD, and He answered me, And delivered me from all my fears.*
>
> *Psalm 34:4*

God is willing to deliver you from every sinful fear, however great or small. This is the verse I say to myself over and over when I am at the dentist's office. When I am afraid, I reassure myself with this verse. Instead of turning to pills or alcohol or some other form of escape, seek the Lord. You can talk to Him anytime. He will talk back to you through His Word which is "alive and powerful" (Hebrews 4:12). He will give you grace to endure any trial or temptation and eventually will give you your "way of escape" (1 Corinthians 10:13).

9. Overcome your fear with love.

> *There is no fear in love; but perfect love casts out fear, because fear involves punishment, and the one who fears is not perfected in love.*
>
> *1 John 4:18*

Perfect love is complete. It involves loving God and loving others. Concentrate on showing love to God and/or others and your fear will subside. You show love to God by obeying His Word whether you feel like it or not. You show love to others by being **"patient, kind, not seeking your own way, etc."** (1 Corinthians 13: 4). Fear is selfish. When you think about yourself, your fear escalates. This is so true that the actual reason for the worry does not even have to be real! For example, a wife who keeps thinking "I just know something horrible is going to happen!" can become completely panicked over absolutely nothing. The key for her to overcome her fear is for her to put on love.

Love looks for opportunities to give. Fear keeps an eye on the consequences to self. Love **"thinks no evil"** (1 Corinthians. 13:6). Fear thinks of little else. Love **"believes all things"** (1 Corinthians. 13:6) while fear is highly suspicious.

> *"Love is so busy doing today's tasks that it has no time to worry about tomorrow. Because it focuses on tomorrow, fear fails to undertake responsibilities today. Love leads to greater love, fulfilling obligations brings peace and joy and satisfaction and greater love and devotion to the work. Fear, in turn, occasions greater fear, since failure to assume responsibilities brings additional fear of the consequences of acting irresponsibly. Those who fear God enough to take His Word seriously, find that this fear develops into mutual love. The way, then, to put off fear is to put on love."*[44]

What about legitimate concerns such as a sick husband? There are two ways to respond to a legitimate concern. One is to focus on the present day and what God considers your responsibility regarding the concern. The other is to focus on the future, jump to a rash conclusion, (usually the worst possible conclusion) and panic.

When you focus on the future, God may not give you grace to respond biblically (see Matthew 6:34.) In fact, God never gives grace for rash conclusions that are not really happening. If it is not happening, then it is not real and God always wants us to live in the light of reality, not in the grip of sinful imaginations. For example, a wife is concerned about her husband's bout with the flu. It seems to her that he is not recovering as quickly as he should. She begins to think about what else might be wrong with him. Before long, she has him terminally ill, dead, his funeral planned, and him buried. Instead of **"thinking on things that are true"** (Philippians 4:8), she has jumped to a rash conclusion based on very little data. God will neither comfort nor give her grace to cope with something that is not happening. He will, however, give her the grace to correct her thinking and to recover from her fear and panic. ✳

✳ On the other hand, suppose that same wife has a legitimate concern about her husband who is not recovering quickly from the flu. Instead of jumping to rash conclusions, she focuses on what God wants her to do *today*. Today she can pray very specifically for her husband. Today she can call his doctor and consider taking him in for an office visit. Today she can be a servant to her husband and care for his physical needs. Today she can notify the prayer chain at church and ask them to pray. Today she can comfort herself with the fact that if he does die tomorrow, God will take care of her. God will give her grace to focus on today. Her love for God and her husband will overcome any fear she may experience.

Showing love to God is accomplished by obeying His Word. In the Word of God, we are instructed to think and act in certain ways. There are specific instructions in Philippians chapter four for us to obey when we are anxious.

> *Be anxious for nothing, but in everything <u>by prayer and supplication with thanksgiving let your requests</u> be made known to God. And the peace of God, which surpasses all comprehension, shall guard your hearts and your minds in Christ Jesus. Finally, brethren, whatever is true, whatever is honorable, whatever is right, whatever is pure,*

*whatever is lovely, whatever is of good repute, if there is
any excellence and if anything worthy of praise, <u>let your
mind dwell on these things</u>. The things you have learned
and received and heard and seen in me, <u>practice these
things</u>; and the God of peace shall be with you.*

Philippians 4:6-9, emphasis added

Let's look more closely at some of the instructions found within
Philippians 4:6-9:

1. Pray a prayer of supplication and thanksgiving (verses six and seven).
2. Replace unbiblical thoughts with biblical thoughts (verse eight).
3. Perform practical acts appropriate for the specific situation
   (verse nine).

Pray a Prayer of Supplication and Thanksgiving

A supplication is a humble request. When you begin to feel even slightly
tense or anxious, take the time to pray and make your request to God. Be
sure to include in your request your gratefulness to God. Consider the following example:

> Lord,
> <u>My request</u> is that my husband will stop running a fever
> and will be well soon. <u>Thank You</u> for what you are wanting
> to teach us and for reminding us how much we need You.
> <u>Thank You</u> for whatever You decide would glorify You the
> most.
> In Jesus Name,
> Amen

Replace Unbiblical Thoughts with Biblical Thoughts

Verse eight in Philippians chapter four tells you what you are to think
about. If you fail to keep your mind directed in these areas, you likely will
fall into the anxiety mentioned in verses six and seven.

True thoughts are valid, reliable, and honest. They are the opposite of false. *Honorable* thoughts are noble and worthy of respect. *Right* thoughts are upright, just, and conformable to God's standards. *Pure* thoughts are morally pure. *Lovely* thoughts are pleasing, agreeable, or amiable. *Good repute* thoughts are attractive and ring true to the highest standards.[45]

Biblical Thoughts that Overcome Fear

1. "This is frightening (**true thought**), but I am going to do the right thing (**honorable and right thought**); and God will, no matter how my husband reacts, give me the grace to get through it" (**true, honorable, and lovely thought**).

2. "If I have to feel anxious, I'll just have to feel anxious (**deny self and honor God**), but I am going to obey God (**right thought**) and show love to God (**right and honorable thought**) by responding in submission to my husband."

3. "My responsibility is to do what is right and God will, *at that time*, give me the grace and wisdom to respond" (**good repute, honorable, and right thought**).

4. "If I get confused or do not know what to say, I can always tell him, 'let me think about how to respond and I'll get back with you'" (**right and honoring to God thought**).

5. "I am afraid he will respond badly, but I don't know that to be a fact (**true thought**). My responsibility is to confront him (**right thought**). When I do God will help me" (**honoring and good repute thought**).

6. "I'm afraid he will hurt my feelings again, but I certainly can't know what he is thinking (**true thought**). Love believes the best (**lovely thought**). My responsibility is to concentrate on showing love to him" (**right thought**).

Perform Practical Acts Appropriate to the Specific Situation

Paul used himself as our example to follow when he wrote **"The things you have learned and received and heard and seen in me,** *practice these things..."* (Philippians 4:9, emphasis added). What the Philippians had seen Paul do probably included such things as pray, seek wise counsel, give a blessing instead of returning evil, express biblical thoughts he was thinking, thank God, and center his life around glorifying God. As a godly wife, you must also practice these kind of things. As you pray, think, and act right —

> *God's peace, incomprehensible in its grandeur, will stand guard at the door of [your] the believer's heart and thoughts, preventing the entrance of fears and doubts.*[46]

Let me summarize this section by urging you to not be anxious. Instead, pray a biblical prayer of supplication with thanksgiving. Pray right away, don't wait. Check your thoughts and make sure they are biblical according to the list in Philippians 4:8. Do whatever would be biblically appropriate at the time. If you persist in your responsibilities, you will experience the **"peace of God which surpasses all comprehension"** (Philippians 4:7) and the **"God of peace shall be with you"** (Philippians 4:9).

It is inherent within the previous three exhortations that perfect love (biblical love to God and others) will overcome your fear. Whether you are anxious over a very small worry or you are experiencing an overwhelming crisis, if you respond in loving obedience to God, He will give you His peace. His peace is supernatural and not dependent on your circumstances. Respond in love by obedience to God's Word and your fear will fade away. If you are a wife in especially frightening circumstances because of your husband, know that you truly can **"do what is right without being frightened by any fear"** (1 Peter 3:6).

Chapter Twenty

The Wife's Loneliness
Overcoming a Lack of Oneness

As I am writing, it is Christmas time. Radios are mournfully blaring "I'll be home for Christmas ... if only in my dreams." Everyone longs to be home with their families. Even the coffee commercials on television picture a young soldier sneaking in on Christmas morning and surprising his younger brother and parents by waking them up with the wonderful aroma of the coffee he has brewing in the kitchen. It is easy to feel the excitement and joy of his parents as they realize he is home. Indeed, not being with family at Christmas can evoke strong feelings of loneliness. I feel sad for some of those who are alone at Christmas.

I also feel sad for those who are not alone, but feel overwhelmingly lonely. There are wives who have husbands with them and yet they are alone. Perhaps their husband is withdrawn, aloof, or hardly ever home. He may be very self-absorbed and inwardly focused. The wife may be bitter and feeling very sorry for herself. Her self-pity may be fueled by an idolatrous desire for intimacy with her husband. Whatever the cause, loneliness is one of the most painful emotions that any of us ever experience.

Scripture abounds with examples of those who are painfully lonely. Elijah had a thrilling mountain top experience as God rained down fire on Elijah's altar in direct challenge to the wicked prophets of Baal. Afterwards, Elijah and the people slew the prophets of Baal. Elijah had just witnessed an incredible miracle from God, but when wicked Queen Jezebel threatened to kill him, he panicked and ran for his life. Exhausted and hiding in a cave, Elijah began to feel isolated and alone. Instead of focusing on the power and protection of God, Elijah whined to God:

> *"I have been very zealous for the Lord, the God of hosts;*
> *for the sons of Israel have forsaken Thy covenant, torn*
> *down Thine altars and killed Thy prophets with the sword.*
> *And I alone am left; and they seek my life, to take it away."*
> *1 Kings 19:10, emphasis added*

Jeremiah was not a popular prophet. His sober warnings from God to the children of Israel went virtually unheeded. People pulled away from him. They thought he was a nut! They mocked him. Jeremiah struggled with intense emotional pain. He felt abandoned by God, forsaken, and isolated. He was burdened down, trapped, and despairing with no hope. Imagine how Jeremiah felt as he described his feelings.

> *In dark places He [God] has made me dwell, Like those*
> *who have long been dead. He has walled me in so that I*
> *cannot go out; He has made my chain heavy. Even when I*
> *cry out and call for help, He shuts out my prayer.*
> *Lamentations 3:6-8, adaptation added*

Jeremiah was lonely. Everyone was against him. No one believed him. He even felt abandoned by God. I cannot think of anything more desperate than to cry out to God for help and to believe God has shut you out. There could not possibly be a greater sense of loneliness.

By far the most poignant and heart-wrenching picture of loneliness is that of the Lord Jesus Christ in the garden of Gethsemane and later on the cross. Jesus asked Peter, James, and John to watch and pray with Him. Yet they slept as He agonized in prayer over His impending trial. His time of greatest need had come and His closest friends slept. He had done so much for them and they could not do this one thing for Him (Matthew 26:37-44).

On the cross, the Lord Jesus endured the most intense experience of loneliness possible. After having had perfect harmony with God the Father for all of eternity, He cried out in anguish from the cross, **"My God, my God, why hast Thou forsaken Me?"** (Mark 15:34). We cannot fathom His agony or His isolation as He bore the sins of the world.

Though nowhere near the degree the Lord Jesus suffered, Paul may have been tempted to fall into loneliness. Paul was imprisoned in Rome. The prison was cold and damp and dark. Paul wrote to his beloved Timothy urging him to come and visit as soon as possible (2 Timothy 4:9). He also warned Timothy to beware of those who had deserted and harmed Paul — Demas deserted him, Alexander the coppersmith did Paul **"much harm"** (2 Timothy

4:14). At the preliminary hearing, no one supported Paul. Unlike Elijah who could leave the cave he was hiding in, Paul was near martyrdom and in prison until the end. He knew he was already **"being poured out as a drink offering, and the time of my departure has come"** (2 Timothy 4:6-7). Abandonment by those you trust and love and have poured your life into may cause deep loneliness. Paul was abandoned and he was cold. It is pitiful that he implored Timothy to bring him his coat before winter. He was going to die. His prison conditions were wretched. He was alone.

Like Elijah, Jeremiah, Jesus, or Paul, you may be experiencing intense loneliness. A woman does not have to be single to be lonely. She can be married and living with her husband. In fact, her loneliness may be exaggerated because of feeling trapped in a marriage with a man who is withdrawn and aloof. Elijah and Jeremiah were overwhelmed with their loneliness. Jesus and Paul were not. The difference is Elijah and Jeremiah felt sorry for themselves while Jesus and Paul sought refuge in God. If you are lonely, who are you most like — Elijah and Jeremiah or Jesus and Paul?

If you are responding like Elijah and Jeremiah, you are likely sinning. Loneliness may be a result of your own sin. Compare the following sinful causes of loneliness to the biblical cures for loneliness.

SINFUL CAUSES OF LONELINESS	BIBLICAL CURES FOR LONELINESS
1. The wife is withdrawn and aloof from her husband. Perhaps she is expecting her husband to do for her what only God can do. She may be withdrawn and lonely because of guilt over some sin in her life or perhaps she is bitter towards her husband or God.	1. Repent of the specific sins. Seek refuge in God through prayer and meditation on His Word. Show love to her husband whether she feels like it or not. Be open and honest with him speaking edifying words. Clear her conscience and then continue to do what is right. **"Draw near to God and He will draw near to you. Cleanse your hands, you sinners; and purify your hearts, you doubleminded."** James 4:8

2. The wife is self-absorbed, vain, prideful, and thinking only of herself. As a result, her husband and others avoid her.	2. Repent of her self love. Put on love to God and to others. **"Do nothing from selfishness or empty conceit, but with humility of mind let each of you regard one another as more important than himself; do not merely look out for your own personal interests, but also for the interests of others."** Philippians 2:3-4
3. The wife is fearful of what her husband might think of her if he knew what she was thinking or was really like.	3. The biblical antidote for fear is love. She will show love to God and to her husband as she speaks the truth in love. **"... but speaking the truth in love, we are to grow up in all *aspects* into Him, who is the head, *even* Christ ..."** Ephesians 4:15
4. The husband is selfishly withdrawn and private.	4. Give him a blessing by trying to talk to him and sharing her thoughts and desires. **"... not returning evil for evil, or insult for insult, but giving a blessing instead ..."** 1 Peter 3:9

5. The wife uses anger and intimidation to manipulate in order to have her own way. Therefore, her husband is afraid to open up to her and share his thoughts and feelings.	5. Be kind and gentle even if he does not open up to her and talk to her. Do what she can to make it easy for him to respond. **"... for the anger of man does not achieve the righteousness of God."** James 1:20

Sin often results in isolation. If you are sinning in any of the above ways, that may explain why your husband is withdrawn and you are experiencing loneliness as a result. Another cause of loneliness is an idolatrous desire for intimacy. It is not wrong for a wife to desire intimacy with her husband unless she desires it so intensely that she sins if she cannot have it. Then her desire becomes idolatrous. In those cases, even if her husband attempts to be more open with her, she is likely to be disappointed no matter how hard he tries. He may give up trying and then her idolatrous desire for intimacy becomes even more intense.

IDOLATROUS DESIRES FOR INTIMACY	BIBLICAL DESIRES FOR INTIMACY
1. Wife longs for, has her heart set on her husband meeting her need for intimate companionship.	1. Long for and set her heart on closeness with the Lord Jesus. Talk to God, share everything with God if her husband will not open up to her. **"As the deer pants for the water brooks, So my soul pants for Thee, O God. My soul thirsts for God, for the living God."** Psalm 42:1-2

2. Wife daydreams about having intimate conversations with other men.	2. Wife thinks about (hence, desires) pure and righteous things instead of sinful imaginations. **"Finally, brethren, whatever is *true*, whatever is honorable, whatever is *right*, whatever is *pure*, whatever is lovely, whatever is of good repute, if there is any excellence and if anything worthy of praise, let your mind dwell on these things."** Philippians 4:8, emphasis added
3. Wife is disrespectful to her husband because he does not meet her expectations.	3. Wife is grateful to her husband for whatever attention he gives her. Therefore, she desires greater closeness with her husband than she would if she were disappointed. **"..in everything give thanks; for this is God's will for you in Christ Jesus."** 1 Thessalonians 5:18
4. Wife feels excessive sorrow because of lack of intimacy with her husband.	4. Wife worships and serves the Lord Jesus Christ whether she ever has an intimate relationship with her husband or not. **"Serve the LORD with gladness; Come before Him with joyful singing."** Psalm 100:2

5. Wife feels intense resentment towards her husband.	5. Wife gives a blessing to her husband instead of dwelling on "hurts." As a result, she will not feel as hurt. So, it will be easier for her to not resent her husband and for her to desire biblically appropriate intimacy with him. **"Love does not act unbecomingly; it does not seek its own, is not provoked,** *does not take into account a wrong suffered,..."*
	1 Corinthians 13:5, emphasis added

Loneliness is exacerbated by self-pity. Regardless of our circumstances, if we feel sorry for ourselves, we are likely to experience intense loneliness. Self-pity will throw a wife into the pit of depression very quickly. Often the intensity of her self-pity does not always correlate to actual circumstances. For example, a wife may have a good husband who loves her and tries hard to please her. On the other hand, she may be very selfish, discontent, and ungrateful for what he does. Hence, she wallows in self pity.

Often the most unstable counselees I have are those who feel the most sorry for themselves. Their lives are not working out as they desire. Thus, they are blatantly ungrateful and not content with what the Lord has given them. Many times, their circumstances do not correspond to the intensity of their painful emotions. They are likely to blame God even if indirectly. For instance, some wives tell me that "I have prayed and prayed and God hasn't changed my husband." (The unspoken implication is that somehow God is not fair or good to them.)

To counter a selfish tendency towards self pity, a wife must cultivate gratefulness to God and to her husband and learn to be content in her particular circumstances. Telling God "Thank You" even when you feel lonely and miserable is an excellent way to begin to **"give thanks in all things..."** (1 Thessalonians 5:18). By an act of your will, think about your particular circumstances. Realize God could remove you from them today. If He does not, He must have some purpose in them for you.

God desires to mold your character to become more like the Lord Jesus Christ (Romans 8:28-29). Perhaps God wants to remind you how much you need Him. It is possible that God wants you to have a special opportunity to glorify Him. Certainly, God has a purpose that is too deep for us to comprehend. In any event, God is good, but you must persuade yourself of His goodness towards you. It may help you to gain the proper perspective if you consider what you truly deserve — death! (Romans 3:23).

God wants you to go against your feelings. Instead of wallowing in self pity, thank Him and remind yourself of God's goodness towards you. Even if your husband is sinning and you must suffer, respond as Peter exhorted, **"For it is better, if God should will it so, that you suffer for doing what is right rather than for doing what is wrong"** (1 Peter 3:17). Cultivate an attitude of gratefulness wholly trusting in the goodness and sovereignty of God.

In addition to thanking God and praising His goodness, adopt a high view of God. You are here to serve God, not God here to serve you. Humbly bow before Him taking the posture of His creature whose chief end is to glorify God. Serve God through your ministry to your husband and your family. Revere God. Think of Him and treat Him as the High and Holy God. The more you serve Him, the less lonely you will feel.

View your time alone as a grace gift from God. Realize you are never really alone. God is always there. Hebrews 13:5 says, **"I will never leave you, nor will I ever forsake you."** So talk to Him in your mind or aloud often during the day. The more lonely you feel, the more you should let God talk to you. He will talk to you through the holy Scriptures either by your reading them, singing them, meditating on them, or recalling previously memorized verses.

Long for God as King David did —

I remember the days of old; I meditate on all Thy doings;
I muse on the work of Thy hands. I stretch out my hands
to Thee; My soul longs for Thee, as a parched land.
Psalm 143:5-6

Nothing that you could possibly desire would be better than a closeness to God. Not silver or gold. Not fame or fortune. Not even a husband who openly and freely shares himself with you. When you experience loneliness, let your emotions be a signal that you need God. Draw close to God in grateful submission to Him.

Seek to know God in an intimate way. Let your knowledge be first hand. Have the Psalmist's attitude:

Whom have I in heaven but Thee? And besides Thee, I desire nothing on earth. My flesh and my heart may fail, But God is the strength of my heart and my portion forever. For, behold, those who are far from Thee will perish; Thou hast destroyed all those who are unfaithful to Thee. But as for me, the nearness of God is my good; I have made the Lord GOD my refuge, That I may tell of all Thy works.

Psalm 73:25-28

You will come to know Christ in a more intimate way by meditating on Scripture and praying. **"The Lord is good to those who wait for Him; to the person who seeks Him"** (Lamentations 3:25).

Realize that you can still be the excellent wife God intends whether your husband is closed off from you or not. Your husband may be a complete failure before God, but you do not have to be. You can respond like the Lord Jesus and the Apostle Paul or you can selfishly respond like Elijah and Jeremiah. The Lord Jesus endured the cross **"for the joy that was set before Him"** (Hebrews 12:2). Elijah had no joy even after the splendid miracle he had just witnessed. The Apostle Paul **"learned to be content ..."** Jeremiah had (at least for the moment) no **"peace."** He had forgotten what it was like to be happy.

Work hard at knowing Christ in a more intimate way and at putting on gratitude and contentment. Thank God often for your circumstances and what God wants to teach you and how God wants to use you for His glory. **Loneliness is painful, but it is not the occasion for sin.** Draw close to God and have the attitude the Psalmist had:

"As for me, I shall be glad in the Lord!"

Psalm 104:34

Chapter Twenty-One

The Wife's Sorrow
Overcoming a Grieving Heart

Recently, I had the opportunity to counsel "Karen," a new Christian. She had learned that her husband was leaving her for another woman. Also, to compound matters, her teenage daughter was sexually active and openly defiant. This wife and mother wanted so much for her husband and daughter to come to know the Lord and to repent. She is doing all that she can, but her whole world is shattering around her. I remember feeling her pain as she told me her story. Her heart was broken.

Sin hurts others. In the case of "Karen," her husband's and daughter's sin had hurt her deeply. So deeply, in fact, that it seemed impossible for her to go on. As she began to face the reality of what was happening, she began to experience intense emotional pain.

Her only hope was in God. Otherwise, her circumstances would have been too difficult to bear. Unfortunately, I have to counsel far too many wives who have allowed their lives to be destroyed by their husband's sin. Fortunately, though, there are answers and a God who desires to reach out to them, to comfort them, to help them, and to use this trial for their good. They do not have to endure their situation alone. He will walk through it with them even if their husband's sin is exceptionally difficult.

Husbands are capable of extremely gross sin such as child molestation, other criminal acts, violence, drug addiction, solicitation of prostitution, adultery, pornography, cruelty, drunkenness, and homosexuality. Any one of these sins is enough to put a wife into a state of hopeless despair and to break her heart.

The disciples experienced a similar emotion. When Jesus told them He was going to be killed, they were devastated. They were overwhelmed with sorrow. Jesus said to them, **"Sorrow has filled your hearts"** (John 16:6). The passage in John 16 does not tell us, but perhaps the reason the disciples were overcome by their sorrow is because their response to their circumstances was sinful. If their sorrow had been godly, their hearts would not have *filled* with sorrow. They would not have been *overcome* by this emotion.

If you are a Christian, God has given you many inward "heart" capacities. For example you now have a capacity to love God and love others you did not have while unsaved. You also have a joy that the world cannot know. In addition, God gave you His peace. You also have the ability to experience godly sorrow or grief. Look over the following diagram of a heart that contains within it a capacity for peace, joy, love, and sorrow.[47]

Godly sorrow is manageable. It does not overwhelm you. It co-exists within your heart along with the peace of God, the joy of God, and love for God and others. The Lord Jesus experienced godly sorrow. Remember when He wept over Jerusalem and wept when Lazarus died? His greatest sorrow, however, was on the cross.

> **Surely our griefs He himself bore, and our sorrows He carried; yet we ourselves esteemed Him stricken, smitten of God, and afflicted.**
>
> **Isaiah 53:4**

In spite of his grief, however, we know that Jesus was never sinfully filled with sorrow.

Being sinfully filled with sorrow is a result of unbiblical thinking or actions. Grief is never a justification for sin. For example, consider "Karen," whose husband is guilty of the painful sin. If she has the right motives and thinks and responds in a godly manner, she will grieve and sorrow but not be overwhelmed. If she has selfish motives and thinks and responds in a sinful manner, she will likely be overwhelmed and unable to function.

Compare the following sinful thought responses to the corresponding godly thought responses:

SINFUL THOUGHT RESPONSES	GODLY THOUGHT RESPONSES
1. "How could he do this to me after all I have done for him?"	1. "He is sinning. How does God want me to respond to his sin?" (1 Peter 3:8ff)
2. "This is more than I can stand."	2. "This feels like more than I can stand, but God will help me get through it." (1 Corinthians 10:13)
3. "I can't take the pressure anymore!"	3. "I can bear up under the pressure for as long as God deems necessary." (1 Corinthians 10:36)
4. "I'll show him what it is like."	4. "I'll develop a biblical plan to fight back with good." (Romans 12:21)
5. "I hate him."	5. "God hates what he is doing. God will avenge his sin. My responsibility is to forgive whether I feel like it or not." (Luke 6:27)

6. "I can't believe what he did to me. First he did _____ to me, then he ..."	6. "Any person is capable of any sin however gross." (Jeremiah 17:9) "His sin is against God. My responsibility is not to compound his sin with my own sin." (1 Corinthians 13:5)
7. "He will never hurt me again."	7. "He may hurt me again. I hope not, but if he does he will just have to hurt me, I am going to glorify God." (1 Corinthians 10:31)
8. "I'm so humiliated. What will others think?"	8. "It is others' responsibility to think about this in a Christian manner, not to gossip or slander my husband or me (James 4:11). If they do gossip and I find out about it, God will give me the grace to handle it at that time."
9. "How could God let this happen to me?"	9. "God is good. He, too, wants my husband to repent. I thank God for reminding me how much I need Him." (1 Thessalonians 5:18)

Sinful thoughts are likely to result in sinful acts. Take a moment and compare the following sinful actions to the following godly reactions.

SINFUL ACTIONS	GODLY ACTIONS
1. Detailed gossiping of his sin to others.	1. Having the right motives, only giving necessary details to those directly involved in helping her biblically to respond.
2. Judging her husband's motives.	2. Assuming the best about his motives unless he tells her otherwise.
3. Exaggerating offenses.	3. Facing the offenses realistically, not exaggerating or minimizing them.
4. Not giving him a chance to repent and re-earn her trust.	4. Going against feelings and working towards reconciliation, realizing she must forgive but it may take time for him to re-earn her trust.
5. Ceasing to attend church because of embarrassment.	5. Continuing to attend church and to fulfill her responsibility.
6. Outburst of anger.	6. Realizing her anger will not achieve God's purposes. Thinking long and hard about how to biblically answer.
7. Seeking solace in another man.	7. Seeking solace in God and His Word, and perhaps, one or two godly women in the church.

8. Sharing deep emotional pain with the children in an intimate fashion that only adults are mature enough to handle.	8. Sharing appropriate factual information with the children and in the process giving them hope that even if their Daddy does not repent, God will take care of them and somehow they will be alright.
9. Wishing she could purchase a gun and kill her husband.	9. Realizing vengeance belongs to the Lord. Praying for and longing for his repentance.
10. Wishing he were dead.	10. Instead of longing for vengeance, putting godly pressure on him to repent by overcoming evil with good and praying for his repentance.
11. Committing suicide.	11. Continuing to fulfill her responsibilities whether she feels like it or not.

When a wife responds sinfully to sorrow, the sorrow that fills up her heart crowds out her God-given peace, joy, and love.[48]

The key to overcoming excessive and sinfully overwhelming sorrow is to repent of any specific sinful motives, thoughts, or actions and to concentrate on showing love to God and others. In the process, the person's capacity to love grows and their sorrow shrinks back down to a level that is manageable.[49]

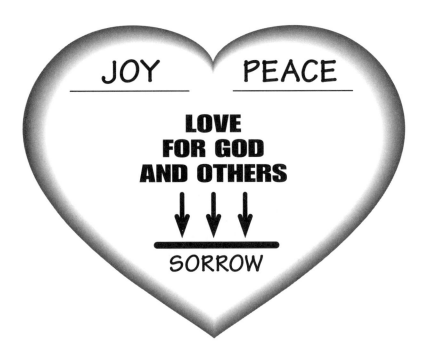

Righteous love will grow within a wife's heart as she is obedient to God's Word. As a rule in a difficult marriage, the more grievous the husband's sin, the harder the wife should fight back. Fighting back, however, is not with evil but good towards her husband. Romans 12:17 is a clear command: **"Never pay back evil for evil to anyone."**

What if the wife fights back in a righteous way and her husband still does not respond positively? If she does what is right and continues to do what is right until God gives her a **"way of escape,"** she will have fulfilled the admonition in Romans 12:18 that says, **"If possible, so far as it depends on you, be at peace with all men."** She will be showing love to God and her husband which will result in a growing capacity in her heart to love biblically.

Paul reminds us that we are not to take our own revenge. Revenge is the prerogative of God.

> *Never take your own revenge, beloved, but leave room for the wrath of God, for it is written, "VENGEANCE IS MINE, I WILL REPAY," says the Lord.*
>
> *Romans 12:19*

God will use biblical means to avenge your husband's sin and protect you. He may choose to use the legal authorities such as the police or courts (see Romans 13:1-3). He may sovereignly choose to take your husband out of this world. He may release you from the bond of marriage. He may choose to wait until eternity to avenge the sin done against you and Him. Regardless, personal revenge is not yours to pursue. The resources God has given to protect you, you are to pursue. If you do not retaliate with evil and if you stay in the battle for as long as God requires, God will apply tremendous pressure on your husband to repent.

> *But if your enemy is hungry, feed him, and if he is thirsty, give him a drink; for in so doing you will heap burning coals upon his head.*
>
> *Romans 12:20*

Paul ends this section with a rousing command to fight.

> *Do not be overcome by evil, but overcome evil with good.*
>
> *Romans 12:21*

In other words, instead of being overcome by your husband's evil, you keep on fighting back until his evil is overcome by the good you do through the power of the Lord Jesus Christ. Fight back diligently until your husband surrenders (repents) or God removes you from the battle. *Good* ways to overcome evil include prayer, speaking the truth in love, giving him blessings, doing kind things, working at getting the **"beam out of your eye"** (Matthew 7:5), and being biblically submissive, respectful, and loving. (For more information on fighting back biblically see Jay Adams' book *How To Overcome Evil.*)

For example, if your husband commits adultery, lovingly confront him according to Luke 17:3ff in the hopes of bringing about forgiveness.[50] If he is unsaved, it may be appropriate to ask him to consider the claims of Jesus Christ. If he explodes in angry rages and yet claims to know Christ, point out his responsibility to speak kind, edifying words. I know it is hard, but keep on fighting back for as long as it takes. Your weapons are much more effective and powerful than any weapon your husband may employ. You are commanded *not* to be overcome by your husband's evil. You *are* to fight back with God's good. As you do, your sorrow will lessen. You may still have grief because of your husband's sin, but sorrow does *not* have to fill your heart.

If you are in an especially difficult situation, you must seek your comfort and hope from God. He is to be your refuge and your strength. Let Him talk to you through His Word. Spend a lot of time in the Book of Psalms. There you will find Psalmists who experienced the same emotions you are feeling. See their thoughts about God and experience the same comfort and hope from God they experienced.

Approach God confidently in order to draw near to Him and find **"grace to help (you) and mercy"** in this your time of need (Hebrews 4:16). If you seek Him humbly, desire to do His will, and ask for help, He will freely give it to you. It does not matter how many times in one day or one week you approach Him, He is there and will have compassion on you and help you.

I remember one particular event in my life that caused me deep emotional pain. While this incident had nothing to do with my husband, the cause of the sorrow was none-the-less overwhelming. It is so easy to sin when you are in pain. I became desperate to seek God's help and strength. I longed to be enveloped in God's arms and there to feel safe and at peace. I went to God through prayer and talked to Him. Over and over I reminded myself of God's goodness. I prayed, "Lord, You are so good. You do all things well." Next I thanked Him for the circumstance. As I continued to hurt, I learned to be very specific about what I was thanking Him for. For example, "Lord, thank You for this particular circumstance. Also, thank You that You are in control, that this is good for me or You would not permit it. Thank You for this special opportunity to glorify You and magnify Your name. Thank You for what you are trying to teach me. Use me for your glory even if I must continue to suffer through this experience." By God's grace, I never came away from this kind of prayer without a renewed hope and my sorrow back down to a manageable level.

In addition to praising God for His goodness and thanking Him for the difficult circumstance, I asked Him to help me not to become angry at Him as well as not to accuse Him of being unjust or unfair to me. Having a grateful, submissive heart towards God is so vitally important that I pray a similar prayer occasionally even when circumstances are going well. My prayer goes something like this, "Lord, my prayer is that no matter what happens to me or to my loved ones, I will not become angry with You. God forbid that I would be anything other than submissive and grateful to You for how You choose to use my life to glorify Yourself."

I know that another's sin (especially if it is your husband's) can hurt deeply. I also know that it is possible for your sorrow to be righteous, godly, and not overwhelming. God is good. We are here to serve and worship Him on His terms. Sometimes, He gives us opportunities to **"share the sufferings of Christ"** (1 Peter 4:13). Find your comfort and refuge in God while continuing to serve Him as He desires. Respond to Him in a humble and submissive way. Fight back with good to overcome your husband's evil. Your hope must be set on the Lord. You can persevere for Jesus' sake.

Your heart may be broken over someone's sin. Remember, though, that you are not alone. God, too, is deeply grieved as well as offended. God is ready and waiting to help you. He will bear this burden with you and lighten your load.

> *Come to Me, all who are weary and heavy-laden, and I will give you rest. Take My yoke upon you, and learn from Me, for I am gentle and humble in heart; and YOU SHALL FIND REST FOR YOUR SOULS. For My yoke is easy, and My load is light.*
>
> *Matthew 11:28-30*

Your sorrow will lessen as you seek refuge in God, as you go against your natural feelings, and as you show love to God and your husband. You do not ever have to be sinfully overwhelmed again. Sarah laughed at the Angel of the Lord when He announced she would bear a son. His response to Sarah was, **"Is there *anything* too difficult for God?"** (Genesis 18:14, emphasis added). Let me ask you the same question, "Is there anything (including your marriage) that is too difficult for God?" The answer is obvious, "Absolutely not! Not then and not now."

Postscript

At the beginning of this book I asked "Who is the excellent wife?" and "What is she like?" Now you know. She loves God with all her heart. She takes the Word of God seriously. She is not ignorant of her biblical responsibilities. She loves, respects, and submits to her husband as God desires. She is growing and learning personally, and she is teaching other women. She loves the role God has given her. She is the glory of her husband. She truly glorifies God.

Also at the beginning of this book, I said, "This is my labor of love for you." And so it has turned out to be! However, I do not regret the work because I want *so much* for every woman who reads this to be godly. I think of some of the young women that I love so much — my daughter Anna Maupin, Stuart Scott's wife, Zondra, my daughter-in-law Jaimee Peace, Lou Priolo's wife Kim, John Crotts' wife Lynn, and the "Legacy" leader at Three Rivers Baptist Church, Ann Graff. I have cried with them, shared their joys, and watched them grow in grace. Their potential to glorify the Lord is so great. There is nothing that can happen to them that God could not use for His *good*. As much as I love them, He loves them more.

What about you? Are you a Christian? Are you willing to obey God and become the wife God wants you to be? Let me encourage you to reread the sections of this book that have convicted you personally. Study the Scriptures and apply them to yourself. Use this material to teach and help other women. Live it out in your life and teach it to your children. Persevere and be faithful. By God's grace, you can become —

An excellent wife, who can find?
For her worth is far above jewels.
Proverbs 31:10

Salvation Work Sheets
"Who is Jesus Christ?"

The Bible tells us much about Jesus and who He is. Many of the claims were made by Jesus Himself and many were made by others about Him. Look up the following references and write down what these claims are. Before you begin your study, say a brief prayer to God and ask Him to show you if these things are true.

1.   What does Jesus call himself?

    a.   John 4:25,26

    b.   John 8:28 and John 9:35-38

    c.   Matthew 27:42,43

"Son of God" and "Son of Man" are Old Testament expressions for the Messiah who was predicted to come. The Prophets in the Old Testament knew that this Messiah was God and that He was worthy of worship. See Daniel 7: 13,14.

2.   What does Jesus claim about Himself?

    a.   John 5:39

    b.   John 6:51

    c.   John 8:12

    d.   John 8:58

    e.   John 10:30 and 14:7-9

3.   The Trinity is three Divine Persons (God the Father, God the Son, and God the Holy Spirit) who are the same in essence and nature yet with distinct personalities. When God the Son, Jesus, lived here on earth for 33 years, He subordinated himself to the will of God the Father. Why? See Philippians 2:5-8.

4.   The Apostle Paul says in his letter to Titus that "God is our Savior" (Titus 1:3).

    a.   Who does Paul then say our Savior is? (Titus 1:3,4).

    b.   What else does Paul say about Jesus? (Colossians 1:15,16).

5.   Who did Peter say that Jesus was?

    a.   Mark 8:27-29

    b.   2 Peter 1:1

6. Who did John the Baptist say that Jesus was?

    a. John 1:29 and 34

7. Who did the Apostle John say Jesus was?

    a. John 1:1,14

    b. Revelation 19:16

8. Who did God the Father say Jesus was?

    a. Matthew 3:17

9. Who has the authority to forgive sins?

    a. Luke 5:21

    b. Who forgave the paralytic's sins? (Luke 5:17-20).

    c. What did Jesus do to prove that He had authority to forgive sins? (Luke 5:21-24).

Summary:

Jesus claimed to be God by saying He:

- was the "Son of God"
- was the "Son of Man"
- was the Savior (the Messiah)
- had authority to forgive sins

Jesus proved that He was God by:

- the works that He did (for example, creation)
- the miracles that He did
- His resurrection from the dead

The teaching of the Bible that Jesus is God is not something that we can explain by human logic. It is a supernatural truth which we believe because God's Spirit illumines the truth to us. Next, we will study in detail what Jesus did on the cross.

What Jesus Did On The Cross

Just about everyone in America has heard of Jesus and knows that He died on the cross. However, they may have many misconceptions about the purpose of His death. So this lesson is a study on "What Jesus Did on the Cross."

1. How was Jesus killed? (Matthew 27:35).

2. What did the sign over His head say? (Mark 15:26).

3. What did the people who were making fun of Jesus say? (Luke 23:35-37).

4. How did the soldiers decide to divide up Jesus' garments? (John 19:24).

5. Which four books in the Bible contain the story of Jesus' death on the cross?

6. Make a list of what Jesus said as He was on the cross:

    a. Luke 23:34

    b. Luke 23:42,43

    c. Luke 23:46

    d. John 19:25,26

    e. John 19:30

    f. Mark 15:37,38

7. What was the purpose of Jesus' death?

    a. 1 Peter 2:24

    b. Hebrews 2:17 ("propitiation" means to satisfy God's wrath).

    c. Ephesians 1:7 ("In Him" refers back to Jesus Christ).

    d. Romans 4:25 ("He" refers back to Jesus).

    e. Romans 5:9

    f. 1 Corinthians 15:3

Jesus told His disciples that the "Scriptures" (The Old Testament) were about Him (John 5:39). Indeed, there are many places in the Old Testament that foretell the coming Messiah and what He will do for the people so they can be reconciled to God. (Sin had put a barrier between people and God because God is holy.) Jesus' death on the cross was God's way of punishing sin so that God's sense of justice could be satisfied. In other words, Jesus was punished in our place.

One of the most detailed descriptions of how Jesus took our punishment is in Isaiah 53. This was written by Isaiah over 700 years before Jesus was born. God gave this information to Isaiah supernaturally and Isaiah doesn't call Jesus by His name but calls him the "Servant".

8. How was Jesus treated by men? (Isaiah 53:3).

9. What did He "bear" for us? (Isaiah 53:4).

10. What happened to Jesus because of our "transgressions" (our sins) and our "iniquities" (also means sins)? (Isaiah 53:5).

11. Isaiah 53:5 says, "The chastening (punishment that we deserve) for our _____ fell upon Him."

12. Isaiah 53:6 says, "But the LORD has caused the iniquity (sin) of us all to _____ _____ _____"

13. What kind of sacrificial offering was Jesus? (Isaiah 53:10).

14. Where was Jesus' anguish? (Isaiah 53:11).

15. What will He bear? (Isaiah 53:11).

16. Isaiah 53:12, "Yet He Himself bore the _____"

17. What was God's motive for sending Jesus to die for our sins? (I John 4:10).

Summary: Jesus died on the cross to take the punishment for our sins. He died in our place. He paid the full penalty and then He said,

"IT IS FINISHED!"

What Does The Bible Teach About Sin?

As we studied Jesus' death on the cross, we learned that He died to take the punishment for our sin. Also, we learned that God was satisfied that sin had been sufficiently punished and that Jesus' resurrection from the dead is proof of that. Now we are going to study about sin—who sinned first, why they did, and why and how we sin today. Some sins are very obvious—for example, murder. Some sins are obvious only to God. Regardless of which kind of sin we commit, all sin grieves God because He is perfectly pure and holy. Therefore, we need to understand just what sin is and how to properly deal with it.

1. The first created being to sin was an angel named Lucifer (later his name became Satan). His problem was pride. He wanted to be worshiped like God was worshiped as some of the other angels. Lucifer made a "power-play" in heaven and God cast Lucifer and all his followers out. What did Lucifer want? (See Isaiah 14:13-14). List the five "I will" statements of Lucifer:

   a.

   b.

c.

d.

e.

2. Lucifer had a real problem with pride. He should have been grateful to worship and serve God. Instead, he wanted all the attention himself. What was the underlying reason he thought he deserved that kind of attention? (Ezekiel 28:17).

3. Lucifer was the first angel to sin and Adam and Eve were the first human beings to sin. When God created Adam and Eve they were innocent and without sin. God put them in the Garden of Eden which had a perfect environment. Then God tested their devotion to Him by telling them they could eat fruit from any tree except one—"the tree of the knowledge of good and evil." God warned them that if they disobeyed, they would die.

   a. Satan was not content to leave well enough alone. He decided to try to get Adam and Eve to follow him by disobeying God. He appeared to Eve in the form of a serpent. (See Genesis 3:1).

      1) How is the serpent described?

      2) What did he ask Eve?

   b. God told Eve if she ate from that tree she would die. What did Satan tell her would happen? (Genesis 3:4).

   c. Whom did Satan tell Eve she would "be like" if she ate? (Genesis 3:5).

   d. What did Eve decide to do? (Genesis 3:6).

   e. Before they sinned, Adam and Eve were very comfortable around God and not afraid of Him. What was their response to God now? (Genesis 3:10).

   f. God confronted them with their sin. Whom did Adam blame? (Genesis 3:12).

   g. Whom did Eve blame? (Genesis 3:13).

4. Because God is holy, He has to punish sin. He pronounced judgment right then on Satan, Eve, and Adam. What was one part of the punishment? (Genesis 3:19).

5. After Adam and Eve sinned, they knew sin in a personal, experiential way. It had become part of their natural nature and was then passed down to their children and their children's children, etc. Also, the consequences of sin were passed down.

   a. Why did "death spread to all men"? (Romans 5:12).

   b. What is the "just" consequence of sin? (Romans 6:23).

6. The Bible classifies sin by different terms such as transgression, iniquity, wickedness, evil, disobedience, and unbelief. Look up the following verses and list what the particular sin is:

   a. Romans 13:1

   b. 1 Corinthians 6:18

   c. Ephesians 4:25-29 (these sins are obvious sins)

   d. Ephesians 4:31 (these sins may be obvious or may be "mental attitude" sins. Mental attitude sins are sins that we "think" which may or may not result in an additional, obvious sin.)

   e. Ephesians 5:18

   f. Philippians 4:6

   g. James 3:6

   h. James 4:17

   i. James 5:12

7. All sin, whether open or hidden, is seen and remembered by God. What does God judge? (Hebrews 4:12).

8. Is there anything hidden from God? (Hebrews 4:13).

9. God is holy. Therefore, He must punish sin. Man sins. Therefore, man is separated from God and the result is death. However, God loves man, so He provided a way for man's sins to be punished and for man to be with Him for all eternity. The way that God provided is "Jesus death on the cross bearing our punishment." How is it that we can know that we, personally, are in a right relationship with God? That *our* sins are taken care of? (See Acts 16:31).

10. People often know about Jesus but they are still depending partly on themselves to be good enough to earn their way into heaven. If that's the case, then they are not really "believing" (trusting) in Jesus' death on the cross to be sufficient to save them. The Bible says that Jesus saves us "not on the basis of deeds which we have done, but according to His mercy" (Titus 3:5). In addition to not trusting the Lord Jesus as their Savior, many people are like Satan in that they do not want God to rule over them. They want to control their own lives, so they do not trust Christ as their Lord. If that is true of you, "God is now declaring to men that all everywhere should repent, because He has fixed a day in which He will judge the world in righteousness through a Man (Jesus Christ) whom He has appointed, having furnished proof to all men by raising Him from the dead" (Acts 17:30-31). Romans 10:9 tells us "if you confess with your mouth Jesus as Lord, and believe in your heart that God raised Him from the dead, you shall be saved" (Romans 10:9).

Assurance of Salvation

Many times when people are asked the question, "Do you know *for sure* that if you died you would go to heaven?" their answer is something like, "I'm not sure but I hope so." Finally, we will focus on what the Bible teaches about "knowing for sure." Because this issue is a critical one, before you begin to answer the ques?tions, say a short prayer and ask God to show you the truth of His Word.

1. A person who is "saved" is going to heaven when he dies. What do you have to "do" to get "saved?"

    a. John 3:16

    b. Romans 10:13

    c. John 1:12

2. Read the following verses and make a chart. On the left side, list what "saves" you and on the right side, list what will not "save" you:

    a. John 14:6

    b. Ephesians 2:8,9

    c. Acts 16:30,31

    d. Ephesians 2:4,5

    e. Colossians 1:13,14

    f. Galatians 1:3,4

    g. Titus 3:4-7

3. People think about their salvation in one of two ways: they must be good and do things to "earn" it, or,

    Jesus did *all* the work necessary and they must put their faith or "trust" in Him (alone) to be their Savior.

    a. *Nowhere does the Bible say that a person is saved by what he does or how good he is!!!* On the contrary, the Bible says that the only acceptable sacrifice or punishment for sins is Jesus' sacrifice on the cross. Why, then, do so many people think they must believe in Jesus *plus* "earn" their way into heaven? Because, it is logical from a human perspective. But God says, "My ways are not your ways and my thoughts are higher than your thoughts" (Isaiah 55:9). We are not holy so we do not think like God thinks. Because He is holy, *all* sin must be punished. It is not enough for us to have done more good things than bad. All the bad had to be dealt with and that's what Jesus declared when He said, "It is finished!"

    b. Look up the following verses and write down what God wants you to know about "assurance of your salvation."

        1). Romans 3:28

        2). Romans 8:1

        3). Romans 10:11

        4). John 5:24

        5). John 6:47

        6). 1 Corinthians 3:15

        7). 2 Corinthians 1:9-10

        8). 1 John 5:11-13

        9). 1 Peter 1:3-5

        10). Titus 1:2

4. There are basically three reasons why people don't have the assurance of their salvation:

    a. They don't know what the Bible teaches.

    b. They have never really *put their trust in Jesus as their Lord and Savior.* Jesus said, "But you do not believe, because you are not of My sheep. My sheep hear My voice, and I know them, and they follow me; and I give eternal life to them, and they shall *never* perish and no one can snatch them out of My hand" (John 10:26-28).

c. There is no evidence of salvation in their life such as a desire for God, a longing to please God, or obedience to Christ's commandments. "And by this we know that we have come to know Him, if we keep His commandments" (1 John 2:3).

Salvation is a work of God not a work of man. So if you are having doubts, ask God to grant you repentance from your sin and faith in His Son.

The
"*Put Off*" - "*Put On*" *Dynamic* [51]
Developed by Martha Peace

This Bible study is for the purpose of teaching Christians how to deal practically with their sin. Many times we are aware that changes need to be made in our lives and we confess the appropriate sins to God. However, we may find ourselves committing those same sins again and again. Habitual sin is especially difficult because we automatically respond wrongly, without thinking. Therefore, it is important to learn exactly what God has to teach us through His Word about establishing new habit patterns.

Before you begin this study, pray and ask God to show you the truth of His Word.

Begin by looking up the following Scriptures and write out the answers to the questions:

1. How do we become aware of sin?
   a) Hebrews 4:12 *the Word of God.*
   b) John 16:7,8 *the Holy Spirit*
2. Do we *have* to sin? Explain. (See Romans 6:6, 7, 14). *No - God's grace* *because of God's grace*
3. Describe what the "old man" was like. (See Ephesians 4:22). *corrupt*
4. Describe what the "new man" is like. (See Ephesians 4:24). *like God.*
5. What are we to "put off" and what are we to "put on"?
   (See Ephesians 4:22,24). *put off old*   *put on new*
6. What are we to "put off" (lay aside) according to Colossians 3:9? *evil practices*
7. What are we to "put on" according to Colossians 3:10? *new self*
8. This "new self" is to be renewed. How? (See Colossians 3:10). *the true knowledge of Christ*

Thus, we see that we are to "put off" our old ways of thinking and acting and "put on" new ways which are like those of Jesus Christ. When sinful ways of thinking or responding have become habitual, just confessing that sin is not enough. The sinful habit pattern must be *replaced* with a righteous habit pattern. It is as if what we are to "put on" is the biblical antidote to what we are to "put off." For example, it is not enough to just stop telling lies. A person must begin (work at) telling the truth, the whole truth. By God's help (grace) he will become a truthful person instead of a liar.

Look up the following Scriptures and fill in the chart:

Scripture Reference	"Put Off" Character Deficiencies	"Put On" Character Qualities
1. Ephesians 4:25	falsehood	truthfullness
2. Ephesians 4:26,27	anger	forgiveness
3. Ephesians 4:28	steal	work/share
4. Ephesians 4:29	unwholesome talk	edification
5. Ephesians 4:31,32	rage, bitterness anger	kind/compassionate forgiving
6. Ephesians 5:11	darkness	expose the darkness/put on the light
7. Ephesians 5:4	obscene speech	thanksgiving
8. Ephesians 5:18	drinking	the spirit
9. Philippians 4:6	worry	faith + thanksgiving
10. Colossians 3:8,12,13,14	anger rage bitterness slander filthy	compassion kindness humility gentleness
11. Romans 13:12-14	drunkenness sexual immorality	put on Jesus Christ

As we have seen earlier, God gives Christians the Holy Spirit to convict them of sin and to help them carry out God's desires. As a result, is there anything that God requires that a Christian cannot do? (See Philippians 4:13.) Hence, God will never ask us to do something that He will not give us the grace to carry out. Sometimes we may not feel like obeying God; however, if we do obey (in spite of our feelings), God will give us grace.

Write down the specific sins in your life you know need to be "put off:"

_____   _____   _____

_____   _____   _____

_____   _____   _____

Take time now to confess these sins to God.

Write down what you are to "put on" (the biblical antidote) in your life in the place of these sins:

_____   _____   _____

_____   _____   _____

_____   _____   _____

Write down some practical actions you can do to "put on" godly character:

1.
2.
3.
4.
5.

Based upon what you have learned in this study, write out your prayer:

Questions & Answers

Q: How did you become a counselor?

A: That's an interesting question because I never wanted to be a counselor. After I was saved, I only wanted to teach ladies' Bible classes. For five years at a solid Bible-teaching church, the pastor helped me prepare to teach the ladies' class. I taught Bible books such as Genesis, John, and Colossians. Then providentially the Lord brought Lou Priolo, a biblical counselor, to our church and I heard him speak. I really liked how practical and biblical he was. So, my husband and I took classes from Lou so that we could learn more personally and so that I could become a better Bible teacher. It was Lou, who after getting to know me, suggested that I take the biblical counseling training. I told him, "No, thanks. I'm a teacher, not a counselor." Later my husband, Sanford, encouraged me to give the counseling a try. That's when I took the training seriously. So, the Lord made me a counselor even though it would not have been the path I would have taken. Of course now I'm glad He did.

Q: What is nouthetic counseling?

A: Nouthetic (pronounced "new-thet-ick) counseling is biblical counseling. The word nouthetic is an English word that Jay Adams coined from the Greek word, *noutheteo*. *Noutheteo* is a New Testament word that means to exhort, admonish, give instruction, or to place or set into the mind. The reason that Jay Adams called biblical counseling "nouthetic" instead of simply "biblical" counseling was to differentiate his view of counseling from those who claimed their model was "biblical" even though they integrate various psychological theories into their beliefs. Nouthetic counseling uses just the Scripture (which is God's inspired Word and absolute truth). It is based on believing that God really has "given us everything we need pertaining to life and godliness" (2 Peter 1:3). It is also based on the belief that when a person has a problem, you cannot go deeper inside that person than the "thoughts and intents of their heart" (Hebrews 4:12). Nouthetic counselors are usually pastors and sometimes lay men and women who exhort and encourage (in love) those who need help with their problems. They give those they work with great hope and, at the same time, accountability. Many unbelievers have come to faith in Christ through biblical counseling, and many believers have, through the sufficiency of Christ and His Word, solved their problems in a short period of time. If you would like to know more about nouthetic counseling and/ or training, see the web site, www.NANC.org.

Q: What does it mean to be trapped by vain regrets?

A: All of us have things that we regret, whether it was something stupid we said or something sinful. We have choices we made in life that if we had it to do over again, we would change. Reliving the past and playing it over and over is not honoring to the Lord. Instead, biblically deal with the past by asking forgiveness or paying restitution when needed, but then honor the Lord by not dwelling on it. Being consumed with past regrets is one way we become very selfishly focused. Instead, we should be focused on the Lord Jesus Christ and honoring Him and graciously accepting the forgiveness we have in Him.

Q: What does it mean in 1 Corinthians 11:7-9 that the "woman is the glory of man"? I thought we were to only give God glory.

A: In the sense of worship and praising His worth as the only true God and our Creator, certainly we are only to give glory to God. In the sense of honoring another person or helping them to succeed in their tasks, we can certainly give glory to man. For instance, children who honor their parents by respectfully obeying are giving their parents glory as others notice. Also a wife who honors her husband through joyful, respectful submission and being a "helper-suitable" is giving her husband glory. She is in that way, as Paul wrote, "the glory of man" (1 Corinthians 11:7).

Q: I read a book that said in order for me to overcome my hurt over what someone did to me in the past, I must come to the point where I forgive God. Is that true?

A: No, it is not true. In fact, it is blasphemous. God hasn't done and cannot do anything wrong. There is nothing that we have to forgive Him for. We should not even think in those terms. Instead, we should be grateful for His blessings and for the trials in our life that can be used for His glory and our ultimate sanctification (making us more like Christ; Romans 8:28-29). Instead of being angry with God, we are to view ourselves as God's creature put on earth by Him to serve Him on His terms. Thus, we are to "in everything give thanks; for this is God's will for you in Christ Jesus" (1 Thessalonians 5:18).

Q: How can a person achieve emotional wholeness?

A: Recently someone asked me this question, and I answered by using biblical terms instead of psychological terms. In order to rephrase this question in biblical terms you might ask, "How can a person be joyful and fulfilled in life?" The answer is by being in a right relationship with God through the Lord Jesus Christ (Romans 5:1-2), by obeying His Word, and thus by His grace manifesting the fruit of His Spirit in your heart and life. His fruit in your life results in "love, joy, peace, patience, kindness, goodness, faithfulness, gentleness, and self-control" (Galatians 5:22-23). I cannot think of anything more joyful and fulfilling.

Q: I work hard taking care of my family but struggle with resentment because I have no time or energy for myself. Is this a sin, or is it all right to desire time for myself?

A: There is nothing wrong with desiring time for yourself (within reason); but there is a difference between desiring time for yourself and being resentful if you cannot have it. This is a difficult question to answer without more details such as—Do you think your husband is being sinfully unreasonable in what he is requiring you to do? Do you have several small children and even with your husband's help you are in "survival mode?" Are your children older but not doing their share of the work? Are you disorganized or lazy and does that create additional, unnecessary work? Have you over-committed to projects outside of your home? If your answer is "yes" to any of these questions, then you should respond appropriately depending on the question.

For instance, if your husband is sinfully unreasonable, appeal to him (gently and respectfully). If he does not change his mind and you are convinced that he is sinning, then with love and respect, reprove him. For what to do further regarding the issue of your husband overloading you with work, I will refer you to chapter 14 in "The Excellent Wife" book.

If the problem is that you have several small children and you are in "survival mode," then pray for wisdom and perhaps ask for some outside help (either paid or volunteer from the church or your family) to help with the work.

If the problem is that the children are untaught and not held accountable, then it is your responsibility to teach them and follow up to see that they have accomplished their chores until it becomes a habit for them.

If the problem is that you are disorganized or lazy, then read some good books on organizing and ask one of the older ladies in the church who is well organized to come over one day and give you some good suggestions. Don't be lazy, get to work, and work "heartily as unto the Lord." If you have over-committed to projects outside the home, then make an assessment about what is really necessary and ask yourself, "What does the Lord want me to concentrate on now?" Often the answer is your family. It would be better to do fewer things, but do them well and not be so overwhelmed.

In addition to all these suggestions, the bottom line for every woman who is struggling with resentment because she does not have time for herself is that she must realize her time belongs to the Lord, and she should desire for Him to use her as He desires. If you feel resentful, then you are sinning. Don't think in terms of "I have my rights or I have to have my time." If you do, you'll continue to struggle with resentment no matter how much time you have. Think instead "How can I use the time that God has given me to show more love to Him and more love to others (including my family)." Certainly, it is not wrong to plan something that you would like to do or ask your husband to help you, but do not set your heart on it so much that you are willing to sin if you do not get it.

Q: Is it all right for women to be elders and deacons in the church? I have heard some women say that "God has called me to this ministry."

A: This is a question that I am asked more and more often. The issue is being debated even among conservative evangelicals. The answer is simple—no, it is not all right for women to be elders and deacons or pastors. The reason is from Scripture. If you were to read 1 Timothy and 2 Timothy and the book of Titus, you would learn much about the role of the pastor. When the word "pastor" is used, the same Greek word is often translated "overseer," "bishop," or "elder." So whether it says "elder" or "pastor," it is the same. Clearly in 1 and 2 Timothy and Titus the elder or pastor is a man. For example, "the husband of one wife" (1 Timothy 3:2) and "if a man does not know how to manage his own house, how will he take care of the church of God?" (1 Timothy 3:5). Concerning the deacons, they are also men. For example, "Deacons likewise must be men of dignity... these men must first be tested..." (1 Timothy 3:8-10). The women have a different role—not inferior, but different. They are to teach the younger women (Titus 2:3-5), and they are to "adorn themselves by means of good works" (1 Timothy 2:10). In addition, the Apostle Paul wrote in his instructions to the churches, "But I do not allow a woman to teach or exercise authority over a man, but to remain quiet." (1 Timothy 2:12). Women have told me that they feel "called" to be ministers or teachers to both men and women. Certainly it is good to desire to minister to others. But when our feelings tell us one thing and the Scripture another, we have to go with the Scripture. God has greatly gifted women as He has men, and it is a joy for all Christians to use the spiritual gifts He has given them. The only way to truly give God glory is to serve Him and use our gifts within the parameters clearly set forth in His Word.

Q: What is the correct way to raise godly children with an unbelieving husband so that they will respect their father?

A: The Scriptures are clear that children are to honor their father and mother whether they are Christians or not. Showing "honor" or "respect" is something that a child can do whether their father is acting as he should or not. Respect is shown in tone of voice, how they look at their father, the attitude with which they obey him, and how they speak of him to others. The child can be taught to do what is right and honor the Lord whether their father does or not. Certainly I do not think mothers should be "bad-mouthing" the child's father to the children (or anyone else for that matter!), but neither should she pretend that the father is a Christian and that his worldly views are alright. The mother has a responsibility to teach her children and bring them up "in the Lord". Part of that teaching is teaching them to be discerning about good and evil and about biblical beliefs and unbiblical beliefs. They need to learn that unbelievers do not think like believers and that only God can change that. So, the child should be praying for their father's salvation, obeying their father graciously unless he is asking them to sin, and giving their father blessings and "overcoming evil with good". Children can be taught to think objectively about others' sin and to respond biblically to it, all-the-while showing respect to their father because of his God-given position in the family. For more information on raising kids, I recommend my tape set "Raising Kids Without Raising Cain" along with the workbook that accompanies the tapes. Also I recommend Ted Tripp's book, "Shepherding Your Child's Heart."

Q: Where do you start to help your husband understand that reading "Playboy" magazine, etc. is bad and not God's way?

A: If your husband says he is a Christian, I would lovingly but in a clear, straightforward manner, tell him "Honey, pornography is a sin. It is this kind of thing that the Lord Jesus was talking about when He said, '...but I say to you that everyone who looks at a woman with lust for her has already committed adultery with her in his heart' (Matthew 5:28). Your thoughts cannot be pure when looking at this, and you must repent. I love you. Is there anything I can do to make it easier for you to give this up?" Then, if he does not repent, proceed with the Matthew 18:15-18 process. For much greater detail, read chapter fourteen in "The Excellent Wife" book.

If your husband is not a Christian, appeal to his conscience to "do what is right." For example, "Honey, it's not right for you to be looking at pornography. It will cause you to be discontent with being married, it costs money, and you run the risk of the children finding it. Is there anything I can do to help you with this?" If an unbelieving husband won't repent, then pray for wisdom as to what to do. If the problem is bad enough that you think you should do something, consult with the elders in your church. Otherwise, keep praying and occasionally appeal to your husband to "do what is right." Also some pornography (such as child pornography) is illegal as well as extremely dangerous. If he will not give up that kind of pornography, I would contact the police (Romans 13:1-3). Your motive in all of this must be one of love and desiring to help your husband.

The Biblical View of Authority

1. God has authority over the earth (Job 34:12-15).
2. Man does not have authority as God does (Ecclesiastes 8:8).
3. Man can abuse his authority and hurt others (Ecclesiastes 8:9).
4. Sometimes God wields His authority in judgment against wicked nations (Isaiah 30:30-31).
5. Sometimes God wields His authority in judgment against His own people when they turn from Him (Jeremiah 5:20-22, 29).
6. Some Priests in the Old Testament abused their authority (Jeremiah 5:30-31).
7. Men are sometimes given authority to rule over others (Daniel 5:16; Matthew 8:9).
8. The Lord Jesus amazed the people as He taught with authority (Matthew 7:29).
9. The Lord Jesus has authority to forgive sins (Matthew 9:6).
10. The Lord Jesus gave His Apostles authority over unclean spirits and to heal disease (Matthew 10:1).
11. The Lord Jesus has authority over all other authorities (Matthew 28:18; Ephesians 1:21; Colossians. 2:10).
12. Instead of fearing man, we should fear God who has authority to cast people into hell (Luke 12:5).
13. Kings and Rulers have authority given to them by God (John 19:11).
14. No one has authority over others unless God gives it to them (Romans 13:1).
15. We are to obey the authorities God gives us (Romans 13:2; 1 Peter 2:13-15).
16. Concerning sexual intimacy, husbands and wives have authority over their spouse's body (1 Corinthians 7:4).
17. In the church in Corinth, a head covering for the woman was a symbol of her being under authority (1 Corinthians 11:10).
18. In the end, God will abolish all earthly rule and authorities (1 Corinthians 15:23-24).
19. In the context of the church, women are not to exercise authority over the men (1 Timothy 2:12).

20. Unrighteous people are described, in part, as despising authority (2 Peter 2:10).

21. In addition to Kings and Governors, certain people are given authority:
    - Parents over children: Ephesians 6:1
    - Masters over slaves: 1 Peter 2:18
    - Husbands over wives: Ephesians 5:23

22. Warnings to be careful with the authority God gives you.
    - Fathers: Ephesians 6:4
    - Masters: Ephesians 6:9
    - Husbands: 1 Peter 3:7

23. God gives authority to man. Man's authority over others is not absolute. God is the higher authority. No man has absolute authority over another. If man's authority would cause the person under his authority to sin, then the person that was asked to sin must respectfully refuse even if it means they suffer consequences. That is the only view that is (1) **consistent with the holiness of God** and the Scriptural teaching that (2) **each person is accountable to God for their own sin** (1 Peter 1:14-16; Ezekiel 18:20; Deuteronomy 24:16).

Meekness Assessment and Homework Assignment

adapted from the book
The Quest for Gentleness and Quietness of Spirit
by Matthew Henry

Instructions: Read carefully each of the following questions or statements. Circle the numbers of those on which you need to work. Go back to those you circled, look up and memorize the Scriptures, spend time in prayer and think about how, by God's grace, you need to change. Show the list to your family and close friends and ask them to hold you accountable when they observe you not having a gentle and quiet spirit.

1. Am I more likely to think "This makes me mad!" or "What might God be doing in this situation?" (Proverbs 19:11).
2. What would more likely come to your mind: "Love is patient. I can respond in a kind way and give glory to God." or "This irritates me!"? (1 Corinthians 13:4-7).
3. Which describes how you would likely react: Sighing and withdrawing in anger or in gentleness trying to help the other person to understand? (Colossians 3:12-13).
4. Do you ever stop and ask yourself:
   - Why am I angry?
   - Why so very angry?
   - Why angry at all?
   - What reason is there for all this emotion?
   - Should I be so strongly reacting because of such a sudden and transient provocation? (Philippians 2:3-5 and 1 Timothy 6:11).
5. While angry do you ever reveal secrets, slander, make rash vows, make railing accusations, use reviling language, call names, or take God's name in vain? (Titus 3:1-2).
6. Are you more likely to play angry thoughts over and over in your mind or to give the other person a blessing by praying for them? (Ephesians 4:31-32).

7. Are you clearing yourself when unjustly accused? Or are you really proud and quarreling? (1 Peter 2:19-23).

8. Is it easy for you to acknowledge your error or do you insist upon your own vindication? (1 Peter 5:5).

9. Will you listen to and consider someone else's reproof of you even if they are your inferiors (such as your child) or do you bully them and blame them? (Psalm 37:5-6, 7-8).

10. Do you struggle greatly with difficult emotions such as anxiety or frustration during the days before your menstrual period? Is it likely your entire family will know your hormones are acting up? (Colossians 3:8-17).

11. Do you think calm thoughts or are you disturbed within? (James 3:13).

12. Do you deal gently with others showing patience and compassion or are you hard and unforgiving? (Colossians 3:13; Philippians 4:5).

13. Do you enjoy life and love life or do you dread each day and fret and worry? (Philippians 4:6-7).

14. Are you easily provoked or slow to anger? (Proverbs 31:26).

15. Are your thoughts calm and rational or do you sometimes overreact to circumstances? (Ephesians 5:2; 1 Peter 2:11-12).

16. Are you more like the high priest in Hebrews 5:1-2 who has compassion on the ignorant and those going astray (since he is also subject to weakness) or more like the wicked servant in Matthew 18:21-35 who would not have compassion and pity on his fellow servant?

17. Do you forbear (put up with others) or are you easily provoked for small cause? (Psalm 78:38-39; Philippians 4:5).

18. Are you fiery and hasty with what you say or do you take great care to think about how to respond? (Ephesians 4:29-30; James 4:1).

19. Do you use anger and threats to manipulate those under your authority or do you give instruction in love? (Psalm 106:32-33).

20. Do you err on the side of mercy when correcting those under your authority or are you harsh? (Psalm 103:8,14).

21. Do you treat others as you wish to be treated or do you treat them with contempt? (Matthew 7:12).

22. Do you grumble and complain at your present circumstances that disappoint you or are you grateful to God for what He is doing? (1 Thessalonians 4:11; Philippians 4:12).

23. Are you quick to imagine injuries or do you assume the best about others unless proven otherwise? (1 Corinthians 13:7-8).

24. Are you envious of the wicked or are you placing your trust in God? (Psalm 73:21-28).

25. Are you becoming more aware of times when you are not gentle with others and you are disputing with God or do you see no need to change in this area of your life? (1 Corinthians 10:12).

26. When it is necessary to reprove (tell them what they are doing wrong) another person, are you more likely to lash out impulsively or more likely to gently try to help them to turn from their sin with good will, soft words, and objective arguments? (Galatians 6:1).

27. Do you pray and ask the Lord to make you a gentle woman or does it not cross your mind? (Zephaniah 2:3).

28. Do you brood and become angry when you are persecuted for your faith or do you rejoice that the Lord counted you worthy to suffer for His sake? (Matthew 5:11-12; Acts 5:41; Psalm 39:1).

29. Do you become aggravated, hurt, or frustrated with God over your circumstances or do you have great joy in serving Him on His terms? (Isaiah 45:9; Proverbs 19:3).

Examples of Not Answering a Fool According to His Folly

1. Wife to unbeliever husband says, "Honey I'm not sure we can afford to purchase a new car now."
    *   Husband says in anger, "I have always wanted a truck like this and you are selfish and don't want me to have it."
    *   Wife says, "I would like for you to consider thinking about this truck for a while and looking at our budget to see if we can really afford it."
    *   Husband says in anger, "I am going to buy this truck. Now sign this loan."
    *   Wife responds, "Honey this is not right. You know we cannot afford an additional payment right now.
    *   Husband says sarcastically, "If you loved me, you would sign this loan for me. I would do this for you."
    *   Wife responds, "Sweetheart the issue is *if* we really can afford this truck. I don't think we can. Therefore, I cannot with a clear conscience sign the loan. Honey, it is your responsibility to protect your family financially and not put us in financial peril." (At this point, whether she signs or not would depend on if she thinks it would be a sin. If she signs a loan knowing full well that they cannot pay it back, it would be a sin. If she refuses to sign, she should clearly and nicely explain why. If he can get the loan on his own, then she will have to trust God with the outcome.)

2. Christian husband comes home from work in a bad mood. The wife has been washing clothes all day and the folded (but not yet put away) laundry is sitting on the kitchen table.
    *   Husband angrily says, "Look at this mess. You are a slob!"
    *   Wife says, "Dear, there is nothing wrong with you asking me to put the clothes away before you get home from work, but as a Christian man you should be patient and kind in your tone and words."

- Husband glares at her and then huffs off refusing to speak for hours.
- The wife puts away the clothes to give a blessing instead. Later she says to him privately, "John, this is not right for you to pout and punish me this way. You should honor God and not take out your bad, sinful mood on me about the laundry."
- Husband glares again and says nothing and walks off.
- Wife prays for him and plans a way to give him a blessing instead.
- If the husband remains unrepentant, the wife should bring in two or more witnesses to exhort him to repent of his sinful bullying.

Loneliness

The chapter on loneliness surprised me as I wrote *The Excellent* Wife because as I wrote it, it became my favorite chapter in the entire book. It was striking because I have never personally struggled with loneliness, even when I have been alone. Sometimes I do get bored and want to do something with somebody but (as my friend Maribeth says) **being alone and lonely is not the same thing. If you are alone (and bored) you can find someone to do something with. If you are lonely, your thoughts are wrong and most always involve self-pity.**

The reason this chapter is my favorite is because it causes you to think about and desire the Lord. When I wrote *the Excellent Wife*, I had worked on it for almost three years and had a goal of finishing it by the end of the year (ten years ago). So, the day after Christmas I got up at 5:30 AM and began to write. I wrote one chapter a day for five days and then I finished the rough draft of the entire book. The next to the last day was the chapter on loneliness. Since the antidote to self-pity is delighting in the Lord, it turned my focus on Him. Since I was writing to tell others how to delight in the Lord, the loneliness chapter became my favorite chapter.

Biblical Principles of Loneliness

A. **We are to take refuge in the Lord when we are lonely regardless of the reason** (Psalm 25:16-22)
B. **God has a special concern for the orphans and widows who are left alone** (Psalm 68:5-6)
C. **Loneliness describes the psalmist whose enemies have turned on him and God is disciplining him until he reminds himself of what God has done** (Psalm 102:1-3, 25-28)
D. **Our sin can isolate us from God just like the sin of the children of Zion isolated them from God** (Lamentations 1:1, 8)
E. **It is all right to ask help from others when we are going through a trial but our greatest strength must come from God** (Mark 14:32-42; 2 Timothy 4:7-22)

The following are some quotes from books of men who had a very high view of God. These are books that I recommend for you to read and meditate upon. They will remind you of God and draw you close to Him:

1. Jerry Bridges (member of the Navigators Community Ministries Group where he has a Bible teaching ministry. This quote is from his book, *The Joy of Fearing God*, page 61). This is a prayer:

"O glorious God! The vast oceans You hold in Your hand and the billions of stars You hold in their courses are but faint pictures of Your infinite greatness. Indeed, You spoke the universe into existence in the beginning and now by Your mighty power You hold it all together from hour to hour. Fill our minds with awe and adoration as we think upon Your greatness. Fill our hearts with gratitude and gladness as we realize that with all Your infinite power and sovereignty, You have condescended to be our God. Through Jesus, Your Son, we praise you. Amen."

2. Walter Chantry (pastor of Grace Baptist Church, Carlisle, Pennsylvania since 1963) from his book, *Praises for the King of Kings*, page 7 and 9.

"To you who believe, He (Jesus Christ, the son of God) is precious" (1 Peter 2:7). Faith and love are twin graces. When trust in Jesus is born within a soul, so too is a holy affection toward the Saviour brought to birth. Every genuine believer cherishes and adores the Lord Jesus. Those who are in love enjoy thinking about and talking about their dearly beloved. Better yet, the amorous heart longs to be in the presence of the one who is endeared. The theme of these meditations is the Delight of every Christian's heart – Jesus, the Lord. He is precious in the sight of God the Father, whose testimony is, 'This is my Son, whom I love; with him I am well pleased' (Matthew 3:17). Our spirits echo this sentiment. He is our lord, whom we love; we are entirely pleased with him.

"Samuel Rutherford once exclaimed, 'black sun, black moon, black stars, but, O bright, infinitely bright Lord Jesus!' Isaiah predicted the coming of our blessed Redeemer with these words, 'the glory of the Lord will be revealed, and all mankind together will see it' (Isaiah 40:5). 'The Son is the radiance of God's glory' (Hebrews 1:3). All of the beauty, loveliness and dignity of the infinite God that can be revealed to the creature man shines from the face of Christ. The person of Jesus Christ constitutes the perfect representation of God. He is the fullest self-manifestation of divine glory. 'In these last days God has spoken to us in his Son' (Hebrews 1:2). We would see more of Jesus! If only God's Spirit would open these Psalms about the Messiah to our hearts as we ponder them, we will be satisfied."

"To behold Jesus, to adore him, and to rejoice in his praises are not means to higher ends. Fixing the eyes of our souls upon the Lamb of God, and bowing before him in joyful, loving worship *is* the highest end of our existence, the only fully satisfying experience of the human heart, the chief ingredient of human blessedness. 'That I may know Him...' (Philippians 3:10) and enjoy Him forever is the end for which every saint lives."

> 3. Charles Spurgeon (pastor of the London Tabernacle in London, 1800's, from his book, *All of Grace*, page 129, the chapter on "Why Saints Persevere").

"God is faithful in His love; He knows no variableness, neither shadow of turning (James 1:17). He is faithful to His purpose; He does not begin a work and then leave it undone. He is faithful to His relationships. As a Father He will not renounce His children; as a Friend He will not deny His people; as a Creator He will not forsake the work of His own hands. He is faithful to His promises and will never allow one of them to fail for a single believer. He is faithful to His covenant, which He has made with us in Christ Jesus and ratified with the blood of His sacrifice. He is faithful to His Son and will not allow His precious blood to be spilled in vain. He is faithful to His people to whom He has promised eternal life and from whom He will not turn away.'

Practical Ways to Repent of Self-pity

1. Be discerning about what you are feeling and thinking. If you feel lonely and it is painful for you, realize what you are thinking. Write your thoughts down and analyze each one of them biblically.
2. Cultivate gratefulness to God and to your husband. Think "thank you" thoughts to God often especially when something doesn't go your way.
3. Learn to be content. There are a lot of material things we can definitely live without and there is a lot of attention from our husbands that we can also live without. Give your husband blessings instead and think about your responsibility before God to be content.
4. Realize that God could remove you from the circumstance today if He wanted to but that God's purposes are higher than yours. And if the Lord does remove you from the circumstance of your husband being aloof or closed off from you, you don't want to be ashamed of yourself before the Lord that you whined and complained and were angry and bitter when (looking back) you can

see how God was working even though you didn't know it.

5. Realize that God has a purpose. Romans 8:28-29 is true.

6. God wants you to go against your feelings and think and do what is right. He will, then, help you not to slip into your self-centered pity-party, "poor me" routine.

7. Adopt a high view of God through reading and thinking about the Psalms and also reading good books by godly men and women who challenge your thinking. Read with a dictionary handy in case you need to look up a word. Read when you are awake and clear-headed. Also underline sentences that stand out to you so that you can refer back to them.

8. View time alone as a grace gift from God to spend more time with the Lord reading His Word and learning about Him and talking to Him.

The Character of God and the Issue of Biblical Submission
Thoughts to Help You be Submissive When You Don't Feel Like It

All day, every day you should be mindful of the Lord and talking to Him. For a wife, the issue of whether to be submissive to her husband or not comes up a lot. She has a choice to make every time her husband tells or asks her to do something or stop doing something such as, "Watch the grocery budget; we are spending too much this month," "Would you mail this letter for me today?" "When you park your car in a public place pick a spot that is away from others so their doors will not bang your car," "We're not going to purchase a new sofa right now because we may need that money for something else," "I prefer my shirts to have no starch in them."

Thoughts to Help You be Submissive

1. "Lord, I know that You are good and I will do this because I know this is what you want me to do."
2. "This is a way that I can show love to my husband because 'Love doesn't seek its own way.'"
3. "Nothing is worth sinning against God."
4. "Lord, thank You for testing me by changing my plans today."
5. "Lord, you know I don't want to do what my husband asked and you know how selfish I am. Help me to put my husband first."
6. "Lord, this is Your plan for my life and I thank you for it."
7. "Lord, help me serve You however You please."
8. "What a joy it is to do this for You!"
9. "Lord, I trust You that you know how You want me to serve You."
10. "If I contend with my husband, I will be out of God's will."
11. "What my friend said about me not being submissive hurt my feelings but she's right and I need to change."
12. "Lord, help me see what my husband asked me to do as rebellion against You if I don't do it."
13. "I am going to do this as 'unto the Lord'."

14. "Lord, teach me to obey with a cheerful heart even with small, seemingly unimportant matters."
15. "Lord, help me right now to think and respond in a way that pleases You."

The Character of God and Biblical Submission

God is:
- Holy – He would never ask me to do anything sinful.
- Faithful to Keep His promises – He promises us rewards for our good works done in His name. Submission to my husband is one of those good works.
- All-Powerful – He has the power to help me obey Him.
- All-Knowing – He knows what I am really thinking and if my actions are really honoring to Him.
- Always present – He is always here with me to help me no matter how tough things are.
- Good – God created me and made my role as a wife. He is good and declared His creation good.
- Sovereign – He is the King of Kings and the Supreme Ruler. He has the right to tell me what my role is whether I like it or not.
- Immutable – God does not change and He hasn't changed His mind concerning the role of the husband and wife even if it is over 2000 years after Christ came to eart
- Patient – God has been incredibly patient with me and is teaching me to be more and more discerning about being submissive.
- Graceful – It is only by God's grace to help me that I could desire to be submissive to my husband.
- Merciful – God's mercies are new every morning. He will help me today to be a godly wife.
- Love – When I think that I am suffering because of my husband, I need to remind myself of the love of God on my behalf. That will give me an entirely new perspective.
- Just – God will discipline me if I rebel and disobey Him through disobeying my husband.

Misperceptions Regarding a Wife's Submission to Her Husband

When *The Excellent Wife* book came out ten years ago, I knew I had written a somewhat controversial book. My Mother said that young women were not going to like what I had written. That did not surprise me because the non-Christian world embraces the philosophies of men and (for the most part) our pagan world has embraced a feminist/politically correct philosophy. What *has* surprised me is the reaction of many dear, Bible-believing, fellow Christians who differ not on the **issue** of submission but on the issue of the **extent of the authority of the husband** (for instance how far does his authority extend if the husband asks his wife to sin or to cover up his sin). As a result, I have found myself challenged to make the issues more clear for the Bible-believing Christian world as well as for the individual ladies I occasionally have the opportunity to counsel concerning biblical submission of a wife to her husband.

First, I would like to cover eleven misperceptions regarding a wife's submission to her husband. We will consider how to refute those misperceptions and then I will explain two illustrations to help a wife (as I believe she rightly should) come forward in love as a witness to try to help her husband who is in unrepentant sin.

Eleven Misperceptions Regarding a Wife's Submission to Her Husband

1. **The Mutual Submission Only View**

   - This is the typical liberal view of those who do not believe the Scriptures are God's Word without error. It fits in nicely with the feminist philosophy and is politically correct. In other words, husbands and wives are equal in authority and are to be submissive to each other.
   - We correct this misperception by explaining the context of Ephesians chapters 5 and 6. In Ephesians 5:21, Paul was giving a generic introduction to the issue of submission. Then he proceeds to tell you "how" to be submissive by explaining specific examples such as wives under the authority of their husbands, children under the authority of their parents, and slaves under the author-

ity of their masters. In other words, Paul was writing, "I want you to be submissive and this is practically how you do it." There are no other Scriptures that reverse these authority structures or even make them equal. Those who use Ephesians 5:21 as proof that husbands and wives are equal in authority and then discount all of the specific examples that follow are reading their own opinions into what they want the Scriptures to say.

2. **The "I wouldn't touch that subject with a ten foot pole" (pastor's) view**

- This is the view of the majority of Bible-believing pastors. Deep down they know that the doctrine of biblical submission of a wife to her husband is biblical but they rationalize not teaching it because it might downsize their church considerably. This likely would account for the fact that so many Christian ladies have never heard of this doctrine before.
- On the rare occasion when I have an opportunity to talk with a pastor with this view, I encourage him to help his ladies by lovingly teaching this doctrine from the pulpit. One pastor told me that he was afraid of the ladies' reaction so he played a section of one of my tapes in one of his sermons – he said, "that way, it was you telling them and not me!"

3. **The "I'm submissive. I would never sell the house without my husband's permission" view**

- Many Christian wives believe themselves to be submissive because they would never "cross" their husband when it comes to big issues – selling the house, buying a car, or having another baby. However if you talked with their husband's, they would say, "She fights me every step of the way (over small as well as large issues).
- Consider the example of a child obeying a parent. Should the child obey only if it is really, really important? Of course it is *not* all right for the one under authority to decide what is important. They are to obey unless providentially hindered, unless asked to sin against God, or unless they make an appeal and the person in authority over them changes their mind.
- Consider the example of obedience to God: Are Christians to obey God in large *and* small matters or are they to obey God based on what *seems to be* really important to them? Of course, God requires and expects all levels of obedience (1 Peter 1:14-15).
- Wives are to be faithful in the small things as well as the large. (See

Luke 16:10).

- Submission is a heart's attitude as well as an outward action. If her motive is right (to show love to God and to her husband), a wife will consider even the small issues to be of paramount importance to God and to her husband (Romans 12:9-10).

- Submission should be from the husband's perspective not from the perspective of what the wife thinks is important. The "spirit of the matter" includes the husband's desires or preferences not just the times when he gives an absolute order or dictate. For example, when a husband says, "Honey, I think I prefer to not have so much starch in the collar of my shirts," compared with "Do not put starch in my collar." The wife should want *so much to please her husband* and *show him love and maintain the "spirit of submission"* that she should be faithful in the least. She should be exhorted to consider even the least requests and opinions of her husband as possibly a submission issue and therefore important – seeing submission from the husband's perspective and being faithful in the least little things.

- Consider a husband asking his wife, "Would you mail this letter for me today?" Later in the day the wife thinks about it and decides it can wait until the next day when she will be running errands anyway. This is assuming that his request is not that important. She is taking matters into her own hands, and she has disobeyed. Instead, she should either go mail the letter as he asked or make an appeal, but she should also be willing to go mail it if it is important to him. Unless her husband releases her from the request or God providentially hinders her, then she should be submissive (not from what *she* might consider important but what her husband does). If she has been providentially hindered, she should explain to her husband what happened and follow through with his original request as soon as possible.

4. The "I can't take it any more and God understands" view

- This sort of thinking comes from a bitter heart. The wife has been "hurt" and she is likely playing those hurts over and over in her mind. Her emotional pain becomes greater and greater and God is further and further away from her thoughts or God may be in her thoughts but in the wrong way. For instance, "Why doesn't God help me with this?" Instead of thinking this way, she should realize that she is sinning and must repent.

- She needs hope (1 Corinthians 10:13, Romans 8:28, Lamentations 3:21-25).

- It is not true that she "can't take it any more" – what is true is that "God *is* faithful and will not allow her to be pressured beyond what she is able to bear."
- One good source of hope is Jay Adams' *Christ and Your Problems* book.
- The wife must forgive her husband (Ephesians 4:31-32), work at overcoming evil with good (Romans 12:21); and give a blessing instead (1 Peter 3:9).
- She must "put on love" to her husband. For example, think, "Love does not take into account a wrong suffered. Instead of sitting here thinking about what he has done to me, I am going to take this time to think of something nice I can do for him and then I'm going to do it." Or "I'm going to take this time and energy to pray for my husband and ask the Lord to grant him repentance and I'm also going to ask the Lord how I can help my husband."
- A wife who thinks God understands that she can't take it any longer has a wrong view of God– instead she should think that God requires that she forgive (in her heart) whether her husband ever changes or not.

5. **The "Obey even if he asks you to sin" view**

- The wife needs to understand the biblical view of authority (Romans 13:1; 1 Corinthians 11:3; Matthew 28:18). God is the highest authority and He is the one who ordains and limits all other lesser authorities – kings or queens/husbands/parents/ slave owners. God is holy and cannot tempt anyone to sin (James 1:13-14). Men are sinful and do, at times, tempt or even command others to sin. However, God has provided several "means of grace" for the Christian to respond when ordered to sin by someone in authority over them. Those "means of grace" are the grace of the indwelling Holy Spirit, the Scriptures, and other brothers and sisters in the Lord helping to "bear their burdens" (Galatians 6:2). The Lord has also provided other resources to protect a wife whose husband is asking her to sin–church discipline if he is a Christian (Matthew 18:15-18) and the governing authorities of whatever country they live in. At times the Lord may give the wife an opportunity to suffer for righteousness sake (1 Peter 4:14-16, 19). For example, if a wife refuses to participate in a sinful sex act with her husband, he may pout or threaten to divorce her or scream at her in a rage. If her motives are pure before the Lord and she is respectful and otherwise submissive to her husband, she is suffering for righteousness sake (1 Peter 3:13-17).

- Some believe that Sarah is praised in Scripture because she obeyed Abraham by lying for him when she said, "I am his sister." (Sarah *was* his half sister but she deliberately deceived the king because Abraham was afraid he would be killed because Sarah was so beautiful.) 1 Peter 3:5-6. Realize that stories in the Old Testament (narrative) are just that—stories. They were never intended for us to personally follow everything we read. Peter nowhere in 1 Peter 3 refers specifically to Sarah lying for Abraham. The context of Peter's letter is suffering. Within the context of suffering for the Lord's sake, women married to unbelievers, as well as believers, would sometimes suffer. If she were a godly woman then her true adornment would show – a gentle and quiet spirit and submission to her husband. Peter does not refer to Sarah's lying as "doing what is right". He does not mention the lying incident. He *does* refer to her being submissive to her husband. In other words, as a pattern in Sarah's life she was submissive to her husband. This reminds me of King David. As a pattern in his life he had a heart for God yet we know there were some things about his life (such as the adultery) that we are not to copy. Narrative stories have legitimate points such as seeing God's providential care or His justice or His mercy. Think of the book of Esther. Esther did a lot of things that God providentially used for His glory and His purposes but there is much in what she did that Christian women today are not to copy. For example, Esther did not tell the king or anyone in the king's palace or harem that she was a Jew yet the Old Testament specifically forbids mixed marriages outside of their faith (Esther 2:10). The fact that Mordecai (her cousin who was her guardian) told her not to tell her nationality still doesn't make it right. Mordecai shouldn't have asked her and Esther should have appealed to try to get out of the king's harem. The point of the story was *God* and **His faithfulness to keep His covenant promises**. The point was not to find your daughter a husband in such a way or for her to be deceptive. God obviously uses people in spite of their sin – Esther, Sarah, you and me.
- So, Peter is saying to do what is right – that is be submissive to your husband and have the right heart's attitude. That's all he's saying and we should not read more into it than God and Peter intended.
- Wives also need to have a right view of suffering. It is a privilege to suffer for the Lord's sake and for truly doing what is right. It is foolish to suffer unnecessarily (asceticism, Colossians 2). That's like shooting yourself in the foot and then expecting to be praised for how terrible it is to suffer in that way. She never has to suffer

for being rebellious or disrespectful but if her husband asks her to sin and she suffers for appealing, and if necessary for refusing, then she is honoring God.

- Be aware that many books dogmatically teach the "obey even if he asks you to sin" view.
- God kept Abraham and Sarah safe *in spite of* their sin not as a reward for it. Wouldn't it have been much more honoring to God if Sarah (as well as Abraham) had not lied and sinned against God? God was not rewarding Sarah's obedience when she lied, He was showing His grace and mercy and faithfulness to keep His promises to them (the promised son, father of a great nation, etc.).He still expects and requires holiness of each individual, even if a person whom God placed in authority over them has asked them to sin. God is the highest authority. Each believer is to be "**holy as He is holy**" (1 Peter 1:15-16). This is the only view that is consistent with the holiness of God and consistent with Scripture.

6. **The "Win him without a word" view**

- This view is often espoused with the previous one, "Obey even if he asks you to sin" view.
- This view is the basis for teaching that a wife is not to reprove her husband or come forward as a witness even if he is in unrepentant sin. Instead, she is to not say anything and thus "win him without a word."
- Again, this is a wrong understanding of 1 Peter 3:1-2
- Two key phrases here are "**disobedient to the word**" and "**may be won without a word**". Peter plainly defines those who are "**disobedient to the word**" and that is a phrase describing unbelievers (See 1 Peter 2:6-9). Peter's point is not about reproof (telling the husband what he is doing wrong) but is about sharing the gospel with an unsaved husband. The wife is to win her husband (evangelize him) by her chaste and respectful behavior and her godly heart's attitudes, not by preaching to him and stuffing gospel tracts under his pillow. In other words, she is not to be a hypocritical Christian who professes Christ and treats her husband in a disrespectful way.

7. **The "I don't have to obey because he is not a Christian" view**

- This is clearly refuted in 1 Peter 3:1-2.
- Some wives' motives are good but they are ignorant of what the Bible really teaches. If ignorance is not the problem, then she is

likely rebellious. Whatever the cause, a woman married to an unbeliever is to be biblically submissive to him unless he asks her to sin.

8. **The "You'd better not tell anyone what I've done" (husband's) view**

    *   This is sinful intimidation/manipulation on the part of the husband.
    *   He is asking his wife to unbiblically cover up for him. She would have to sin if she did not come forward as a witness (if necessary).
    *   If he is a Christian (or says he is) then it *is* the responsibility of the church to judge those within the church (1 Corinthians 5:9-13).
    *   The wife or family may be the only ones to know since many people put on a good front in public and at church. For example, I once counseled a wife whose husband was a pillar in their church – a deacon, taught the adult Sunday School class, and was a well-known businessman in his community. At home, he was a tyrant with an extreme anger problem. He bullied his wife and children. She reached a point where she (wrongly) threw in the towel on their marriage. Instead of a "win him without a word" philosophy which she had sinfully allowed to drive her to despair, her responsibility was to confront her husband with his sin and exhort him to repent. If he did not, she should have brought two or more witnesses in. If he still did not repent, then she should have taken it to the pastor and/or elders in the church. (See Matthew 18:15-18.)
    *   It is understandable why a wife who has been threatened or intimidated would say nothing. However, she not only runs the risk of disobeying God by not coming forward as a godly witness but she runs the risk of becoming so embittered that she compounds her husband's sin by leaving him or divorcing him.
    *   If her husband is an unbeliever, the church has no jurisdiction. Certainly they can pray for her husband's salvation and perhaps it may be appropriate for the pastor or one of the men in the church to talk with him. However, the wife should not pressure her husband with the gospel or expect him to love the Lord; but when her husband has a pattern of sin in his life that is detrimental to himself or his family and friends, she should appeal to his conscience to do what is right. If necessary, she should bring in the governing authorities such as the police (Romans 13:1-2).

9. **The "I'll divorce you if you don't submit" (husband's) view**

    *   Certainly this threat is always wrong but do make sure that what the wife is refusing to do is really a sin and not just "differentness."

For example, it is a sin to knowingly sign a joint income tax statement that has false information. It is not a sin to go out to eat in a restaurant that serves alcohol as long as the husband is not requiring her to get drunk.

- This is also intimidation/manipulation on the part of the husband. Often he makes threats if she won't cover up for his sin or if she refuses to participate in sinful sexual acts. Instruct her to say something like this, "It would be very difficult for me if you divorce me. That's not right and that's not what I want. But if you do, God will give me the grace to go through it.

10. The "Nowhere in the Bible does it say for a wife to reprove her husband" view

- Nowhere in the Bible does it *not* say for a wife to reprove her husband.
- The Bible *does* say for the wife: to be respectful (Ephesians 5:33); to have a gentle and quiet spirit (1 Peter 3:4); to be under her husband's authority (Ephesians 5:22); and to love her husband (Titus 2:4). These *specific* mandates apply to a wife but so do all the other mandates regarding conflict-solving biblically and dealing with other people's sin.
- The Bible often instructs us in areas that apply to all Christians. Each and every possible contingency is not spelled out. Often we are left to make the appropriate application. In addition to specific mandates, there are general mandates for every Christian such as "Overcome evil with good," "Bear one another's burdens," "If your brother sins go to him privately," "Put off anger and put on kindness." We are all (and this includes husband and wife) to try to help each other become as much like the Lord Jesus Christ as possible.

11. The "I'll come forward as a witness if my husband commits adultery, sexually molests the children, or commits murder" view

- This is a common misconception of biblical submission. Some think that the wife is not to be her husband's judge. I agree that the husband is accountable to God as his ultimate judge; but God *did* make a wife her husband's judge in the sense that she is to make righteous, godly, objective judgments. She is not to make self-righteous, pharisaical judgments or be judgmental. She is to make judgments concerning outward statements and behavior. For example, it is wrong to scream at the children in anger. It is wrong for a husband to bully his wife through sinful intimidation. These are judgments that all Christians are to make and (if appropriate) to act upon.

- Sin is sin and whether you are talking about anger, lust, murder or adultery. God has given clear instructions for what to do when someone sins against you (that includes a husband against a wife or a wife against a husband). I don't believe we are to arbitrarily choose which sins we consider the greater sins and which the lesser. Certainly some sins are of such magnitude that they must be dealt with very quickly while others can be with dealt with more patiently, but a wife is still to come forward as a witness to try to help her husband if he will not turn from his sin.

Advice for Women Married to Unbelievers
Biblical Principles for a Wife to Follow

A. Pray for him (1 Timothy 2:1-3).

B. Be prepared to give him the gospel or answer his questions about the Lord (1 Peter 3:13-17).

C. Have extra special compassion; he does not know the Lord and if he dies in his sins, he'll spend eternity in hell (2 Corinthians 5:14; Romans 2:4).

D. Live out the biblical principles on being a godly wife: love your husband, be biblically submissive to him, and show respect to him (Titus 2:3-5; Ephesians 5:22:33).

E. Do not expect him to think or act as a Christian. He does not have that capacity (1 Corinthians 2:14).

F. Plan and do things he would like: go fishing, have sex, invite his friends over, surprise him with his favorite dinner or a sweet note tucked under his pillow (Proverbs 31:10-12).

G. Instead of thinking of him as the man who ruined your life or public enemy number one, think of him in endearing terms: the father of my children, my husband, the man who provides for me and the children, the man who stuck by me even when I didn't deserve for him to ... 1 Corinthians 13:7 ("Love bears all things, believes all things, hopes all things, endures all things.")

H. Socialize with his friends but draw the line at personal sin. If he and his friends want to do something you cannot do (for instance, go to an X rated movie), graciously bow out but do offer to do something else with them instead. For instance, "Let's go bowling." Ahead of time prepare interesting topics that would not be offensive to talk about. Don't be a stick in the mud, be gracious if they say something that is not purely biblical, be patient with them. Remember when you were not saved and the probably thousands of foolish things you said and did, be warm and gracious, having "speech seasoned as it were with salt," to them. There's no reason that you cannot have a good time. Show affection to your husband and treat him with respect. Wear a toe ring if he likes it! Your warmth and enjoyment of his friends will be, in a sense, "being all things to all people" (1 Corinthians 9:12, 23).

I. Evangelize him with your chaste and respectful life (1 Peter 3:1, 2). The context of 1 Peter 3:1-2 is evangelism. Those who are "disobedient to the word" are unbelievers (see 1 Peter 2:7-8). It doesn't mean the wife cannot ever talk about the Lord to her husband, especially if he asks or it is in the natural flow of conversation.

Chaste comes from the root word for holy. You should be pure in your thoughts and actions. He should never have to be offended or embarrassed because you are sensuous toward other men or look at them with a lingering gaze or dress immodestly (you don't have to look like *Little House on the Prairie* either!)

Respectful comes from the word that means fear, to be in awe of, to reverence. This is how the wife is to act regardless of what the husband does. It doesn't mean living in some sort of non-reality when he is sinning or when she would like to give her opposing opinion, it does mean she uses a gracious and warm tone of voice and looks at him respectfully.

This chaste and respectful life is one of active, aggressive evangelism. To talk him to death about the Lord or kneel by his bed and pray out loud for his salvation while he's trying to go to sleep would be the opposite of "win him without a word." It would be very disrespectful as would five Christian bumper stickers on your car that he would see every time he opened the garage door.

J. Work hard at being a good wife. Unless providentially hindered, get out of the bed and fix his breakfast in the mornings, leave whatever you are doing when he returns home, greet him cheerfully, and ask about his day. Be a good cook and work hard at maintaining an organized, loving home. Even if he is an unbeliever, you should be a ray of sunshine in his life. Remember that this may be the only happiness he ever experiences for all of eternity. Proverbs 31:27

K. Consider your husband as more important than yourself. Philippians 2:3-4 He is your primary ministry and if you are restricted in what you can do for the Lord because of your husband, that does not mean that you are any less of a Christian or any less being used of God. Having fun with an unsaved husband and enjoying him (as far as possible) can also be considered by God to be a "work of righteousness."

L. If you must reprove your husband (tell him what he is doing wrong), do it with a respectful tone. The motive is to help him, (whether he perceives it that way or not), and appealing to his conscience to do *what is right*. All men are born with a conscience but not all men born again! (Genesis 2:18; Proverbs 31:26; 28:23;27:5-6). He doesn't have to be a believer for you to be a "helper-suitable" for him.

M. Do not make your husband's becoming a Christian an idol in your heart. While it is a good desire and good prayer, if God doesn't save him and the wife becomes bitter, angry, or self-pitying, then she is setting her heart on her husband's salvation instead of setting her heart on living her life for the glory of God (Hebrews 12:1-3).

N. Do not have unrealistic expectations. Even if he does become a Christian, he will still have irritating mannerisms and sin issues to work on (Ephesians 4:1-3).

O. Do not fall into the trap of day-dreaming about other men and how wonderful it would be to be with them (Ecclesiastes 5:7).

P. Do not take it as a personal offense when your husband does not see anything wrong with a certain movie (1 Corinthians 2:14).

Q. Do not have a wrong view of God. Here are some examples:

    1. "Name it and claim it!" This is a wrong view because God is sovereign and rules over His creation whether those of us in His creation believe it or not. We are not sovereign and God does not have to obey us! (Psalm 99:1; Psalm

29:10; 47:7-8; Isaiah 40:21-26).

2. Do everything just right and your husband will be saved. It is not true that the husband's salvation depends on the wife doing everything perfectly. Certainly her desire should be to please God and for her husband to be saved, but God can save a husband even if the wife is terrible! God is sovereign in her husband's salvation, not her. Thinking that she must do everything just right or she's ruined her husband's chances puts a great and unnecessary burden on the wife.

3. God is sitting in heaven almost wringing His hands because He hopes that the husband will make a decision for Him. (See Ephesians 2:4-9).

4. Somehow God gave her a raw deal in giving her an unbelieving husband. God is not good or fair. (Job 1:21-22).

R. Some women married to unbelievers have a wrong view of the grounds for divorce. Some men are so difficult and mean that there have been many times that I (Martha) wished a wife did have biblical grounds for divorce, but verbal or physical abuse are not one of those grounds. However she should take full advantage of all the resources God has given to protect her. See Chapter 14 in *The Excellent Wife* book. In addition to thinking that they have biblical grounds for divorce and not having them, there are those who think that there are no grounds. However, there are two – 1 Corinthians 7:15, "let the unbeliever depart" and Matthew 19:9 "…for the cause of immorality." For more information on the subject of divorce, I recommend Jay Adams' book, *Marriage, Divorce, and Remarriage.*

S. Do not think that you cannot be used of the Lord because your husband is an unbeliever. That's simply not true. Think of Timothy's mother who was married to an unbeliever, yet God used her to greatly influence her son's life.

T. Be careful not to share intimate details of your marriage in the form of prayer requests because he is not a Christian Proverbs 31:11). This is inappropriate no matter whether your husband is a believer or not. Stop and think how he would feel if he found out.

U. Do not think that it's all right to complain about your husband to friends and family because he is not a Christian. To do that is slander and gossip and a lack of love. Instead, have compassion instead of grumbling and complaining.

V. If you are struggling with loneliness, it may be due to your own sin. This often results in being caught up in self-pity and anger at God. Do not think and say things like, "He'll never change. He'll never be saved. I'm trapped and there is no hope" (Romans 8:28; 1 Corinthians 7:16).

W. It may be tempting but do not withdraw from him and basically live a private life in reaction to his being the same way. Instead, fight back with "good" instead of more evil (Romans 12:21).

X. Do not think that God could never bless your marriage because you married your husband in disobedience. Remember 1 John 1:8. You should humble yourself and admit your sin to God, ask His forgiveness, and realize that God is faithful to forgive sin and not hold it over your head in a cruel, vindictive way.

Y. Do not think it's all right to express and vent anger at God over your circumstances. This is blasphemous thinking. Instead, humbly submit to your circumstances and be grateful to God for how He is using you even when you are suffering for the Lord's sake (1 Peter 5:6-10).

Endnotes

1 Robert Thomas, ed., *New American Standard Exhaustive Concordance of the Bible* (Nashville: Holman Bible Publishers, 1981), #1128, p.1640.

2 Stuart Scott, "Biblical Relationships," Sunday School material, 1993.

3 Robert Thomas, #259, p.1486.

4 Stuart Scott, Class notes on "Relationships," (Grace Community Church), 1994.

5 Ibid.

6 Lou Priolo, "A Biblical Alternative to Criticism," *The Journal of Biblical Counseling*, Vol. 10, #4 (1992), p.15.

7 Ibid.

8 Buck Hatch, "God's Blueprint for Biblical Marriage," Class videotape, 1980.

9 Lou Priolo, Class notes on "Idols of the Heart," (Atlanta Biblical Counseling Center), 1994.

10 Robert Thomas, #3626, p.1669.

11 Robert Thomas, #3616, p.1669.

12 W. E. Vine, *Vine's Expository Dictionary of New Testament Words* (McLean, Virginia: MacDonald Publishing Co.), pp.702-703.

13 Ibid., p.703.

14 Ibid.

15 Jerry Bridges, *Transforming Grace* (Colorado Springs, Colorado: Nav Press, 1991), p. 138.

16 *Webster's Seventh New Collegiate Dictionary* (Springfield, Massachusetts: G.& C. Merriam Company, 1963), p.171.

17 A. T. Robertson, *Word Pictures in the New Testament* (Grand Rapids, Michigan: Baker Book House, 1931), p.547.

18 Ibid.

19 Ed Sherwood, "A Biblical View of Sex in Marriage," 4-2-93.

20 Robert Thomas, #1692, p.1507.

21 Ed Sherwood, "A Biblical View of Sex in Marriage," 4-2-93.

22 Ibid.

23 Ed Wheat, *Intended for Pleasure* (Grand Rapids, Michigan: Fleming H. Revell, 1977).

24 Bob Smith, "Book Review," *The Journal of Pastoral Practice*, Vol. 8, #3 (1989), pp.52-58.

25 Jay Adams, *The Christian Counselor's Manual* (Grand Rapids, Michigan: Zondervan Publishing House, 1973), p.392.

26 *Webster's Dictionary*, p.51.

27 Robert Thomas, #987, p.1638.

28 *Webster's Dictionary*, p.989.

29 Lou Priolo's tape "Biblical Resources for a Wife's Protection" may be obtained from Sound Word Ministries. Tel: (219) 879-7753.

30 The NATIONAL ASSOCIATION OF NOUTHETIC COUNSELORS (NANC) certifies biblical counselors and is a training organization. The word "nouthetic" comes from the Greek word *noutheo* which means to counsel, exhort, or admonish. This group believes that the Scriptures are sufficient and they use only the Scriptures to counsel. You can determine the location of a certified NANC counselor by calling NANC at (317) 337-9100 or accessing the website at www.nanc.org.

31 Jay Adams, *The Handbook of Church Discipline* (Grand Rapids, Michigan: Zondervans, 1986).

32 Robert Thomas, #692, p.1635.

33 John MacArthur, *Colossians and Philemon* (Chicago, Illinois: Moody Press, 1992), p.144.

34 Wayne Mack, Cassette tapes "Conflict Resolution in Marriage - Part I and II." These tapes may be obtained from Sound Word Ministries. See endnote #29.

35 Wayne Mack, Cassette tapes "Getting Along With In-Laws, Parent-Side" and "Getting Along With In-Laws, Child-Side." These tapes may be obtained from Sound Word Ministries. See endnote #29.

36 W. E. Vine, p.579.

37 Homer A. Kent, Jr., *The Freedom of God's Sons* (Winona Lake, Indiana: BMH Books, 1976), p.162.

38 Lou Priolo, Cassette tape, "How to Improve Your IQ - Impatience Quotient." See endnote # 29.

39 W. E. Vine, p.57.

40 Robert Thomas, #3709, p.1656

41 Ibid., #2372, p.1673.

42 Ibid., #3950, p.1673.

43 Lou Priolo, Client homework handout at The Atlanta Biblical Counseling Center. See endnote #29.

44 Jay Adams, *The Christian Counselors Manual*, p.413.

45 Homer A. Kent, Jr., *Expositor's Bible Commentary Vol. V* (Grand Rapids, Michigan: Zondervans, 1978), p.152.

46 William Hendricksen. *Philippians, Colossians, and Philemon*, (Grand Rapids, Michigan: Baker, 1962), p.201.

47 Lou Priolo, The Atlanta Biblical Counseling Center.

48 Ibid.

49 Ibid.

50 Dr. Wayne Mack has two excellent tapes on "Rebuilding a Marriage After Adultery." To obtain the tapes contact Dr. Wayne Mack, The Master's College.

51 This Bible study may be reproduced for the purposes of counseling, Bible studies, academics, or personal use.

Biographical Sketch of Martha Peace

Martha was born, raised, and educated in and around the Atlanta area. She graduated with honors from both the Grady Memorial Hospital School of Nursing 3 year diploma program and the Georgia State University 4 year degree program. She has thirteen years work experience as a Registered Nurse, specializing in pediatric burns, intensive care, and coronary care. She became a Christian in June, 1979. Two years later, Martha ended her nursing career and began focusing her attention on her family and a ladies' Bible study class. For five years she taught verse-by-verse book studies. Then she received training and certification from the National Association of Nouthetic Counselors. N.A.N.C. was started by Dr. Jay Adams for the purpose of training and certifying men and women as biblical counselors.

Martha is a gifted teacher and exhorter. She worked for eight years as a counselor at the Atlanta Biblical Counseling Center where she counseled women. She instructed for 6 years at Carver Bible Institute and College in Atlanta where she taught women's classes including "The Excellent Wife," "Raising Kids Without Raising Cain," "Introduction to Biblical Counseling," and "Advanced Biblical Counseling." Martha is the author of two books in addition to *The Excellent Wife*. The books are *Becoming a Titus 2 Women* and *Attitudes of a Transformed Heart*. She is currently part time adjunct faculty at The Master's College in Valencia, California. Her books and tapes are available through Bible Data Services, 1119 Montclair Drive, Peachtree City, Georgia (770-486-0011 or www.marthapeace.com.

Martha is active with her husband at Faith Bible Church in Sharpsburg, Georgia where she teaches ladies' Bible study classes. In addition, she conducts seminars for ladies' groups on topics such as "Having a High View of God" and "Problems Women Face Today."

Martha has been married to her high school sweetheart, Sanford Peace, for thirty-nine years. He is an air traffic controller with the FAA but his real work is as an elder at Faith Bible Church. They have two children, Anna who is married to Tony Maupin and David who is married to Jamee Peace. In addition to their children, they have ten grandchildren, Nathan, Tommy, twin girls - Kelsey and Jordan, Caleb, Cameron, Carter, Matthew, Kylee, and Noah.

- Pray that God will soon provide the needed resources so that **Tim and Mary Sue Austin and their family** can move to Dakar, Senegal where Tim will teach at Dakar Academy. Also, Mary's dad, Gail Ohren, is in pretty poor health. He is at his home in Hibbing. The hospice nurse estimates he has only a few days to live. Pray for grace and courage for all as they face the uncertainties of the days ahead.
- Please continue to pray for **George Stull** who was hospitalized this past week and is now home. Pray for wisdom for the doctors as George undergoes a series of medical tests.
- Please pray for **Nick Nicholas,** brother-in-law to Terry & Mary Makings who is hospitalized in critical condition. Pray for healing for Nick and peace for the family.

CALVARY MISSIONARY: Ted & Jean Miller, Design engineer with HCJB Global

SISTER UKRAINIAN CHURCH ~ Church of Evangelical Christian Baptists at Velikodolinskoye and Pastor Vladimir Korbut.

COMMUNITY: Peace Presbyterian Church

CONVERGE HEARTLAND DISTRICT: West Point Baptist Church, West Point, NE, Pastor Curtis Hineline

UNITED STATES: Church Planters Pat & Winnie Barnes are planting Faith Mountain, Lakewood, CO, Converge Rocky Mountain region

WORLD: Missionaries John & Elaine Mehn are church planting in Tokyo.

PRAISES

*Congratulation to **Jeremy & Heather Budihas** the proud parents of Easton James who was born at 7:20 a.m. Thursday morning. Easton weighed in at 7# 9 oz. and is 20" long.*

*Praise God for **Kari Swensen's newborn niece, Rory**. After a rocky start Rory was able to go home this past week*

JOIN US IN PRAYER

CHURCH FAMILY: Please pray for the following needs:
Andrea Wright, Carol Reisner, Bob Chabane, Kay Knodel, George Stull, Carol Vining, Bob Schwenk, Dan Ehrismann's brother, Don, Larry Boyd's brother, Shawn ~ struggling with ongoing health concerns.

- Pray for **Jon and Jessica Reed** as they live a life of major transition to a new culture and language in Brazil and most recently, parenting, following the birth of daughter **Kezia**.
- Pray for **John, Jennie and Ella Warden** as they relocate to Sucre, Bolivia. They will be living with a Bolivian family, and as such will be immersed in a new language and culture. Pray for language aptitude and the grace to face many changes.
- Pray for **Jeremy and Trina Hamilton and their family** as they also adapt to a new language, culture and ministry setting in Belgium. Pray for them as they begin a new ministry with university students in Gent.
- Pray for strength and comfort for many within our church body who are **concerned and/or caring for aging parents.**
- Pray for a **positive transition** as we move from a Sunday school class model to a community model in our adult education ministry on Sunday mornings beginning September 13. Pray for those who will give leadership to these developing communities of faith.
- Pray for **DJ Jons** who has been undergoing tests at Mayo Clinic in Rochester, MN. Pray for a clear diagnosis and for God's healing through whatever means he chooses.
- Pray that God will be preparing the hearts of those who will be participating in the **GriefShare, DivorceCare and DivorceCare4Kids ministries** that begin in September.
- Pray that God will provide the needed staff for the **AWANA** ministry this fall. There is no shortage of kids. We do not want a shortage of staff!
- Pray that God will enable **our sister church in Big Valley** to complete their construction phase with the monies we have sent to them this summer. This completes the $15,000 commitment we made to them three years ago, $5,000 each year for three years.
- **Alice Anderson (Pastor Bruce's wife)** had a stroke Tuesday evening. She seems unable to control her right side and is having great difficulty with clear speech. The family has seen a great deal of progress with her speech already. They would greatly appreciate your prayers. She is a patient at Sanford Hospital in Sioux Falls, SD.

June 28, 2009